Endorsements for Angelika Kratzer's Modals and Conditionals

'... Kratzer's classic work on modality and conditionals is one of the major
... of contemporary formal semantics. This collection of six of her
...aking papers on the topic is invaluable. But what is most gratifying is
...zer substantially revised the papers, updating them and providing a
... retrospective comments. An indispensible resource for anyone inter-
...emantics or the philosophy of language.'

François Recanati, Institut Jean Nicod

'...k collects and revises two decades of the work that has shaped the
...iew of the language of modals and conditionals: an invariant, univocal
...y that is variously understood with shifts in the conversational back-
...syntax that identifies *if*-clauses as the relative clauses restricting modal
... and a semantics that discerns in the conversational background what
...d what would be best, given what is given. Just for the argument on
...s foundation rests, the book deserves frequent and close study. The
...ell another compelling story in which rivals for the meaning of
...s are reconciled in a wedding of situation and thought—facts, so-
...e rival pleads that an *if*-clause is premise to reasoning of which the
...i is report. The other, in a familiar metaphysical turn, has suppressed
...f reasoning in favour of an assertion about ordering relations among
...rlds. Although it has been said (Lewis 1981) that formally there is
... choose between them, Angelika Kratzer demonstrates that only a
...hat includes premises gains a purchase on how and why the words
...xpress a conditional affect judgments about its truth. So, in repre-
... foundations for the modern view, the author also offers a radical
... reform it. This book is a treasure of the puzzles, illustrations and
...t have informed the subject. It defines the standard against which all
...on modals and conditionals is to be measured.'

Barry Schein, University of Southern California

'...d conditionals lie at the center of philosophical inquiry. In work
...n the 1970s, Kratzer proposes a vantage point from which it can be
...modals and conditionals share a common logical structure, that of
...on generally. This work collects and dramatically expands upon
Angelika Kratzer's now classic papers. There is scarcely an area of philosophy
that remains or will remain untouched by their influence.'

Jason Stanley, Rutgers University

OXFORD STUDIES IN THEORETICAL LINGUISTICS

GENERAL EDITORS
David Adger, Queen Mary University of London; Hagit Borer, University of Southern California

ADVISORY EDITORS
Stephen Anderson, Yale University; Daniel Büring, University of California, Los Angeles; Nomi Erteschik-Shir, Ben-Gurion University; Donka Farkas, University of California, Santa Cruz; Angelika Kratzer, University of Massachusetts, Amherst; Andrew Nevins, University College London; Christopher Potts, Stanford University, Amherst; Barry Schein, University of Southern California; Peter Svenonius, University of Tromsø; Moira Yip, University College London

For a complete list of titles published and in preparation for the series, see pp 204–5.

Modals and
Conditionals

ANGELIKA KRATZER

OXFORD
UNIVERSITY PRESS

OXFORD
UNIVERSITY PRESS

Great Clarendon Street, Oxford OX2 6DP
United Kingdom
Oxford University Press is a department of the University of Oxford.
It furthers the University's objective of excellence in research, scholarship,
and education by publishing worldwide. Oxford is a registered trade mark of
Oxford University Press in the UK and in certain other countries

First published 2012
Reprinted 2013

British Library Cataloguing in Publication Data
Data available

Library of Congress Cataloging in Publication Data
Data available

ISBN 978-0-19-923469-1

Contents

Detailed Contents

General preface

The theoretical focus of this series is on the interfaces between subcomponents of the human grammatical system and the closely related area of the interfaces between the different subdisciplines of linguistics. The notion of 'interface' has become central in grammatical theory (for instance, in Chomsky's recent Minimalist Program) and in linguistic practice: work on the interfaces between syntax and semantics, syntax and morphology, phonology and phonetics, etc., has led to a deeper understanding of particular linguistic phenomena and of the architecture of the linguistic component of the mind/brain.

The series covers interfaces between core components of grammar, including syntax/morphology, syntax/semantics, syntax/phonology, syntax/pragmatics, morphology/phonology, phonology/phonetics, phonetics/speech processing, semantics/pragmatics, intonation/discourse structure, as well as issues in the way that the systems of grammar involving these interface areas are acquired and deployed in use (including language acquisition, language dysfunction, and language processing). It demonstrates, we hope, that proper understandings of particular linguistic phenomena, languages, language groups, or inter-language variations all require reference to interfaces.

The series is open to work by linguists of all theoretical persuasions and schools of thought. A main requirement is that authors should write so as to be understood by colleagues in related subfields of linguistics and by scholars in cognate disciplines.

The present volume collects a number of Angelika Kratzer's fundamental contributions to the linked phenomena of modality and conditionality over the last thirty years or so. Each paper is prefaced with an introduction setting it in its larger context and linking it to current concerns, and most of the papers have been extensively re-edited so as to clarify how they connect to current work, while preserving the original line of argumentation. The intellectual narrative of the resulting volume takes the reader from empirical issues in the semantics of modals, through logical questions about how semantic theory should be set up, to philosophical concerns in the semantics of knowledge and belief.

David Adger
Hagit Borer

Preface and acknowledgments

The plan was to have a collection of old papers. But when asked to look at the project, Barry Schein sent comments that sounded as if the papers were new. They had to be rewritten, then, and that's what happened.

If there is anything worth reading in the chapters to come, it's because I have been lucky in life. I am fortunate to have the spouse I do. In fact, I am fortunate to live in a place where I can marry at all. I am fortunate to have the extended family I do, spread over two continents, from Mindelheim to Sedgwick, Maine. I am fortunate to have had the teachers I did: in Konstanz, and in Wellington, on the other side of the world. I am fortunate to have the friends I do, some of them from way back when. I am most fortunate to have had the students I did: in Berlin, before the wall came down, and after that, in the Pioneer Valley. I have been lucky to get away from time to time: Paris, Brazil, Hungary, Scotland, California, the mountains, back to Berlin, now Somerville. The incredible team from OUP treated me better than I deserve. But, best of all, I have been paid handsomely during all those years—for doing nothing but what I like best.

Amherst and Somerville, Massachusetts, January 2011.

The research leading to this book has received funding from the European Research Council under the European Community's Seventh Framework Program (FP7/2007–2013) / ERC grant agreement n° 229 441 – CCC awarded to François Recanati.

The published book chapters and articles listed below have been used for this collection with the kind permission of de Gruyter (chapters 2, 4) and Springer (chapters 1, 3, 5, 6), the latter representing rights originally granted to Reidel and Kluwer Academic Publishers. For chapter 6, I also used passages from my Stanford Encyclopedia of Philosophy article on Situations in Natural Languages, for which I retained the rights for non-electronic publications.

1. What 'Must' and 'Can' Must and Can Mean. *Linguistics and Philosophy* 1 (1977), 337–55.
2. The Notional Category of Modality. In H. J. Eikmeyer and H. Rieser (eds.), *Words, Worlds, and Contexts.* Berlin and New York: de Gruyter (1981), 38–74.
3. Partition and Revision: The Semantics of Counterfactuals. *The Journal of Philosophical Logic* 10 (1981), 201–16.
4. Conditionals. Chapter 30 in Arnim v. Stechow and Dieter Wunderlich (eds.), *Handbuch Semantik/Handbook Semantics.* Berlin and New York: de Gruyter (1991), 651–6.
5. An Investigation of the Lumps of Thought. *Linguistics and Philosophy* 12 (1989), 607–53.
6. Facts: Particulars or Information Units? *Linguistics and Philosophy* 25 (2002), 655–70.

Introducing Chapter 1

My goal for *What "Must" and "Can" Must and Can Mean* was to give a truth-conditional account of modals based on a mechanism for drawing conclusions from premises. Premise sets can be inconsistent, so the mechanism I was after had to be able to resolve inconsistencies. I believed then, and still believe now, that the semantics of modals and conditionals offers an ideal window into the way the human mind deals with inconsistencies. There are many areas in human cognition where inconsistencies arise and need to be resolved. Theories of belief revision have attracted most of the attention here, beginning with Veltman (1976) and culminating in the 1980s with Alchourròn, Gärdenfors, and Makinson (1985).[1] As Makinson (2003) explains, he and his co-workers were motivated by David Lewis's work on counterfactuals (Lewis 1973a), but they found possible worlds semantics ontologically unacceptable. My work from the 1970s also took off from Lewis (1973a), but I saw no need to escape from possible worlds. I was interested in the meanings of modals and counterfactuals, and hence in truth-conditional semantics. I was convinced by Lewis's argument that the truth of a counterfactual like (1)

(1)   If I looked into my pocket, I would find a penny.

depends on whether or not there is a penny in my pocket and not whether or not I believe there to be one. Yet there is a close connection between truth-conditional theories of counterfactuals and theories of rational belief change on my account. What I set out to show was that there could be truth-conditional theories of modals and conditionals that are based on the same principles for reasoning from possibly inconsistent premises that are at work in rational belief revision. I believed that such theories could yield analyses of counterfactuals that, as far as their logical properties were concerned, were as good as the similarity based theory of Lewis. This program was shown to be successful in Lewis (1981). As Lewis (1981) concluded, formally, there was nothing to choose.

---

[1] Hansson (2006) has an overview of theories of belief revision, including the possible worlds version of Grove (1988).

My own interests in modals and conditionals have always been primarily empirical. I was looking for the kind of empirical generalizations that have made syntax in the Chomskyan tradition such a rewarding field for linguists. Conflict resolution is a phenomenon that affects many modules of grammar, and it looks like a phenomenon that is amenable to theoretically ambitious empirical inquiry. Gerald Gazdar explored conflicts between presuppositions and implicatures in his (1976) dissertation, published as Gazdar (1979). Sauerland (2004), Fox (2007), and Alonso-Ovalle (2008) posit similar mechanisms for resolving inconsistencies generated during the computation of scalar implicatures. The realization that phonological constraints may be in conflict with each other was the force that created Optimality Theory in the 1990s. Optimality Theory is presented as a theory of conflict resolution in Prince and Smolensky's (1993) manifesto *Optimality Theory* (emphasis mine):

Departing from the usual view, we do not assume that the constraints in a grammar are mutually consistent, each true of the observable surface or of some level of representation. On the contrary: we assert that the constraints operating in a particular language are highly conflicting and make sharply contrary claims about the well-formedness of most representations. The grammar consists of *the constraints together with a general means of resolving their conflicts.* We argue further that this conception is an essential prerequisite for a substantive theory of UG.

Quoted from the ROA version (2002: 2).

Within a premise semantics, modality can be seen as relying on principles of theory construction and mechanisms of conflict resolution that are shared with other cognitive domains. Interestingly, there are also domains where inconsistencies can't seem to be resolved, but lead to breakdown. Abrusán (2007) identifies certain presupposition conflicts that are resistant to resolution and produce a type of deviance that comes across as ungrammaticality. She observes that in those cases, the contradictions are of the kind Gajewski (2002) characterized as L-analytic. L-analyticity singles out the logical vocabulary of a language, and hence leads to a notion of contradiction that is syntactically defined at the level of logical forms, rather than semantically at the level of propositions. Against the background of Gajewski (2002) and Abrusán (2007), we may wonder whether the availability versus unavailability of mechanisms for resolving inconsistencies might be diagnostic of grammatical versus non-grammatical processes in the construction of meaning. The issue is highly relevant for the status of scalar implicatures, which

Gennaro Chierchia has argued to be computed in grammar (Chierchia 2004; also Chierchia, Fox, and Spector, forthcoming). Potential implicatures can conflict with each other, with presuppositions, or with standard at issue meanings. If the computation of scalar implicatures is part of grammar, we might expect to see cases where conflicts triggered by potential implicatures result in ungrammaticality, rather than in the removal of the culprits to restore consistency.

The original version of chapter 1 appeared in 1977 in *Linguistics and Philosophy* 1, 337–55. The article is reproduced here with many stylistic revisions, clarifications, and occasional glimpses into the more recent literature while leaving the original storyline intact. An earlier German predecessor of the 1977 paper was distributed in 1975 as a report of the *Konstanz Sonderforschungsbereich* 99, and another German predecessor appeared in 1976 as an article in *Linguistische Berichte* 42, 128–60.

Chapter 1

What *Must* and *Can* Must and Can Mean*

1.1 *Must* and *can* are relational

Words, phrases, and sentences acquire content when we utter them on particular occasions. What that content is may differ from one context to the next. It is the task of semantics to describe all those features of the meaning of a linguistic expression that stay invariable in whatever context the expression may be used. This invariable element is the meaning proper of an expression. All of this is a simplification, of course, that abstracts away from many complications. Here is one: nobody would claim that a semantic analysis of the words *must* and *can* should try to capture whatever is common to the meanings of the two respective occurrences of these words in (1):

(1) You must and you can store must in a can.

The two occurrences of *must* in (1) are usually not taken to be occurrences of the same word, but are considered accidental homonyms. The must you can store in a can has nothing to do with necessity, and the can you can store your must in has nothing to do with possibility. The word *must* in English has at least two different meanings, then, and the word *can* does, too. So far, we have seen that there is a noun *must* and a modal *must*, and a noun *can* and a modal *can*. I think everyone will accept this. But many scholars have claimed that even if we take just the modals *must* and *can*, they are ambiguous too; there are really many modals *must* and many modals *can*. To justify such claims, sentences like the following four might be offered:

(2) All Maori children *must* learn the names of their ancestors.

(3) The ancestors of the Maoris *must* have arrived from Tahiti.

* I thank John Bigelow, Max Cresswell, Urs Egli, Irene Heim, David Lewis, and Arnim von Stechow for comments on the original paper, and Barry Schein and many generations of students for explicit and implicit hints about how I could have written a better one.

(4)   If you *must* sneeze, at least use your handkerchief.

(5)   When Kahukura-nui died, the people of Kahungunu said: Rakaipaka *must* be our chief.

The *must* in sentence (2) is a deontic *must*: it invokes a duty. The *must* in sentence (3) is an epistemic *must*: it relates to a piece of knowledge or evidence. The kind of *must* in sentence (4) has been called a "dispositio-nal"[2] *must*: it helps us talk about dispositions people have—when they can't help sneezing or must die, for example. The *must* in (5) is sometimes called a "preferential" or "bouletic" *must*: it relates to preferences or wishes. Maybe the classification should be refined. Maybe we should consider other kinds of *must*. How many? Look at the following four fragments of conversation:

You: The Maori children must learn the names of their ancestors.

I: Do they really? Is there a law in New Zealand that provides that the Maori children learn the names of their ancestors?

You: No, of course there is no such law in New Zealand. At least no official law. But the Maoris have their tribal laws, and it was these laws I had in mind when I said that all Maori children must learn the names of their ancestors.

You: The ancestors of the Maoris must have arrived from Tahiti.

I: No, they could have arrived from somewhere else. We know that their technical means permitted them much longer trips. They could have even arrived from Peru.

You: But we know that they did not arrive from Peru. We know it from their tribal history. We know it from Polynesian mythology. We simply know it; they must have arrived from Tahiti.

You: I must sneeze.

I: Don't be silly. You must not. Everyone knows how to prevent sneezing. You feel that something fuzzy is going on in your nose. You feel it a good time in advance. And you can suppress it. That's all.

You: But once I have missed the right moment, I cannot help sneezing any more. It just comes out. It is too late to suppress it. I simply must sneeze.

You: Rakaipaka must be our chief.

I: No, he must not. The Queen does not like him particularly. She does not dislike him particularly, either. He could be our chief, but there are others who could be just as well.

---

[2] See Grabski (1974), for example.

You: I do not care whether the Queen likes Rakaipaka. I only care about our tribe. I only consider what is good for our tribe. That is why Rakaipaka must be our chief.

How many kinds of *must* do we have to distinguish? How many deontic ones? How many epistemic ones? How many dispositional ones? And how many preferential ones? Obviously many in each group. We do not just refer to duties. We refer to duties of different kinds; to different duties different persons have towards different persons at different times. We do not simply refer to a piece of knowledge or information—once and for ever the same. We refer to different kinds of knowledge or information in different situations. We do not simply consider dispositions. Dispositions change. My dispositions now are not the same as my dispositions two minutes ago. We do not always refer to the same wishes or preferences when we use a bouletic *must*. Sometimes it is the wish of the Queen, sometimes it is the wish of our tribe, and sometimes we even consider what we want ourselves. This leaves us with many different *must*s and *can*s. What produces this variety?

If we look at the four different occurrences of the word *must* in sentences (2) to (5), we see that there is something in their meaning that stays invariable. There is a connection between those four occurrences that is much stronger than the connection between any of those occurrences and the word *must* that stands for the must we can store in a can. The connection between the occurrences of *must* in (2) to (5) can be brought out more clearly when we try to paraphrase what might be conveyed by possible utterances of those sentences. Consider the paraphrases (2′) to (5′), for example:

(2′)   In view of what their tribal duties are, the Maori children must learn the names of their ancestors.

(3′)   In view of what is known, the ancestors of the Maoris must have arrived from Tahiti.

(4′)   If—in view of what your dispositions are—you must sneeze, at least use your handkerchief.

(5′)   When Kahukura-nui died, the people of Kahungunu said: in view of what is good for us, Rakaipaka must be our chief.

What happened to the four occurrences of *must* in those paraphrases? In each case a substantial part of the meaning the modal had in the original sentence has been transferred to an *in view of* phrase. The four occurrences of *must* in (2′) to (5′) now all have the same meaning. That meaning seems to be the common core we perceive in each occurrence of *must* in (2) to (5). It is that

common core that stays the same whenever *must* is used. It is therefore that
core that a semantic analysis of *must* should capture. On such an account,
there is only one modal *must*. If we insisted on keeping the many different
musts that are traditionally distinguished we would be forced to accept yet
another *must*: the neutral *must* of (2′) to (5′). (2′) to (5′) are English sentences,
too, and any adequate account of *must* must therefore recognize a neutral
must.

Let us now take a closer look at the semantic core of modals like *must*. That
core seems to be inherently relational. What has emerged in (2′) to (5′) is not
an absolute *must* but a relative *must in view of* that has two arguments: a free
relative, like *what is known* or *what is good for us* etc., and a sentence. Figure 1
is a rough representation of the three crucial components that enter into the
composition of the meaning of (3′).

The neutral *must* in (2′) to (5′) requires two arguments: a modal restriction
and a modal scope. The modal restriction can be provided by a free relative
clause like *what is known*. The modal scope can come from a sentence like *the
ancestors of the Maoris have arrived from Tahiti*. If the neutral *must* in (2′) to
(5′) requires two arguments of a certain kind, the common semantic core of
the four occurrences of *must* in (2) to (5) should require two arguments of
the very same kind. Sentences (2) to (5) only deliver one such argument
explicitly, however. Only the modal scope is overtly represented. The modal
restriction is missing and whatever entity it could have contributed to
semantic composition seems to have been provided by the context of utterance. The impression that the occurrences of *must* in (2) to (5) were deontic,
epistemic, dispositional, and bouletic respectively seems to have been due to
the fact that when I uttered those sentences, a contextually provided modal
restriction merged with the common semantic core whose presence we feel in
all occurrences of *must*. In other words, a particular contextually provided
modal restriction combined with the meaning proper of the modal *must*. It

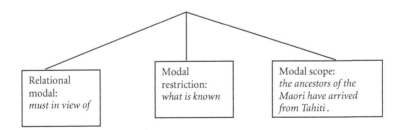

Figure 1

was a fusion of meanings that created the impression that different kinds of *must* were present.

The discussion so far led to the following conclusion: relative modal phrases like *must in view of* and *can in view of* should be considered as representing the semantic core of the modals *must* and *can* respectively. Modals are inherently relational. To be semantically complete, a modal requires two arguments: a restriction and a scope. The restriction may be represented overtly or may be provided by the context of utterance.

The insight that the core of modality is always relative modality is not new.[3] We find the following thoughts in Peirce's Collected Papers, for example:

> ...first let me say that I use the word *information* to mean a state of knowledge, which may range from total ignorance of everything except the meanings of words up to omniscience; and by *informational* I mean relative to such a state of knowledge. Thus by *informationally possible*, I mean possible so far as we, or the person considered know. Then the *informationally possible* is that which in a given information is not perfectly known not to be true. The *informationally necessary* is that which is perfectly known to be true...
>
> The information considered may be our actual information. In that case, we may speak of what is possible, necessary or contingent, *for the present*. Or it may be some hypothetical state of knowledge. Imagining ourselves to be thoroughly acquainted with all the laws of nature and their consequences, but to be ignorant of all particular facts, what we should then not know not to be true is said to be *physically possible*; and the phrase *physically necessary* has an analogous meaning. If we imagine ourselves to know what the resources of men are, but not what their dispositions and desires are, what we do not know will not be done is said to be *practically possible*; and the phrase practically necessary bears an analogous signification. Thus the possible varies its meaning continually.[4]

To limit the scope of this chapter, I will in what follows only consider examples where the modal restriction is overtly represented. In real life, this is very seldom the case, however, even though being aware of a missing modal restriction might help us avoid or settle misunderstandings. Consider, for example, the following case. Many years ago, I attended a lecture in ethics given by a man called "Professor Schielrecht." Professor Schielrecht is a third-generation offspring of the Vienna Circle, so his main concern in philosophy is to show that most of what most people say most of the time does not make sense. Suppose a judge asks himself whether a murderer could have acted

---

[3] Kratzer (1978: part 2, ch. 4) has a detailed discussion of predecessors.

[4] Peirce (1883); quoted from Peirce (1933: 42, 43).

otherwise than he eventually did. Professor Schielrecht claimed that the judge asks himself a question that does not make sense. Why not? Professor Schielrecht's answer was: given the whole situation of the crime, which includes of course all the dispositions of the murderer, this man could not have acted otherwise than he did. If he could have acted otherwise than he eventually did, he would have. So the answer to the question is trivial; there is no need to spend a single second on the problem. There is really no problem. But there IS a problem. The answer to the question of the judge is not trivial. The judge asked himself: could this murderer have acted otherwise than he eventually did? Professor Schielrecht claimed that the judge asked himself whether—given the whole situation of the crime—the murderer could have acted otherwise than he eventually did. The judge did not make explicit the modal restriction for the modal *could* he used. Professor Schielrecht provided the restriction *given the whole situation*, but that restriction trivialized what the judge said. Rather than ridiculing the judge in this way, Professor Schielrecht should have asked him: in view of WHAT could the murderer have acted otherwise than he did? Maybe the judge would not have been able to answer the question. Maybe what he meant was genuinely underdetermined. This made it possible for Schielrecht to fill in an obviously unintended interpretation and thereby submit the judge to ridicule.

Since I will be explicit about modal restrictions in the remainder of this chapter, I will largely abstract away from context-dependency. The context-dependency of modal expressions and the resulting indeterminacy is central to Kratzer (1978), though, and was also the driving force behind my work on conditionals. The topic was taken up again in my 2009 *Context and Content Lectures* (to be published as *Modality in Context* (Kratzer, forthcoming)).

1.2 *Must* and *can* in a premise semantics

This section presents a first analysis of relational modals like *must* and *can* within what Lewis (1981) called a "premise semantics."[5] The meaning of *must* is related to logical consequence: a proposition is necessary with respect to a premise set if it follows from it. The meaning of *can* is related to logical compatibility: a proposition is possible with respect to a premise set if it is

---

[5] The term "premise semantics" is used in Lewis (1981) to refer to the semantics for conditionals presented in Kratzer (1979) and (1981a). Since Kratzer (1979) is just an extension of Kratzer (1977) to conditionals, the term "premise semantics" is applicable to my earliest work on modality as well. My approach to relative modality via premise sets took its direct inspiration from Rescher (1973); see also Rescher (1964). Veltman (1976) developed a formally parallel premise semantics at around the same time, but only considered the special case where premise sets are taken to represent beliefs.

compatible with it. All analyses in this book are cast within a possible worlds framework where possible worlds are assumed to be particulars, as advocated in Lewis (1986), rather than maximal consistent sets of sentences, for example. But the guiding ideas of a premise semantics for modals can be implemented in any framework that provides suitable notions of logical consequence and compatibility. In fact, one of the main virtues of a premise semantics for modality is that it links the semantics of modals to general principles of rational inquiry that apply whenever we reason from a set of premises.

In the possible worlds semantics assumed here, propositions are identified with sets of possible worlds. If W is the set of possible worlds, the set of propositions is $P(W)$—the power set of W. The basic logical notions can now be defined as follows:

DEFINITION 1. A proposition p is true in a world w in W iff $w \in p$.

DEFINITION 2. If A is a set of propositions and p is a proposition, then p follows from A iff $\cap A \subseteq p$, that is, iff there is no possible world where all members of A are true but p is not.

DEFINITION 3. A set of propositions A is consistent iff $\cap A \neq \emptyset$, that is, iff there is a world where all members of A are true.

DEFINITION 4. A proposition p is compatible with a set of propositions A iff $A \cup \{p\}$ is consistent.

With those set-theoretic tools in hand, we can go back to figure 1 in the previous section, and think about the three crucial pieces that enter into the computation of the meaning of a modalized sentence like (3′) above, repeated here as (6):

(6)   In view of what is known, the ancestors of the Maoris must have arrived from Tahiti.

Abstracting away from context dependency, and shamelessly neglecting all matters of tense, the meaning of the modal scope of (6) is the proposition p that is true in exactly those possible worlds where the ancestors of the Maoris have arrived from Tahiti. What is the meaning of the free relative *what is known*, then? What is known may change from one world to the next. If Lord Rutherford had not existed, we would not know many things we do in fact know. If Darwin had never traveled with Captain Fitzroy, our close connection to the great apes might not yet be known. We can imagine worlds where people know more than we do. There are possible worlds where it is known who made the statues on Easter Island, for example. We can conclude, then, that the meaning of a free relative like *what is known* is an individual concept—that is, a function that assigns to every possible world whatever it is that is known in that world. What is it that is known in a world? In our world it is known, for example, that Lord Rutherford was a physicist, that Darwin visited New Zealand, that 1 plus 1 equals 2, and so on. What is known in a possible world is a set of propositions, then, a premise set. Consequently, the meaning of the phrase *what is known* is a function from possible worlds to sets of propositions. To be more specific, it is that function *f* from *W* to $P(P(W))$ (the power set of the power set of *W*) that assigns to every possible world *w* the set of propositions that are known in *w*.

We are now in a position to say what the meaning of the relational modal *must in view of* is. In figure 1, *must in view of* semantically composes with two arguments: the modal scope, which denotes the proposition *p*, and the modal restriction, which denotes the individual concept *f*. The meaning of *must in view of* must then be a function that maps pairs consisting of a proposition and a function of the same type as *f* to another proposition. In the case of (6) that other proposition is the set of possible worlds *w* such that *p* follows from $f(w)$. In other words, the proposition expressed by (6) is true in those worlds *w* such that it follows from what is known in *w* that the ancestors of the Maoris arrived from Tahiti.

If we replace *must* in (6) by *can*, the proposition expressed by the resulting sentence would be true in a world *w* just in case it is compatible with what is known in *w* that the ancestors of the Maori arrived from Tahiti. These considerations lead to the following definitions for the meaning of relational *must* and *can*:

DEFINITION 5. The meaning of *must in view of* is that function v that satisfies the following conditions:

  (i) The domain of v is the set of all pairs $<p, f>$ such that $p \in P(W)$ and f is a function from *W* to $P(P(W))$.
  (ii) For any *p* and *f* such that $<p, f>$ is in the domain of v:

$$v(p, f) = \{w \in W : \cap f(w) \subseteq p\}.$$

DEFINITION 6. The meaning of *can in view of* is that function μ that satisfies the following conditions:

  (i) As in Definition (5).
  (ii) For any *p* and *f* such that $<p, f>$ is in the domain of μ:

$$\mu(p, f) = \{w \in W : \cap(f(w) \cup \{p\}) \neq \varnothing\}.$$

The general idea behind these definitions is simple. The semantics of *must in view of* and *can in view of* is given by means of a function *f* that assigns sets of propositions to every possible world. A proposition is necessary in a possible world *w* in view of *f* if it follows logically from the set of propositions that *f* assigns to *w*. A proposition is possible in a possible world *w* in view of *f* if it is logically compatible with the set of propositions that *f* assigns to *w*. Since the set of propositions a given *f* assigns to a world may vary from one world to the next, there could be worlds *w* and *w'*, such that a proposition *p* follows from *f* (*w*), but not from *f* (*w'*), or is compatible with *f* (*w*), but not with *f* (*w'*). This feature of the analysis has the important consequence that sentences like (2) to (6) can express contingent propositions.

1.3 Inconsistent premise sets

I have given an account of the meaning of relational *must* and *can* in terms of logical consequence and compatibility. In so doing I must be prepared to face all the old paradoxes connected to these notions. For example, *ex falso quodlibet* rules that any proposition whatsoever follows from an inconsistent set of propositions. This section argues that we need not, and should not, accept this paradox. We have clear intuitions about what does or does not follow from an inconsistent set of propositions, and we also have the technical tools to model those intuitions in a precise way.[6]

Imagine a country where the only source of law is the judgments that are handed down. There are no hierarchies of judges, and all judgments have equal weight. There are no majorities to be considered. It does not matter whether a judgment has a hundred judgments against it—a judgment does not have less importance for all that. Let New Zealand be such a country. Imagine that there is one judgment in New Zealand legal history that provides that murder is a crime. Never in the whole history of the country has anyone dared to attack that judgment. No judgment in the whole history of New Zealand has ever suggested that murder is not a crime. There are other judgments, however. There were judges who did not agree on certain matters and handed down judgments that were in conflict with each other. Here is an example of such a disagreement. In Wellington a judgment was handed down that ruled that deer are not personally responsible for damage

---

[6] The method for making the best out of an inconsistent set advocated here was inspired by the account of relative modalities in Rescher (1973), but is different in a number of respects. On the analysis proposed here, *must* and *can* are duals, sentences with modals can be contingent, and the definitions do not assume compactness for premise sets. See Kratzer (1978) for more discussion.

they inflict on young trees. In Auckland a judgment was handed down that ruled that deer ARE personally responsible for damage they inflict on young trees. As a consequence, the set of propositions picked out by the phrase *what the New Zealand judgments provide* in the actual world is inconsistent.

The situation I have just presented is not unusual. It may happen every day that two judges disagree. But the meaning definitions for relational *must* and *can* that I proposed earlier cannot cope with such a situation. According to those definitions, the propositions expressed by sentences (7) and (8) below should be true on the scenario I designed (I put *must be that* in place of *must* so as to get the scope of the negation right in (8)):

(7)   In view of what the New Zealand judgments provide, murder must be a crime.

(8)   In view of what the New Zealand judgments provide, it must be that murder is not a crime.

That (7) should come out true on our scenario is right. But that both (7) and (8) should wind up true is very wrong. Unfortunately, we are committed to this consequence if we accept the definitions I gave for *must*. Since the set of propositions that correspond to the New Zealand judgments in our world is inconsistent, both the proposition that murder is a crime and the proposition that murder is not a crime follow from that set. Although no New Zealand judgment has ever questioned that murder is a crime, our semantic analysis forces us to accept that murder must be a crime and not a crime in view of New Zealand common law.

The situation is no better when we consider the personal responsibility of deer. Since the set of propositions that correspond to the set of judgments in New Zealand history is inconsistent on our story, no proposition can be compatible with it. As a consequence, the propositions expressed by (9) and (10) are both predicted to be false (I am using *it is possible* to fill in for *can* to get the scope of negation right in (10)).

(9)   In view of what the New Zealand judgments provide, it is possible that deer are personally responsible for damage they inflict on young trees.

(10)   In view of what the New Zealand judgments provide, it is possible that deer are not personally responsible for damage they inflict on young trees.

We have run into an odd situation. Our semantic analysis forces us to conclude that, given our scenario, murder must be both a crime and not a crime in view of New Zealand common law. And it tells us moreover that both a ruling in favor of deer responsibility and a ruling against it would go against the law. Maybe the oddest aspect of our current analysis is that a single disagreement is enough to get us into such trouble.

To clear our path towards a possible way out of the dilemma we ran into, let us simplify our scenario a bit further. Suppose that the whole content of New Zealand common law—that is, the collective content of all the judgments that have been handed down in New Zealand legal history—is the set of propositions expressed by (11) to (13):

(11)   Murder is a crime.

(12)   Deer are personally responsible for damage they inflict on young trees.

(13)   Deer are not personally responsible for damage they inflict on young trees.

In a situation like this, an adequate analysis of modals should predict that the proposition expressed by (7) is true, and that expressed by (8) is false. Likewise, the proposition expressed by (14) should come out false:

(14)   In view of what the New Zealand judgments provide, it is possible that murder is not a crime.

As for the personal responsibility of deer, there is a judgment that says that deer are personally responsible for damage they inflict on young trees, and there is another judgment that says they are not. These are two incompatible opinions, and we should be free to go along with either one. That is, we would want the propositions expressed by (9) and (10) to both come out true on our scenario. Since intuitions about the truth of sentences (7) to (10) and (14) on our scenario are completely clear and uncontroversial, we have to aim for an analysis of modals that captures those intuitions. This means that we have to give up our earlier proposal for *must* and *can*.

Some abbreviations will be useful for the considerations that follow. Let A be the set of propositions provided by the New Zealand judgments in our world. In our simplified example, this set has just three members: p (the proposition expressed by (11)), q (the proposition expressed by (12)), and $\neg q$ (the proposition expressed by (13)). The reason why Definition (5) did not yield the right result was because it was based on a relation between a premise set and a proposition that was simply logical consequence. Since A is inconsistent, the relation specified in Definition (5) holds between A and any proposition whatsoever. In particular, it holds between A and p and A and $\neg p$. What we are looking for is a meaning definition for *must* that is based on a more discriminating relation. That relation should hold between A and p, but not between A and $\neg p$. One method of coming to terms with the inconsistency of A would look at the set of all consistent subsets of A. Let X be that set. We have then:

$$A - \{p, q, \neg q\}$$
$$X = \{\varnothing, \{p\}, \{q\}, \{\neg q\}, \{p, q\}, \{p, \neg q\}\}$$

Maybe the relation we are looking for could be one that holds between a proposition and A just in case the proposition follows from every set in X. To be sure, $\neg p$ does not follow from every set in X. It does not follow from the set that contains q as its only member, for example. But, unfortunately, p does not follow from every set in X, either. This shows that the relation we have just came up with is too strict. Here is another attempt. Suppose the relation we are after holds between A and a proposition just in case for every set in X there is a superset in X from which that proposition follows. This relation seems to do the job we want it to do. For every set in X, there is a superset in X from which p follows. But not for every set in X is there a superset in X from which $\neg p$ follows. To see this, consider $\{p, q\}$. Since $\{p, q\}$ is consistent, it is a member of X. But there is no superset of $\{p, q\}$ in X from which $\neg p$ follows. This is a promising result. We seem to have found a method that allows us to draw conclusions from an inconsistent set of propositions while staying as close as possible to the information it contained. In the hope that the method generalizes to the full range of more complicated examples, I want to propose the following revised meaning definition for relational *must*:

DEFINITION 7. The meaning of *must in view of* is that function v that satisfies the following conditions:

   (i) As in Definition (5).
   (ii) For any p and f such that $<p, f>$ is in the domain of v:

$$v(p, f) = \{w \in W: \forall A[A \in X_{f(w)} \rightarrow \exists B[B \in X_{f(w)} \ \& \ A \subseteq B \ \& \ \cap B \subseteq p]]\},$$
$$\text{where } X_{f(w)} = \{A: A \subseteq f(w) \ \& \ \text{consistent } (A)\}.$$

Similar considerations lead to an improvement of Definition (6). Definition (6) was inadequate because it required logical compatibility between a premise set and a proposition. Since A is inconsistent, the required relation does not hold between A and any proposition. What we are looking for is a relation that holds between A and q and A and $\neg q$, in our example, but not between A and $\neg p$. If X is again the set of all consistent subsets of A, we should say that the relation we are after holds between A and any proposition just in case the proposition is compatible with some set and all of its super-sets in *X*. In our case, we can easily find a set in *X* such that *q* is compatible with all of its supersets in *X*. The singleton set {*q*} is such a set. Since *q* is in *A* and {*q*} is consistent, {*q*} is a member of *X*, and obviously, *q* is compatible with every superset of {*q*} in *X*. Likewise, there is a set in *X* such that ¬*q* is compatible with all its supersets in *X*. The singleton set {¬*q*} is such a set. What about ¬*p*? The proposition ¬*p* is consistent, but it is not in *A*, and therefore not a member of any set in *X*. As a matter of fact, ¬*p* is compatible with both {*q*} and {¬*q*}, but each of those two sets has a superset in *X* that implies *p*, and hence is no longer compatible with ¬*p*: the two relevant sets are {*q*, *p*} and {¬*q*, *p*}. Hoping again that the idea we developed on the basis of a simple example generalizes to more complicated cases, I would like to propose the revised meaning definition 8.

DEFINITION 8. The meaning of *can in view of* is that function μ that satisfies the following conditions:

(i) As in Definition (5).
(ii) For any *p* and *f* such that <*p*, *f*> is in the domain of μ:
$$\mu(p,f) = \{w \in W : \exists A[A \in X_{f(w)} \ \& \ \forall B[\ [B \in X_{f(w)} \ \& \ A \subseteq B] \rightarrow$$
$$\text{consistent}(B \cup \{p\})] \ ]\}, \text{where } X_{f(w)} = \{A : A \subseteq f(w)$$
$$\& \text{ consistent}(A)\}.$$

1.4 Structuring premise sets

Our hopes that the semantics of relational *must* and *can* proposed in the previous section might be general enough to cope with the problem of making the best out of inconsistent sets of propositions seem to vanish under the impact of the following example.[7]

The story of Te Miti and Te Kini

The pupils of a Whare Wananga, which was a kind of University in Maori Society, have to be educated according to the recommendations of the former principals of the school. As is to be expected, those principals had different opinions about what is good for a student to learn. There was, for example, Te Miti, who recommended that students practice striding and flying. And there was Te Kini's recommendation, which didn't allow students to practice

---

[7] I am indebted to Irene Heim (personal communication) for raising a related objection against the analysis of modals presented in section 1.3.

striding under any circumstances. In Te Kini's opinion, the practice of striding overstrained the students' legs. He had no objections to the practice of flying.

If the two recommendations mentioned in our story were the only ones those two principals gave during the relevant time period, sentences (15) and (16) can be taken to express the complete content of Te Miti's and Te Kini's respective recommendations.

(15)   The pupils practice striding and flying.

(16)   The students do not practice striding.

If p is the proposition that the students practice striding, and q is the proposition that the students practice flying, the proposition expressed by (15) seems to be $p \cap q$, and the proposition expressed by (16) is $\neg p$. Assuming furthermore that Te Miti and Te Kini were the only principals our Whare Wananga has ever had, we would now want the propositions expressed by (17) to come out true:

(17)   In view of what the former principals of the Whare Wananga recommended, the students must practice flying.

Does our current analysis of *must* match our intuitions about the truth of (17) on our scenario? It seems that it does not. Let A be the set of propositions that form the content of the recommendations of the two former principals. On our scenario, A contains only two members: $p \cap q$ and $\neg p$. The set X of all consistent subsets of A is then:

$$X = \{\emptyset, \{p \cap q\}, \{\neg p\}\,\}$$

Not every set in X has a superset in X from which q follows. The set $\{\neg p\}$ does not, and this means that our analysis of *must* seems to predict (17) to be false on the assumed scenario. We have run into a problem. To escape from it we may try to improve our definitions, or else check our intuitions again. The definitions do not match our intuitions. Either the definitions are wrong or our intuitions are misguided. I opt for looking into the second possibility and propose to re-examine the reasoning that led to the impression that our analysis has a problem in the first place.

Te Miti recommended that students practice striding and flying. Te Kini recommended that students do not practice striding under any circumstances. In such a situation, I argued, we certainly wanted to preserve Te Miti's recommendation about the students' flying. This recommendation was obviously not contradicted by what Te Kini recommended. "Certainly," I just said, and "obviously," but I think we cannot be certain about this at all, and our claim is far from being obvious. Look at the following elaboration of our original scenario.

Te Miti's recommendation fleshed out

Suppose, as we did before, that Te Miti recommended that students practice both striding and flying. But he really wanted them to do both together. Here are his reasons: striding stretches the legs and flying stretches the arms. If you do both, that's a good combination. But if you practice striding without flying, or flying without striding, the proportions of your body become distorted. Your legs get stretched and your arms remain short, or else your arms get stretched and your legs are left behind. Neither is good. Practicing both sports together leads to a good shape for your body.

If the motivation just mentioned was behind Te Miti's recommendation, Te Kini's view that striding is bad under any circumstances challenges Te Miti's recommendation as a whole, not just the part about striding. If the students do not stride any more, Te Miti would not want them to practice flying either. Representing Te Miti's recommendation as a single proposition $p \cap q$ correctly captures the intent behind his recommendation. Our analysis handles this case correctly, then: it does not preserve the students' flying. If striding needs to be given up, flying must be too.

There are subtly different scenarios, however, where we would want to say that Te Kini's recommendation does not contradict Te Miti's recommendation as a whole, but only the part about striding. These would be scenarios where what Te Miti recommended is naturally individuated as two recommendations. He recommended that students stride and also recommended that students fly. He thought that each of those activities was also beneficial on its own. In such cases, we may interpret Te Miti as not recommending the single proposition $p \cap q$, but the pair of propositions $\{p, q\}$. This makes all the difference on our account. If one of Te Miti's recommendations is challenged, we would still want to keep the other one. Our analysis of *must* matches this intuition as well. If the set of propositions that correspond to the content of what the former principals of our Whare Wananga recommended is $A = \{p, q, \neg p\}$, then the set X of all consistent subsets of A looks as follows:

$$X = \{\emptyset, \{p\}, \{q\}, \{\neg p\}, \{p, q\}, \{q, \neg p\}\}$$

For every set in X there is now a superset in X from which q follows. Our analysis of *must* is correct after all, then, once we acknowledge the difference between giving a single conjoined recommendation and giving a pair of recommendations. There is a subtle, but momentous, distinction here that is all too easy to overlook. Sentence (18) is ambiguous, then.

(18)   Te Miti recommended that students practice striding and flying.

The phenomenon we discovered is expected to be very general and should be found with any speech act or attitude whose content can plausibly be thought of as a premise set. For example, if Te Miti believes about a particular student that he practiced striding and flying, what he believes about that student can be individuated as one or two (or more) beliefs. The difference matters when Te Miti's beliefs are challenged. Suppose Te Kini pointed out to Te Miti that the student in question did not actually practice striding. If Te Miti had just a single belief about that student's athletic activities, Te Kini's objection would challenge the whole of what Te Miti believed on that matter. On the other hand, if there were two or more relevant beliefs, Te Kini's objection would only affect part of what his colleague believed.

We have just seen an example of two consistent premise sets that are true in the same set of possible worlds, and hence have the same "deductive closures," but behave differently when consistency needs to be restored after one of the premises has been challenged. That is, even though $\bigcap\{p, q\} = \bigcap\{p \cap q\}$ for any propositions p and q, the premise sets $\{p, q\}$ and $\{p \cap q\}$ might have to be distinguished in the theory of modality. This is an important property of premise sets that has recently been exploited for theories of rational belief change (see e.g. Rott 2001). To have another, even more striking, illustration of the same phenomenon, imagine a situation where the content of a given belief state might be represented as one of the two premise sets $\{p, q\}$ or $\{p, p \leftrightarrow q\}$.[8] Even though $\bigcap\{p, q\} = \bigcap\{p, p \leftrightarrow q\}$, the two sets behave differently in situations where p has to be given up and is replaced by $\neg p$. Rational restoration of consistency yields different results for the two sets. In the first case, we give up p, retain q, and add $\neg p$, and hence end up with $\{\neg p, q\}$. In the second case, we give up p, add $\neg p$, and retain $p \leftrightarrow q$. The result is the set $\{\neg p, p \leftrightarrow q\}$, which implies $\neg q$. Representing the content of recommendations, claims, beliefs, orders, wishes, etc. as premise sets thus offers the priceless opportunity to represent connections between propositions in a given premise set. The content of such speech acts and attitudes can

---

[8] S. O. Hansson (2006) presents such an example. I have been using $\neg$ to stand for set complementation, and I am using $p \leftrightarrow q$ as an abbreviation for $(\neg p \cup q) \cap (\neg q \cup p)$.

now be seen to have an inherent structure that encodes which propositions stand and fall together under challenge. This structure is lost if information contents are directly represented as sets of possible worlds, as is common in possible worlds semantics, following the lead of Hintikka (1962).

In conclusion, I have argued for a unified analysis of modals like *must* and *can* where the observed variety of uses is due to their relational nature. Modals require two arguments to be complete: a proposition (their scope) and a function from worlds to premise sets (their restriction). Such functions are often called "conversational backgrounds." That the premise sets provided by a modal restriction depend on worlds makes sure that modal statements can be contingent. A proposition is necessary or possible if it bears a particular relation to the relevant premise set in the world of evaluation. Since premise sets are not always consistent, the relation between a proposition and a premise set cannot simply be logical consequence or compatibility. We had to design a method that allowed us to model robust intuitions about reasoning from inconsistent sets. This method turned out to be sensitive to subtle potential differences between deductively equivalent premise sets. To quote Rescher (1979: 31), who talks about premise sets that are sets of sentences, not propositions, there is a crucial difference between "juxtaposing commas" and "conjoining ampersands." Much of my work on modals and conditionals since 1977 has exploited that difference. The difference between {p, q} and {p∩q} is not just senseless "notional bondage" (Belnap 1979: 23). It makes all the difference in the theory of modality. "If they are separate items juxtaposed by a comma, the fates of *p* and *q* are independent of one another, unless there is additional information to the contrary...; if they are conjoined by an ampersand, they stand and fall together" (Rott 2001: 81).

INTRODUCING CHAPTER 2

The original version of *The Notional Category of Modality* is 30 years old. I gave it a thorough makeover for this collection, but left the original storyline intact. Among all the papers collected in this book, *The Notional Category of Modality* is the one that had the most impact on subsequent work in the semantics of modality and has triggered the most responses. This made it very difficult for me to update the old manuscript without dramatic changes. I decided to be responsive to at least some recent developments that go to the very core of the semantics of modals and thus present potential challenges for the analysis put forward in the original paper.

One of the conclusions of *What "Must" and "Can" Must and Can Mean* that was carried over to *The Notional Category of Modality* was that the interpretation of modals is relative to a conversational background that might be made explicit by adverbial phrases of various kinds. What I overlooked in the earlier work was that there are important differences between different adverbial phrases contributing conversational backgrounds for different types of modals. This is illustrated by the difference between the English sentence (1a) versus the German sentence (1b):

(1) a. Given the article in the Hampshire Gazette, Mary Clare Higgins must have been re-elected.

   b. Dem Artikel in der Hampshire Gazette nach, soll   Mary Clare
      The article in the Hampshire Gazette after modal Mary Clare

      Higgins wiedergewählt worden sein.
      Higgins re-elected   been   be.
      'According to the article in the Hampshire Gazette, Mary Clare Higgins was reportedly re-elected.'

An assertion of (1a) would commit me to the truth of what the article says, and continuing with (2) would be infelicitous:

(2) ...but I wouldn't be surprised if she wasn't. The Gazette is usually too quick to draw conclusions from projected election results.

In contrast, an assertion of (1b) would not commit me to the truth of the report in the Gazette, and I could continue with (2) without contradicting myself. The difference between (1a) and (1b) points to two different ways of interpreting modals in the "epistemic" or "evidential" family. In (1b), the accessible worlds are worlds that are compatible with the content of the report. The accessible worlds for (1a) are worlds with certain kinds of counterparts of the article in the Hampshire Gazette. The counterparts should have the same content as the original article and relate to reality in the same way. If the actual article was based on unreliable election projections, for example, so were all of its counterparts in the accessible worlds. The accessible worlds are also worlds that, by and large, function normally from the point of view of the actual world. For example, just as in the actual world, reports based on unreliable election projections might or might not be true. With accessibility relations of this kind, then, the truth of (1a) depends on how good the evidence for the Hampshire Gazette report actually was. If the evidence was shaky, Mary Clare Higgins became mayor in some, but not all of the accessible worlds. Only flawless evidence guarantees her being elected in all accessible worlds. As a consequence, I shouldn't assert (1a) unless I believed the evidence for the Gazette report to be highly reliable.

(1a) and (1b) show that modals in the epistemic/evidential family can have two types of interpretations: "strong" interpretations, which—at least with necessity modals—commit the speaker to the truth of the proposition the modal scopes over (von Fintel and Gillies 2010), and "weak" interpretations, which are relativized to the content of some source of information that may or may not be faithful to reality. Those two types of interpretations have figured prominently in the recent literature on the connection between epistemic modals and evidentials (Izvorski 1997; Faller 2002; Matthewson et al. 2007; Rullmann et al. 2008). For example, Rullmann et al. (2008) construe the modal alternatives for the St'át'imcets reportative modal *ku7* as the set of worlds where a relevant report was made, rather than the set of worlds where the content of such a report is true.[1] The result is a "given the report," rather than an "according to the report," interpretation, and *ku7* comes out as a "strong" epistemic modal that doesn't allow the speaker to distance herself from the content of the report. St'át'imcets *ku7* thus contrasts with the German reportative modal *sollen* illustrated in (1b), which relies on alternatives where the content of the relevant report is true, and hence is "weak."

Cross-linguistically, the invariant job of an evidential is to classify evidence for what is being said as direct, indirect, or hearsay (Willett 1988; de Haan

---

[1] Page 350, definition 82.

1999; Garrett 2001; Faller 2002; Aikhenvald 2004; Speas 2008; Murray 2010). Direct evidence may come from direct perception or first-person experiences, like skin itching or headaches. Indirect evidence may come from reports, or inferences drawn from direct or indirect evidence. Rumors or legends may be classified as hearsay. The cross-linguistically invariant job of an epistemic modal is not to classify evidence, but to assess the truth of a proposition against a range of possibilities projected from a body of evidence. There are two distinct semantic jobs to be done, then: classify evidence versus assess the truth of a proposition against possibilities projected from a body of evidence. The two jobs often end up being carried by a single portmanteau item that might then be arbitrarily cataloged as modal or evidential. That evidential meaning components are in principle independent of modal meaning components, but can be bundled together with other meaning components in a single lexical item, was emphasized in Izvorski (1997). Izvorski points out that with finite verbs in the present tense, the Turkish perfect morpheme *mış* is interpreted as an indirect evidential. In non-finite environments and with future or past tense, *mış* only has a perfect, non-evidential, meaning. The evidential meaning component can't be contributed by *mış* itself, then, but seems to be a separate component spelled out in a portmanteau with the present tense. In Quechua and Korean, too, evidential meaning components can be attached to items that are commonly categorized as tenses (Faller 2004; Chung 2005, 2007; Lee 2009).

As a number of authors have pointed out, the English epistemic modal *must* also has evidential characteristics (Westmoreland 1998; Drubig 2001; von Fintel and Gillies 2010). Epistemic *must* excludes direct perceptual or irreducibly first-person evidence, for example, as illustrated by (3) and (4):

(3)   a.   # Your nose must be dripping. I can see it.
        b.   You must have a cold. Your nose is dripping.

(4)   a.   # I must have a terrible headache. I feel lousy.
        b.   The baby must have a terrible headache. He is screaming and pressing his hands against his temples.

English spells out evidential, modal, and temporal meaning components together as the single lexical item *must*, resulting in what we call a "present tense epistemic modal."

Natural languages show a grammatically significant split between so-called "root" and "epistemic" modals. Syntactically, root modals appear in low positions in the line-up of verbal inflectional heads; epistemic modals appear in high positions. Semantically, root and epistemic modals differ with respect to the kinds of facts they depend on. The nature of that difference was a puzzle raised, but essentially left unsolved, in the original *The Notional Category of Modality*. I now believe that the impasse the older paper ran into was due to the erroneous assumption that the two types of modals semantically select modal bases with distinctive semantic properties: circumstantial backgrounds for root modals and epistemic backgrounds for epistemic modals. It now seems to me a hopeless enterprise to try to characterize formal objects like conversational backgrounds as "circumstantial" versus "epistemic." Both types of backgrounds are functions that map possible worlds to sets of factual premises. What is it that would allow us to single out some of those functions as epistemic, but not circumstantial, or the other way round? There don't seem to be any characteristic properties that could produce such a distinction (see Nauze (2008) for an insightful objection along those lines). We need to tell a different story about the source of the differences between root and epistemic modals. Hacquard (2006, 2010) has told such a story.

According to Hacquard, modal bases are projected from event arguments following very general recipes. Different types of possibilities become available in different places of the verbal projection spine because different types of event arguments appear in those places. The lower regions of the verbal projection spine provide access to the participants and spatio-temporal locations of the events described. According to Hacquard, the higher regions provide access to speakers' knowledge via a representation of the speech situation. Hacquard's work presents a major breakthrough in the theory of natural language modality. Her proposal does not only explain the existence of a surprising split between root and epistemic modals in the languages of the world. It also tells us how modal base dependencies might be represented in grammar: possibly only indirectly, via event arguments providing "anchors" from which modal bases can be projected. Hacquard's general vision can be fruitfully supplemented with insights from Hackl (1998), who shows that there is also syntactic variation within the class of root modals. Root modals, according to Hackl, may project control or raising structures, and may be anchored to entities of various types that are represented in the modals' specifier position, possibly as a result of overt or covert movement. Modal anchors do not necessarily have to be events, then, but can be entities of diverse types, including individuals and their stages, spatio-temporal locations, or situations—whatever entities might be represented in a modal's domain in the verbal projection spine.

The original version of *The Notional Category of Modality* accounted for graded and comparative notions of possibility by using ordering sources to induce orderings on the set of accessible worlds and the set of propositions, but didn't make any explicit connections with quantitative notions of probability or desirability. This shortcoming is repaired in the current version, which shows how quantitative notions of probability and desirability can emerge from comparative notions in a natural way: we need to look for suitable probability or desirability measures that preserve suitable relations of comparative possibility that an ordering semantics for modals provides. We may not necessarily find any such measures, but if we do, there are typically many that are potential candidates. This is as it should be, and no reason for concern. Our semantic knowledge alone does not give us the precise quantitative notions of probability and desirability that mathematicians and scientists work with. It seems to provide no more than conceptual launch pads for mathematical explorations to take off from. In fact, as Yalcin (2010) reminds us, Charles Hamblin (1959) thought that natural languages might not truly go beyond merely comparative notions of probability:

Metrical probability-theory is well-established, scientifically important and, in essentials, beyond logical reproof. But when, for example, we say "It's probably going to rain", or "I shall probably be in the library this afternoon", are we, even vaguely, using the metrical probability concept?[2]

In modal logic, modal operators come in duals. But even languages like English or German have modals without duals. The possibility of modals without duals was invoked by Robert Stalnaker (1981) for counterfactual *would*, and by Veronika Ehrich (2001) for the German weak necessity modal *sollen* ('be supposed to'). The issue rose to prominence when Hotze Rullmann, Lisa Matthewson, and Henry Davis (2008) reported that the Salish language St'át'imcets lacks dual modals altogether. The current version of *The Notional Category of Modality* suggests that at least some modals without duals might be neither possibility nor necessity modals, but degree expressions describing a high degree of desirability or probability.

At the time the first version of *The Notional Category of Modality* was written, the goal of compositionally interpreting hierarchical line-ups of inflectional heads was not yet commonly recognized. The theoretical landscape has changed dramatically in this respect. The place of modals in the verbal projection spine and their interactions with neighboring inflectional heads related to voice, aspect, tense, and mood is now much better understood

---

[2] Hamblin (1959: 234).

through the work of Virginia Brennan (1993), Roumyana Izvorski (1997), Paul Portner (1998, 1999, 2003, 2009), Martin Hackl (1998), Rajesh Bhatt (1999 [2006]), Sabine Iatridou (2000), Veronika Ehrich (2001), Cleo Condoravdi (2002), Michela Ippolito (2002), Jonny Butler (2004), Tom Werner (2003), Timothy Stowell (2004), Ana Arregui (2005, 2007, 2009, 2010), Maria Bittner (2005, forthcoming), Cleo Condoravdi and Stefan Kaufmann (2005), Stefan Kaufmann (2005), Valentine Hacquard (2006, 2009, 2010), Kai von Fintel and Sabine Iatridou (2007, 2008), Lisa Matthewson et al. (2007), Hotze Rullmann et al. (2008), Katrin Schulz (2008), Elisabeth Villalta (2008), Henry Davis et al. (2009), Rebecca Cover (2010), Amy Rose Deal (2010a), Dorit Abusch (forthcoming), Aynat Rubinstein (forthcoming), among many others. I could not implement a truly compositional perspective in the new *Notional Category of Modality* without turning it into a book-sized manuscript. The hope is that whatever we may learn about modality all by itself may ultimately be of help when figuring out interactions with other inflectional heads.

Apart from a few stylistic changes, the sections on practical reasoning and conditionals of the original *The Notional Category of Modality* have been left intact, even though the discussion of conditionals is shorter and more condensed than it should be. Chronologically, it was preceded by Kratzer (1978), my dissertation, and by Kratzer (1979). To avoid too much overlap with later papers that share the same general approach to conditionals, but are more interesting from a modern point of view, I did not include Kratzer (1979) or passages from Kratzer (1978) in the present collection. Instead, I expanded and updated the (1986) paper *Conditionals,* which is based on a Chicago Linguistic Society paper and came out of the first seminar I taught on my older work on modals and conditionals after moving to the United States in 1985. The new version of *Conditionals* appears here as chapter 4.

There are three earlier published versions of *The Notional Category of Modality.* The first one appeared in H. J. Eikmeyer and H. Rieser (eds.), *Words, Worlds, and Contexts,* Berlin and New York: de Gruyter (1981), 38–74. The paper was reprinted unchanged in P. Portner & B. Partee (eds.), *Formal Semantics: The Essential Readings,* Oxford: Blackwell (2002), 289–323, and then again in Javier Gutierrez-Rexach (ed.), *Semantics: Critical Concepts,* London: Routledge (2003), vol. iv, 365–403.

Chapter 2

The Notional Category of Modality

It would be considered naïve today to attempt, as did Wegener (1885), to describe the semiotic stratification of human language with examples restricted to German, Greek and Latin. But it is remarkable how well Wegener's theory stands up now that the range of our evidence has been vastly broadened. It takes only a slightly more flexible calculus, I believe, to accommodate all the varieties of semiotic structure evident in ordinary discourse.

Uriel Weinreich

2.1 Introduction

This chapter explores the notional category of modality as reflected in the modal vocabulary of German.[3] The main danger for anyone working on modals is to get utterly lost in the variety of interpretations one and the same expression can receive in different contexts. As a result, we may be tempted to develop sophisticated classifications and study the characteristics of major types of modals including ability, epistemic, or deontic uses. I am not really interested in such classifications. My main concern is to find answers to questions like the following:

- What is the logical nature of modal interpretations?
- What is their variability due to?
- How is the variability of modal interpretations restricted by the vocabulary of a language?
- How do graded and comparative notions of modality come about?
- How do graded and comparative notions of modality relate to quantitative notions of probability and desirability?
- What is the connection between modals and conditionals?

---

[3] Many of the German examples in this article are directly inspired by, or adapted from, sentences and stories in Oskar Maria Graf's *Das Leben meiner Mutter* (*The Life of my Mother*, Graf 1946).

Traditionally, investigations of modality have focused on expressions like *necessarily, possibly, must, can, should,* or *may.* Little attention has been paid to the fact that natural languages have ways of grading and comparing possibilities and the path that leads from graded and comparative notions of possibility to the related quantitative notions of probability and desirability. Furthermore, conditionals are usually not considered in connection with modality. Yet, *if*-clauses often serve to restrict modals explicitly or implicitly (Kratzer 1978, 1979). In what follows, I will present a unified analysis of graded and non-graded varieties of modality that not only accounts for the variability and indeterminacy of modals, but also sheds light on the equally mystifying variability and indeterminacy of conditionals: since *if*-clauses often restrict modals, and since those modals are often unpronounced, complex modalized conditionals may be mistaken for simple conditionals consisting of just a binary connective joining two clauses. The variability and indeterminacy of modals and the variability and indeterminacy of conditionals have a common source. Once this possibility is recognized, insights gained in separate examinations of modals and conditionals fall out as special cases from a general theory of restricted modality.

2.2 Expressing modality in German

Modality has to do with necessity and possibility. In German, as in other languages, modal notions can be expressed in many ways.

Inherent modality

(1)   Niemand läuft in zehn Minuten von   Andechs nach Aufhausen.
       Nobody   runs in ten   minutes from Andechs to   Aufhausen.

(2)   Dieses Auto fährt zwanzig Meilen pro Stunde.
       This   car goes twenty   miles per hour.

(1) and (2) have modalized readings that can be paraphrased as in (1′) and (2′):

(1′)   Nobody is able to run from Andechs to Aufhausen in ten minutes.

(2′)   This car can go twenty miles an hour.

Suffixes on adjectives

German has two suffixes with modal meanings: *-lich* and *-bar*. Here are a few examples, some of which are borrowed from Paul (1920):

-lich

erblich	hereditary
umgänglich	sociable
zugänglich	accessible, approachable
käuflich	purchasable
zerbrechlich	fragile
sterblich	mortal
unsterblich	immortal
vergesslich	forgetful
untröstlich	inconsolable

-bar

zahlbar	payable
unfehlbar	infallible
brauchbar	useful, practicable
brennbar	combustible, inflammable
dehnbar	stretchable
denkbar	conceivable
essbar	eatable, edible
tragbar	portable, wearable
waschbar	washable

In general, the suffixes *-lich* and *-bar* express possibility. There are apparent exceptions like *zahlbar*:

(3)   Die Miete für das Haus auf dem Leoni-Acker beträgt
      The rent   for the house on the   Leoni-Field   amounts to

      zwanzig Gulden, zahlbar am ersten   Januar.
      twenty   guilders, payable on the first of January.

According to (3), it's not that the twenty guilders *can* be paid, they defini-
tively *have to* be paid on the first of January.

Modal auxiliaries

must	muss	müsste
can	kann	könnte
may	darf	dürfte
shall	soll	sollte
will	wird	würde
may	mag	möchte

The exact meaning of some of these auxiliaries will be discussed in more detail as we go along. *Müsste, könnte, dürfte, sollte, würde, and möchte* are subjunctive forms of the corresponding verb on their left. They often have an independent, non-compositional, meaning, though.

Sentence adverbs and impersonal constructions

möglicherweise	possibly
notwendigerweise	necessarily
wahrscheinlich	probably
es ist möglich dass	it is possible that
es ist notwendig dass	it is necessary that
es ist wahrscheinlich dass	it is probable that

Adjectival phrases

imstande sein	to be able
in der Lage sein	to be in the position

The selection of modal expressions in this section makes clear that there is no syntactic category corresponding to the notional category of modality. What, then, is modality?

2.3 Basic notions

The following story highlights the core ingredients of the notional category of modality.

The murder

Much-Girgl has been murdered on his way home. There is an ongoing investigation. Conclusions about the circumstances of the crime are being drawn from the available evidence, and utterances of the following sentences might have occurred:

(4)   Der Kastenjakl kann der Mörder   sein.
      The Kastenjakl can   the murderer be.
      Kastenjakl may be the murderer.

(5)   Der Gauzner-Michl muss der Mörder   sein.
      The Gauzner-Michl must the murderer be.
      Gauzner-Michl must be the murderer.

In uttering (4), a police inspector may have claimed that given the available evidence, it is possible that Kastenjakl committed the murder. More evidence might have become available at a later point, and the same inspector might then have been in a position to assert (5), expressing the opinion that the available evidence warranted the conclusion that Gauzner-Michl was indeed the murderer. The example shows that there are at least two ingredients involved in the interpretation of modals like *kann* or *muss*: a *conversational background* contributing the premises from which conclusions are drawn, and a modal relation determining the *force* of the conclusion. In his second utterance, the inspector drew a stronger conclusion than in his first. To make all of this more precise, I have to review a few notions from possible worlds semantics.

When Lenz says

(6) Bis jetzt   hab' ich dir genug   Bier weggesoffen.
    Up to now have I   you enough beer boozed away.

to the owner of Fink's pub, he expressed a proposition. Possible worlds semantics identifies propositions with subsets of a given universe of possible worlds W. Here are some standard definitions:

Definitions of the basic logical properties and relations

A proposition p is *true* in a world $w \in W$ iff $w \in p$. A proposition p *follows* from a set of propositions A iff $p \subseteq \cap A$. A set of propositions A is *consistent* iff $\cap A \neq \emptyset$. Finally, a proposition p is *compatible with* a set of propositions A iff $A \cup \{p\}$ is consistent.

In the imagined context for (6), the proposition expressed by Lenz's utterance is the set of possible worlds where Lenz has drunk enough of Fink's beer up to the day of his utterance. The meaning of a sentence is described by specifying which proposition(s) it expresses depending on relevant features of the utterance situation.

As in chapter 1, I take conversational backgrounds to be functions mapping possible worlds to premise sets—that is, sets of propositions. In a first approximation, modals express relations between conversational backgrounds and propositions. The most familiar modal relations are what we may call "simple" necessity and possibility. If f is a conversational background, a proposition is a *simple f-necessity* in a world w iff it follows from $f(w)$; it is a *simple f-possibility* iff it is compatible with $f(w)$.

The meanings of individual modals need to be linked to the right modal notions. For *necessarily*, for example, the link could be established as follows:[4]

---

[4] Strictly speaking, rules like this would have to apply at a level of Logical Form, where all modal operators are propositional operators.

Necessarily

Suppose *u* is an utterance of a sentence of the form *necessarily* α such that the proposition *p* is expressed by α. Then

(i) *u* expresses a proposition only if there is a unique conversational background for *u*

(ii) if *u* expresses a proposition and *f* is the conversational background for *u*, then the proposition expressed is $\{w \in W: p$ is a simple f-necessity in $w\}$.

We may wonder why there should be a unique conversational background for a modalized sentence to express a proposition. This seems too strong. More often than not, conversational backgrounds for modals remain genuinely underdetermined and what speakers intend to convey is compatible with several choices of conversational backgrounds. In those cases, we might want to say that there are several propositions expressed—one relative to each background. It would then be part of the vagueness of modal expressions that, sometimes, it remains genuinely underdetermined which proposition was expressed (Lewis (1979a) and Pinkal (1977, 1979) have relevant proposals; now also von Fintel and Gillies (forthcoming)). There might also be problems if a sentence contains more than one modal, each requiring a conversational background of its own. To account for this, we would have to split up utterance situations further and consider separate utterances for each modal. The issue will be set aside here—in Kratzer (1978) I made an attempt to spell out the details of such an approach.

As is, the proposed analysis of modals allows for one modal parameter to be fixed by the context of use. It implies that that parameter is responsible for the variety of interpretations modals can receive. In the murder example, a conversational background representing a piece of evidence created an epistemic interpretation of the modals in question. For further reference, I want to draw attention to a few kinds of conversational backgrounds that play a distinguished role in the semantics of modal constructions.

a. Realistic conversational backgrounds

A realistic conversational background is a function *f* such that for any world *w*, $w \in \cap f(w)$. That is, *f* assigns to every possible world a set of propositions that are true in it.

b. Totally realistic conversational backgrounds

A totally realistic conversational background is a function *f* such that for any $w \in W$, $\cap f(w) = \{w\}$. That is, *f* assigns to any world a set of propositions that characterizes it uniquely. For each world, there are many ways of characterizing it uniquely. This is a major source of vagueness for counterfactuals, as argued in Kratzer (1981a; also section 2.9 below and chapter 3).

c. The empty conversational background

The empty conversational background is the function f such that for any w $\in W$, $f(w) = \emptyset$. Since $\cap f(w) = W$ if $f(w) = \emptyset$, empty conversational backgrounds are also realistic.

Realistic backgrounds for modals in natural languages all seem to track particular bodies of facts in the world of evaluation: that is, we invariably have functions f such that for each world w in the domain of f there is a particular body of facts in w that has a counterpart in each world in $\cap f(w)$. For so-called "root modality," the targeted facts relate to inherent properties or circumstances of individuals or spatio-temporal locations. It is those properties and circumstances that are "kept constant" in all accessible worlds. For so-called "epistemic modals" the targeted facts might correspond to what Hacking (1975) calls "evidence of things." Hacking illustrates this notion with an example by J. L. Austin, where pig-like marks in the ground, buckets of pig food, noises, and smell are taken to be evidence for the presence of pigs. Evidence of things consists of things in the world, including olfactory and auditory objects, which, according to Hacking, "are not private experiences, but rackets and stenches as public as pigsties."[5] However, private experiences should be able to function as evidence of things, too: experiences of seeing, hearing, or smelling—even experiences of illusions and hallucinations—can be actual events. Whatever exists in a world, including individuals, eventualities, and the world itself, should in principle qualify as potential evidence of things of that world.

Modals can also rely on backgrounds that are not realistic. They can depend on *informational backgrounds*, for example. Informational backgrounds represent the intentional content of sources of information.

d. Informational conversational backgrounds

An informational conversational background is a function f such that for any w in the domain of f, $f(w)$ represents the propositional content of some source of information in w.

Possible sources of information are things with intentional content: words, stories, books, reports, maps, testimony, perceptual experiences, and what have you. Sources of information have a double nature. They can function as

---

[5] Hacking (1975: 32).

evidence of things for realistic backgrounds, or as sources of intentional content for informational backgrounds. To illustrate, if a testimony is the salient body of facts that a realistic background is about, the accessible worlds are those that have counterparts of that testimony. The actual existence of the testimony makes it a body of facts, and thus evidence of things, even if it is packed with lies. If that same testimony is the salient source of information feeding an informational background, the accessible worlds are those that are compatible with the intentional content of the testimony.

The distinction between realistic backgrounds representing evidence of things and informational backgrounds representing information content plays an important role for so-called "evidentials" in natural languages. For example, the German reportative evidential *sollen* depends on informational conversational backgrounds: it reports the content of hearsay. In contrast, according to the characterization of Rullmann et al. (2008), the reportative evidential *ku7* of the Salish language St'át'imcets seems to depend on realistic backgrounds.[6] They give the example in (7):

(7)   *Context: There is a rumor going around that Roger was elected chief. Sometimes that kind of rumor is right, sometimes it's wrong. You really have no idea whether it's likely to be right or wrong. You tell me:*

    % aw-an-ém   **ku7**   kw s-Roger   ku cuz' kúkwpi7
    choose-DIR-PASS **REPORT** DET NOM-Roger DET going.to chief
    'Roger was reportedly elected to be chief.'
    Rullmann et al. (2008: example 79, 349)

Rullmann et al. report that judgments for (7) are variable and seem to depend on whether speakers think the rumor could be true. This would be unexpected if (7) just reported the content of the rumor, which is made clear in the example. What kinds of claims do sentences like (7) make, then? Contrasting the English example (8a) with the German example (8b) may point to a possible answer: they bring out the subtle difference between realistic

---

[6] Once we make a distinction between modal bases and ordering sources, as proposed in 2.4, informational conversational backgrounds should be ordering sources, rather than modal bases, since they do not necessarily represent consistent information. If epistemic modals always have realistic modal bases and empty modal bases are special cases of realistic ones, German reportative *sollen* should have a realistic modal base and an informational ordering source. In contrast, St'át'imcets *ku7* would have a realistic modal base representing a salient piece of information functioning as evidence of things and an empty or stereotypical ordering source. As suggested in the original version of this chapter, we should also not exclude the possibility that the meanings of certain types of modals may have to be characterized by more than a single ordering source. Normalcy assumptions, for example, seem to play a role for informational modals, too.

backgrounds representing evidence of things and informational conversational backgrounds representing information content:

(8) a. Given the rumor, Roger must have been elected chief.

     b. Dem Gerücht nach, soll   Roger zum Häuptling gewählt
       The rumor   after, MODAL Roger to-the chief   elected
      worden sein.
      been   be.
      'According to the rumor, Roger was reportedly elected chief.'

(8b) merely reports what the rumor says and allows the speaker to distance herself from it. (8a) suggests that the speaker considers the rumor a reliable source of information. This means that for (8a), the rumor is seen as feeding a realistic conversational background representing available evidence, not an informational one representing the content of the rumor. The claim is that in all relevant worlds that have a counterpart of that rumor, a counterpart of Roger was elected chief. In evaluating (8a) we seem to assume that the relevant worlds are worlds where the counterparts of the actual rumor not only say the same thing as the actual rumor does, but also were produced in the same way. Let me illustrate.[7] Suppose the rumor is a plain lie in the actual world. Its counterparts in the relevant accessible worlds should then be plain lies, too, and (8a) should wind up false. (8b) could still be true, as long as the rumor says that Roger was elected chief. Suppose now that the rumor happened to be true, but was based on shaky evidence, as rumors often are. Maybe your neighbor, who started the rumor, saw a banner with the words "Congratulations Roger," not knowing that it was for Roger's 70th birthday. The counterparts of such a rumor in the relevant accessible worlds would come into existence in the same way as the actual rumor in the actual world, with (a counterpart of) your neighbor spotting (a counterpart of) that sign and concluding that (a counterpart of) Roger was elected chief. The accessible worlds will differ in countless ways, but, most importantly for us here, they will differ as to whether or not Roger's counterparts did become chiefs. In some of the accessible worlds they did, in others not: shaky evidence might or might not produce a true rumor. (8a) winds up false, then. If the actual rumor is from a 100% reliable source, its counterparts in the relevant accessible worlds are, too, and (8a) is true.

Perceptual experiences, too, can feed both realistic and informational backgrounds. If the backgrounds are realistic, the accessible worlds all contain counterparts of the actual experience that come into existence in the

---

[7] I am indebted to Seth Cable for his discussion of the analysis of evidentials in Rullmann et al. in his Fall 2008 UMass Amherst seminar.

same way and have the same content as the actual experience:[8] if the actual experience was an illusion or hallucination, so are all of its counterparts. On the other hand, if perceptual experiences feed informational backgrounds, the accessible worlds are worlds that conform to the information content of the experience. For instance, if I hallucinate unicorns that are approaching, the informationally accessible worlds determined by my hallucination are all worlds that have unicorns that are approaching.

If sources of information function as evidence of things feeding a realistic background, their counterparts in the relevant accessible worlds have to satisfy certain conditions, as we have seen: they have to carry the same information as the actual piece of information, and they have to come into existence in the same way. When sources of information function as evidence of things, their status as evidence is a highly relevant property and should thus play an important role in the choice of counterparts. Take Sewall's *Life of Emily Dickinson*, for example. If the corresponding accessible worlds were simply required to contain, say, duplicates of actual copies of Sewall's book, there would be some accessible worlds where the book is a piece of fiction, rather than a biography. If the book functions as evidence of things, the fact that it is a biography is essential, and hence should be preserved by all relevant counterparts. Moreover, if Sewall's book was based on authentic or forged letters, its counterparts should be based on counterparts of those letters, which would have to be authentic or forged just in case the corresponding actual letters were. All those properties of the actual book are essential for its status as evidence of things, hence need to be preserved by all relevant counterparts.

Informational backgrounds are not the only backgrounds that are not necessarily realistic. Other not necessarily realistic backgrounds may relate to norms of various kinds, and among those, backgrounds representing the normal course of events in the world of evaluation play a privileged role:

---

[8] Lewis (1996) uses modal alternatives of this kind for his analysis of knowledge. "When perceptual experience E (or memory) eliminates a possibility W, that is not because the propositional content of the experience conflicts with W. (Not even if it is the narrow content.) The propositional content of our experience could, after all, be false. Rather, it is the existence of the experience that conflicts with W: W is a possibility in which the subject is not having experience E. Else we would need to tell some fishy story of how the experience has some sort of infallible, ineffable, purely phenomenal propositional content … Who needs that? Let E have propositional content P. Suppose even—something I take to be an open question—that E is, in some sense, fully characterized by P. Then I say that E eliminates W iff W is a possibility in which the subject's experience or memory has content different from P. I do not say that E eliminates W iff W is a possibility in which P is false" Lewis (1996: 553).

e. Stereotypical conversational backgrounds

A stereotypical conversational background is a function f such that for any world w, $f(w)$ represents what is normal in w according to some suitable normalcy standard for w.[9]

What is to count as normal? Definition (e) is deliberately vague and non-committal about what suitable standards of normalcy are and where they may come from. A simple illustration will have to do for now: in the world we live in, people normally die if they are exposed to certain amounts of arsenic. We might want stereotypical conversational backgrounds to represent this kind of normalcy. An example could be some background f such that $f(w_0)$ is consistent and all $w \in \cap f(w_0)$ are worlds where everyone dies who takes the critical amount of arsenic. Since there are a few actual people who have managed to build up tolerance for arsenic, the actual world w_0 itself is not a member of $\cap f(w_0)$, and f is not realistic. A person like Urquhart, who was able to consume large amounts of arsenic and survive in comfort, is not normal. That made him a very unlikely suspect in the murder case of Philip Boyes.[10]

Other instances of normative, and thus potentially non-realistic, conversational backgrounds are *deontic*, *teleological*, and *bouletic* conversational backgrounds:

f. Deontic conversational backgrounds

A deontic conversational background is a function f such that for any world w, $f(w)$ represents the content of a body of laws or regulations in w.

Teleological conversational backgrounds are related to goals and *bouletic conversational backgrounds* have to do with wishes.

It may now be tempting to try to characterize the semantic field of modal expressions along two axes: one specifying a modal relation (the modal force), and the other one specifying restrictions for admissible conversational

---

[9] There is a legitimate question whether the best way to represent normalcy is via premise sets, rather than relying on basic, irreducible, relations that order worlds according to how normal they are from the point of view of a designated world. There is a related question about similarity: should similarity relations between worlds be induced via premise sets, or should they be basic and irreducible? The first question is raised in Yalcin (2010) and is still wide open. Counterfactuals have been a testing ground for the second question and answers have begun to emerge. Are empirical constraints on counterfactual reasoning best stated as constraints on premise sets or as constraints on orderings among worlds? It seems that, within a premise semantics, we can realistically aim for a theory that does not only cover the truth-conditions of counterfactuals, but also the process of drawing conclusions from inconsistent premises more generally, e.g. in completely unrelated areas like the computation of implicatures or the balancing of conflicting constraints in phonology.

[10] Dorothy Sayers: *Strong Poison.*

backgrounds. The following sections will show that this view is too simple. Realistic and normative conversational backgrounds need to be kept separate. They play distinct roles in generating the full range of possible modal meanings in natural languages. The most important argument in favor of such a separation is the fact that natural languages can express graded and comparative notions of possibility. Graded and comparative notions of possibility emerge when we rank worlds that are compatible with a body of facts according to how close they come to some norm or ideal. The gradability of modal notions is not only reflected in a range of different degree constructions that modal auxiliaries and adjectives participate in (2.4). It may also produce certain types of modals without duals (2.5).

2.4 Grades of possibility

Instead of sentences (4) or (5), the police inspector from the previous section might have uttered one of the following sentences:

(9)   Es **kann gut** sein, dass der Gauzner-Michl der Mörder   war.
      It can   well be   that the Gauzner-Michl the murderer was.
      There is a good possibility that Gauzner-Michl was the murderer.

(10)   Es besteht aber immer noch eine **geringe Möglichkeit**, dass der
       There is however still   a   slight   possibility   that the
       Kastenjakl der Mörder war.
       Kastenjakl the murderer was.
       There is, however, still a slight possibility that Kastenjakl was the murderer.

(11)   Der Gauzner-Michl **kann eher**   der Mörder sein als der Kastenjakl.
       The Gauzner-Michl can   rather the murderer be than the Kastenjakl.
       Gauzner-Michl is more likely to be the murderer than Kastenjakl.

(12)   Es ist **wahrscheinlich**, dass der Gauzner-Michl der Mörder war.
       It is   probable   that the Gauzner-Michl the murderer was.
       It is probable that Gauzner-Michl was the murderer.

The police inspector does not know what the real world is like. But he can draw conclusions from the growing evidence available to him. At any given time, this evidence partitions the set of worlds W into two subsets separating those worlds that are compatible with that evidence from those that are not. In the light of our earlier discussion, we know that compatibility with evidence can be understood in one of two ways. If the evidence has propositional content, compatibility is logical compatibility with that content. With "evidence of things," compatibility amounts to co-existence with a counterpart of that evidence. Be this as it may, among the worlds that are compatible with the evidence in our case (in one sense or the other), some are more far-fetched than others. A world where Kastenjakl is the murderer is more far-fetched than one where Gauzner-Michl killed Girgl. Gauzner-Michl couldn't stand Girgl, but Kastenjakl got along very well with him. Even more far-fetched are worlds where someone from the other end of the world committed the crime. Far-fetched with respect to what? With respect to what is the case in the real world? No! Something that was almost impossible might very well turn out to be the case. This is precisely what happens in good detective stories. The most unlikely candidate turns out to be the murderer. What is far-fetched about someone from the other end of the world having killed Girgl is that such things do not correspond to the normal course of events. Normally, you don't meet people from the Antipodes in Girgl's village. And should someone show up who does not actually live in the neighborhood, he wouldn't just go and kill Girgl. Normally, people need a motive for killing someone. It couldn't have been for money, since Girgl wasn't robbed: all his money was found on him. Considering the normal course of events, it is far-fetched that someone from the other end of the world killed Girgl. And considering the normal course of events it is more far-fetched for Kastenjakl to be the murderer than for Gauzner-Michl.

In our example, let's assume that we have a realistic conversational background that determines the set of accessible worlds by tracking the actually available evidence in closely related worlds. It forms the *modal base*. There is a second, stereotypical, conversational background involved in the police inspector's uses of modals in (7) to (10). Stereotypical conversational backgrounds can be used to rank worlds according to how close they come to the normal course of events in the world of evaluation, given a suitable normalcy standard. In that case, they function as *ordering sources*.[11] Quite generally, a set of propositions A can induce an ordering $\leq_A$ on W in the following way:[12]

Inducing the ordering $\leq_A$

For all worlds w and $z \in W$: $w \leq_A z$ iff $\{p: p \in A$ and $z \in p\} \subseteq \{p: p \in A$ and $w \in p\}$.

According to this definition, a world w is at least as close to an ideal or norm determined by a set of propositions A as a world z iff all propositions of A

---

[11] The term is inspired by what Raynaud (1974) calls "source" in French.
[12] The idea comes from David Lewis's work on ordering semantics; personal communication. Lewis's work on ordering semantics has since been published as Lewis (1981).

that are true in z are true in w as well. The relation $\leq_A$ is reflexive and transitive, but not necessarily connected. Technically, $\leq_A$ is a partial preorder, then. It is *partial* because worlds don't have to be comparable, and it is a *preorder* because it is not necessarily antisymmetric. The related relation $<_A$ is defined in the usual way: $w <_A z$ iff $w \leq_A z$, but not $z \leq_A w$. We can now define some additional modal relations that depend on a world w, a modal base f, and an ordering source g:

Necessity

A proposition p is a *necessity* in w with respect to f and g iff for all $u \in \cap f(w)$, there is a $v \in \cap f(w)$ such that

(i) $v \leq_{g(w)} u$

and

(ii)   for all $z \in \cap f(w)$: *if* $z \leq_{g(w)} v$, *then* $z \in p$.

Simplifying slightly, a proposition is a necessity just in case it is true in all accessible worlds that come closest to the ideal determined by the ordering source. Since the definition is neutral with respect to the so-called "Limit Assumption" (Lewis 1973) and thus does not presuppose that there are closest worlds, the definition of necessity is more complicated than might seem necessary. It is modeled after a definition David Lewis gives for counterfactuals.[13] Possibility is the dual of necessity:

Possibility

A proposition is a *possibility* in w with respect to f and g iff its negation (that is, its complement) is not a necessity in w with respect to f and g.

The new notion of necessity is weaker than the earlier notion of simple necessity. A necessary proposition is no longer required to be true in all accessible worlds. It is now sufficient for it to be true in the closest accessible worlds. On the other hand, the new notion of possibility is stronger than our earlier notion of simple possibility. For a proposition to be possible it is now no longer sufficient for it to be true in just some possible world.

Having ordered sets of accessible worlds makes it possible to define various notions of comparative possibility for propositions. There are many candidates and finding definitions that are right for different types of modals is not at all straightforward.[14] Notions of comparative possibility relating to probability

[13] Lewis, personal communication; now Lewis (1981). See also Burgess (1981).
[14] Halpern (1997, 2003) and Yalcin (2010) have extensive discussion; see also Lassiter (2010). However, the critical assessments in Yalcin (2010) and Lassiter (2010) are not yet sufficiently respon-

are unlikely to be the same as notions of comparative possibility relating to desirability, for example. In the way of illustration, let us look at a notion of comparative possibility that establishes a connection to a plausible quantitative notion of probability, as we will see shortly: when comparing two propositions p and q, we disregard the worlds p and q have in common and compare $p - q$ and $q - p$ by checking whether there is any world in $q - p$ that is higher ranked than every world in $p - q$. If not, p is at least as good a possibility as q. If q logically implies p, $q - p = \emptyset$ and p is automatically at least as good a possibility as q. More formally:

Comparative possibility (one option among many that should be considered)

A proposition p is *at least as good a possibility as* a proposition q in w with respect to f and g iff

$$\neg\exists u(u \in \cap f(w) \ \& \ u \in q\text{-}p \ \& \ \forall v((v \in \cap f(w) \ \& \ v \in p\text{-}q) \to u <_{g(w)} v))$$

A proposition p is a *better possibility* than a proposition q in w with respect to f and g iff p is at least as good a possibility as q with respect to f and g, but the reverse does not hold.

The relation "is at least as good a possibility as" considered in the original 1981 version of this chapter was based on a different intuition: for p to be at least as good a possibility as q, it was required that for every world where q is true, there be a world where p is true that comes at least as close to the ideal provided by the ordering source. This definition has consequences that might be unwelcome for certain applications.[15] Suppose, for example, that there is a world w that is better than any other world. We would now predict that all propositions containing w are equally good possibilities. W and $\{w\}$ should be equipossible, then. The old definition may still do well in certain cases where the propositions to be compared can be assumed to be mutually disjoint, as is common in moral reasoning. We are assuming disjoint alternatives, for example, when we say that praying and doing good is better than *just* praying. The new definition is not without problems either. It might not deliver the desired result if the ordering of worlds allows ties or is not connected. Suppose three worlds w_1, w_2, and w_3 are all equally close to the ideal established by the ordering source. Then our (new) definition classifies $\{w_1\}$ and $\{w_2, w_3\}$ as equipossible, for example, which might or might not be a

---

sive to the important fact that we are very likely to need different notions of comparative possibility to account for different types of comparative modal operators in natural languages.

[15] See the critical and insightful discussion in Yalcin (2010).

welcome consequence. Or suppose that there is even a single world in q - p that is not connected to any world in p - q. In that case, there cannot be a world in p - q that is better than every world in q - p, and, consequently, p can never be a better possibility than q according to our definition. There may be good reasons, then, to carefully watch the kind of orderings among worlds that we may want to admit for modal expressions, a topic addressed for counterfactuals in Lewis (1981). The question of which notions of comparative possibility provide the best match with natural language expressions relating to comparative modal notions related to probability and preference is still open and in need of clarification.[16]

Portner (2009) observes that modal auxiliaries and adjectives like *possible* are not gradable in English. This is a language-specific fact, however. Modal auxiliaries and the counterpart of *possible* are gradable in German and other languages. German productively uses the adverb *eher* ('earlier') in comparative constructions with both the modal auxiliary *kann* ('can'; see examples (11) above and (58) below) and the modal adjective *möglich* ('possible'). There is also a corresponding superlative form *am ehesten*. Moreover, modal adjectives like *useful, stretchable, fragile, inflammable, soluble, prone to, able, capable,* etc. are all gradable even in English, and this means that any semantics for modals must in principle allow for graded notions of possibility.

A second issue raised by Portner (2009) is how notions of comparative possibility might relate to quantitative notions of probability. From the current perspective, we would want to understand under what conditions quantitative notions of probability can emerge from orderings induced by ordering sources. The project would be to try to find suitable probability measures that preserve suitable comparative possibility relations. Here is a toy example illustrating how the (new) notion of comparative possibility defined above might be linked to a plausible probability measure.

Suppose $\cap f(w_0) = W = \{w_0, w_1, w_2, w_3\}$ and $g(w_0) = A = \{ \{w_3\}, \{w_2, w_3\}, \{w_1, w_2, w_3\} \}$. The ordering $\leq_A$ induced on W is connected and has no ties, and we have: $w_3 <_A w_2 <_A w_1 <_A w_0$. We can now define a plausible probability measure P on the set of propositions $\wp(W)$ as follows:

$P(\emptyset) = 0$	$P(\{w_2\}) = 4/15$	$P(\{w_3\}) = 8/15$	$P(\{w_2, w_3\}) = 12/15$
$P(\{w_0\}) = 1/15$	$P(\{w_0, w_2\}) = 5/15$	$P(\{w_0, w_3\}) = 9/15$	$P(\{w_0, w_2, w_3\}) = 13/15$
$P(\{w_1\}) = 2/15$	$P(\{w_1, w_2\}) = 6/15$	$P(\{w_1, w_3\}) = 10/15$	$P(\{w_1, w_2, w_3\}) = 14/15$
$P(\{w_0, w_1\}) = 3/15$	$P(\{w_0, w_1, w_2\})$ $= 7/15$	$P(\{w_0, w_1, w_3\})$ $= 11/15$	$P(\{w_0, w_1, w_2, w_3\})$ $= 15/15$

---

[16] I am grateful to Aynat Rubinstein for discussion of those issues.

P is one of many probability measures that preserve the relation "is a better possibility than" defined above and satisfy the standard conditions on probability measures: *P* assigns a number between 0 and 1 to every proposition in $\wp(W)$, it assigns 1 to *W*, and for any disjoint propositions $p, q \in \wp(W)$, $P(p \cup q) = P(p) + P(q)$. Using the table above, the reader can verify that for all $p, q \in \wp(W)$, *p* is a better possibility than *q* iff $P(p) > P(q)$.

To turn our toy example into a more realistic example, we could think of the four worlds w_0, w_1, w_2, w_3 as representatives of suitably chosen equivalence classes. Suppose the possible suspects in Girgl's murder case are Michl, Jakl, Hansl, and Seppl. The set of possible worlds that are compatible with our evidence can then be partitioned according to which one of the four men killed Girgl. If the question "who did it?" is the only issue we are interested in, all other differences between accessible worlds can be neglected, and we end up with a four-cell partition of the set of accessible worlds. Suppose furthermore that, given certain normalcy standards, Michl is the most likely murderer, Jakl is next, Hansl is third, and Seppl is last. To find a plausible probability measure in this case, we can pick one representative from each of the four cells in the partition of accessible worlds and proceed as illustrated above: w_3 could represent the worlds where Michl murdered Girgl, w_2 could stand for the Jakl-worlds, w_1 for the Hansl-worlds, and w_0 for the Seppl-worlds. The probabilities that *P* above assigns to the singletons $\{w_0\}$, $\{w_1\}$, $\{w_2\}$, and $\{w_3\}$ could now be taken to correspond to the probabilities of the four respective cells in the partition of accessible worlds.

This section showed how a separation of realistic and normative backgrounds can in principle lead to plausible comparative and quantitative notions of possibility, probability, and preference. We saw that comparative notions of possibility might provide conceptual jump-off points for the development of corresponding quantitative notions by experts able to push beyond the limits of what the faculty of language provides for everyone.

2.5 Modals without duals

According to the definition in the previous section, the orderings premise sets induce on sets of possible worlds are allowed to be partial and to have ties. Worlds can come equally close to the ideal or norm represented by the ordering source, and they are not even required to be comparable at all. Do modals ever truly care about such properties of orderings? Are there any modals that do not tolerate incomparabilities or ties for the orderings they rely on, for example? These are momentous questions, because disallowing both incomparabilities and ties might mean loss of the distinction between necessity and possibility as we have defined it. If we add the Limit Assumption, which many authors accept, the distinction between necessity and possibility collapses. The toy example from the previous section is a good illustration: all propositions with a probability of 8/15 or higher wind up as both possible and necessary; all propositions with a probability of 7/15 or lower come out as neither possible nor necessary. There is no longer a distinction between what is possible and what is necessary, then. Stalnaker (1981) argues that English counterfactual *would* is a collapsed possibility/ necessity modal in this sense: contrary to appearance, *might* is not the dual of counterfactual *would* for Stalnaker—*would* has no dual. For Stalnaker, a conditional is true in a world w just in case its consequent is true in the closest world to w where its antecedent is true. The assumption is that there is just one such closest world, and this leaves no room for distinguishing counterfactual necessity and possibility.

Both Stalnaker (1981) and Lewis (1981) emphasize that, at least for counterfactuals, the difference between systems that allow orderings with incomparabilities and ties versus those that do not is not as dramatic as it may seem. An order that has incomparabilities or ties can be matched with a multiplicity of orders that disagree precisely in how they resolve those incomparabilities or break those ties. It would then be part of the notorious context dependency of counterfactuals that there might be unresolved indeterminacy about which ordering was intended.

To see what indeterminacy of orderings might mean for the typology of modals more generally, let's construct another toy example. As before, assume that $\cap f(w_0) = W = \{w_0, w_1, w_2, w_3\}$, but we are now comparing a single ordering O_3, which has a tie, with a pair of orderings O_1 and O_2, which resolve the tie of O_3 in opposite ways:

Option 1: indeterminacy between two orders without ties:

O_1: $w_3 < w_2 < w_1 < w_0$

O_2: $w_2 < w_3 < w_1 < w_0$

Option 2: order with a tie:

O_3: $w_2, w_3 < w_1 < w_0$

Assuming O_3, the following propositions wind up as necessary according to our definition: $\{w_0, w_1, w_2, w_3\}$, $\{w_1, w_2, w_3\}$, $\{w_0, w_2, w_3\}$, and $\{w_2, w_3\}$. Those are also the propositions that are necessary with respect to *both* O_1 and O_2— that is, those are precisely the propositions that wind up as necessary, regardless of how we resolve the indeterminacy between O_1 and O_2.

The situation is different for possibility, however. For possibility, option 1 and option 2 truly come apart. On option 1, the necessary propositions are the same as the possible ones. Consequently, the propositions that are necessary regardless of how the indeterminacy between O_1 and O_2 is resolved are precisely the propositions that are possible regardless of how the indeterminacy is resolved. Option 2 presents a rather different picture. According to our definitions, the following propositions come out as *merely* possible: $\{w_0, w_1, w_3\}, \{w_1, w_3\}, \{w_0, w_3\}, \{w_3\}, \{w_0, w_1, w_2\}, \{w_1, w_2\}, \{w_0, w_2\}, \{w_2\}$. Only on option 2 can we draw a distinction between necessary and possible propositions, then. The two notions collapse into each other on option 1. Crucially, this is so even on a super valuation approach, where modal claims are true just in case they wind up true no matter how ordering indeterminacies are resolved.[17] Whether we can or cannot have the familiar dual pairs of modals in a language crucially depends on the orderings the modals tolerate, then.

Rullmann, Matthewson, and Davis (2008) document that not every language draws a lexical distinction between possibility and necessity modals of the kind found in the familiar Indo-European languages. From the current perspective, this could mean that some languages might generally disallow incomparabilities or ties for their ordering source induced orderings. It would then be literally impossible for those languages to have the familiar dual necessity and possibility modals. But there are other possibilities that need to be considered for modals without duals.

In an ordering semantics for modals, ordering sources are used as domain restrictions for the set of accessible worlds: not all, but only the "closest" accessible worlds matter for what is possible or necessary. As the domain of accessible worlds shrinks, necessity modals become weaker and possibility modals become stronger. In the most extreme case, the distinction between necessity and possibility collapses. In less extreme cases, necessity and possibility may still be formally distinguishable, but a language may nevertheless choose not to lexicalize dual pairs of modals in some or all modal domains. The retained modals might all be possibility modals, for example. Being weaker than the corresponding necessity modals, possibility modals could be used to describe situations where English might use *must* or *may*. Peterson (2008) proposes that the modals in the Tsimshianic language Gitksan (spoken in North-Western British Columbia) are possibility modals of precisely this kind. Deal (2010b) makes a similar point for the modal suffix *o'qa* in Nez Perce.

---

[17] Stalnaker (1981) made this point for counterfactuals.

Rather than being just a possibility modal or a collapsed possibility/ necessity modal, a modal without dual could also be a degree expression covering the upper end of a scale of degrees of probabilities or preferences. Such upper-end degree modals could correspond to notions like, "it is (somewhat) probable," or, "it is (somewhat) desirable." We would then expect there to be a certain amount of vagueness with respect to the lower bound of the range of probabilities allowed. For epistemic degree modals admissible probabilities might range from, say, around 50% to 100%, for example.[18]

Here is a toy example illustrating what an upper-end degree modal may do. As before, suppose $\cap f(w_0) = W = \{w_0, w_1, w_2, w_3\}$, but this time round, $g(w_0) = A = \{ \{w_2, w_3\}, \{w_1, w_2, w_3\} \}$. The ordering $\leq_A$ induced on W is O_3 from option 2 above: $w_2, w_3 < w_1 < w_0$. There is a tie between w_2 and w_3, then, which has the consequence that the distinction between necessity and possibility does no longer collapse. Below is a table displaying a probability measure P on $\wp(W)$ that assigns probabilities to the singleton sets in a way that respects O_3. However, since there are ties, P no longer preserves the O_3-induced notion of comparative possibility between propositions defined above.

$P(\varnothing) = 0$	$P(\{w_2\}) = 4/11$	$P(\{w_3\}) = 4/11$	$P(\{w_2, w_3\}) = 8/11$
$P(\{w_0\}) = 1/11$	$P(\{w_0, w_2\}) = 5/11$	$P(\{w_0, w_3\}) = 5/11$	$P(\{w_0, w_2, w_3\}) = 9/11$
$P(\{w_1\}) = 2/11$	$P(\{w_1, w_2\}) = 6/11$	$P(\{w_1, w_3\}) = 6/11$	$P(\{w_1, w_2, w_3\}) = 10/11$
$P(\{w_0, w_1\}) = 3/11$	$P(\{w_0, w_1, w_2\})$ $= 7/11$	$P(\{w_0, w_1, w_3\})$ $= 7/11$	$P(\{w_0, w_1, w_2, w_3\})$ $= 11/11$

As before, P is just one of many probability measures satisfying our current, rather weak, requirements on suitable probability measures. In this example, the necessary propositions are all those that contain both w_2 and w_3. Those are the propositions whose probability is at least 8/11. The possible propositions are all those that contain w_2 or w_3. Those are the propositions whose probability is at least 4/11. An upper-end degree modal might cover a probability range from, say, 5/11 or 6/11 to 11/11. Such a modal could thus be

---

[18] The official weather forecast for Bergen (Norway) extends *somewhat probable* even further: "Within these fields, it is considered most probable (50 percent) that the development hits the dark part. Still it is somewhat probable (30 percent) that it hits the lighter part outside the dark." <http://www.yr.no/place/Norway/Hordaland/Bergen/Bergen/long.html>. A systematic investigation of the probability ranges people attach to expressions of uncertainty in English is Mosteller and Youtz (1990). They report, for example, that the unmodified adjective *probable* tends to be associated with a probability range of about 60 to 80 percent.

used in situations where English would sometimes use *must*, and at other times *may* or *might*. Marginally, such a modal might even be used with two propositions that are negations of each other. In the way of illustration, consider the propositions $p = \{w_0, w_3\}$ and $\neg p = \{w_1, w_2\}$ from our toy example. The probability of both propositions is around 50%: $P(p) = 5/11$ and $P(\neg p) = 6/11$. Marginally, they could both be said to be somewhat probable, then.

The data and observations presented in Rullmann et al. (2008) invite the conjecture that in the modal system of the Salish language St'át'imcets, upper-end degree modals with the force of (*somewhat*) *probable* or (*somewhat*) *desirable* might take the place of necessity and possibility modals. The St'át'imcets modal system lacks a lexical distinction between necessity and possibility modals. The distinction is not only missing for epistemic modals, but for all modals, including deontic, irrealis, and future modals.[19] Here are some of Rullmann et al.'s examples with the inferential epistemic modal *k'a*:

(13)   *apparently / it seems:* **k'a**
     Wa7 **k'a** qwenúxw.
     'He must be sick.' or *'I guess that he is sick.'*
     Rullmann et al., example (4): 320.[20]

(14)   a. t'ak   **k'a**   tu7 kents7á ku míxalh
       go.along INFER then DEIC   DET bear
       'A bear **must** have gone by around here.'

     b. nilh **k'a**   kw s-Henry   wa7 pegwpegwtsám'
       FOC INFER DET NOM-Henry IMPF knock.repeatedly
       'That'll be Henry knocking.'

     c. *Context: You have a headache that won't go away, so you go to the doctor. All the tests show negative. There is nothing wrong, so it must just be tension.*
       nilh **k'a**   lh(el)-(t)-en-s-wá (7)-(a)   ptinus-em-sút
       FOC INFER from-DET-1SG.POSS-NOM-IMPF-DET think-MID-OOC
       'It **must** be from my worrying.'

     d. wa7 **k'a**   séna7   qwenúxw
       IMPF INFER COUNTER sick
       'He **may** be sick.' (*Context: Maybe that's why he's not here.*)

---

[19] See 2.7 for an illustration of how ordering sources produce graded notions of possibility for root modals, too. We would then expect to find upper-end degree modals among the root modals as well.

[20] Rullmann et al. credit the example to Alexander, C., B. Frank, G. Ned, D. Peters Sr., C. Shields, and R.A. Whitley. 2006. In Henry Davis (ed.), *Nqwal'luttenlhka'lha: English to St'át'imcets Dictionary*, vol. ii: *Intermediate*. Lillooet, BC: Upper St'át'imc Language Culture and Education Society.

  e. *Context: His car isn't there.*
   plan   k'a   qwatsáts
   already   INFER   leave
   'Maybe he's already gone.'
   Rullmann et al., example (5): 321.

(15) is particular telling, since it involves two incompatible propositions:

(15) k'a   lh-zúqw-as   tu7 ni7   na núkw-a   qelhmín
     INFER   COMP-die-3CONJ   then DEMON DET other-DET old.person
     smúlhats k'a   lh-mím'c-as   tu7 nka7
     woman   INFER   comp-move-3CONJ then where
     'Maybe the other old woman died or maybe she moved somewhere.'

     Rullmann et al., example (13): 324.

Rullmann et al. take St'át'imcets modals to be necessity modals that can be contextually weakened by domain restrictions. They do not discuss the hypothesis that St'át'imcets modals might be possibility modals that can be contextually strengthened by domain restrictions. And they do not consider the possibility for languages to have upper-end degree modals, which are neither possibility nor necessity modals. Rullmann et al. posit a special mechanism of domain restriction via choice functions, but since ordering sources already function as domain restrictors and are independently needed, the default assumption would be that they are the main source for additional domain restrictions, and thus the main source for variable modal force in St'át'imcets. No further mechanism for domain restriction seems to be needed. An analysis of St'át'imcets modals as upper-end degree modals seems to predict the data and observations presented in Rullmann et al. correctly. First, bilingual speakers translate St'át'imcets modals as English possibility or necessity modals, depending on context. Second, conjunctions of impossibles, as in (15) are acceptable, but only marginally so. Rullmann et al. report that speakers' judgments are not consistent with examples of this kind. This would not be expected if St'át'imcets modals were simply possibility modals. And, finally, there is a clear preference for St'át'imcets modals to describe necessary, rather than merely possible, states of affairs. This preference would again be surprising for possibility modals, but is expected for upper-end degree modals. As illustrated in our last toy example, all necessary, but not all possible, propositions are clear cases of somewhat probable propositions. Quite generally, necessary propositions are always covered by an upper-end degree modal. Since the lower bounds of what are acceptable degrees of probabilities, preferences, tendencies, propensities, etc.

are genuinely underdetermined, there might be questions about which possible propositions are covered, too.

The interpretations of the modals discussed in this section depend on two conversational backgrounds, rather than just one. Does this mean that for different types of modals, a different number of parameters has to be fixed by the utterance context? Would we still want to say that there is a class of modals that express relativized "simple necessity" or "simple possibility," as hypothesized in 2.3? In other words, are there any modals whose interpretations depend on just a modal base, rather than on both a modal base and an ordering source? We will see shortly that the interpretations of apparently "simple" modals like *muss, kann, it is necessary that*, etc. can depend on ordering sources, too. So a better view would be to assume that, quite generally, the interpretations of modals depend on both a modal base and an ordering source, but either parameter can be filled by the empty conversational background. The full range of possible modal meanings expressed in natural languages can now be characterized by conditions on three parameters: modal base, ordering source, and modal force. The available modal forces depend on the properties of the orderings induced by the interaction of modal base and ordering source, as we have seen: apart from the familiar dual pairs of possibility and necessity modals, languages may also have "collapsed" possibility/necessity modals, just existential modals, or simple or complex degree modals with modal forces derived from some notion of comparative possibility in one way or other: *is a better possibility, is a good possibility, is a slight possibility, is somewhat probable, is somewhat preferable*, and so on. Given the rich inventory of possible modal meanings, figuring out what kind of meaning is suitable for a particular modal in a given language is now no longer a simple task. The lack of dual pairs is an important clue for both the researcher and a language-learning child, and so is apparently variable modal force, as documented in the St'át'imcets examples. If, depending on context, a modal shows chameleon-like behavior in allowing both possibility and necessity interpretations, but with a preference for necessity interpretations, a degree modal might be your best bet.

2.6 Root versus epistemic modals

The previous section suggested that in modal reasoning, a conversational background may play the role of a modal base or an ordering source. The modal base determines the set of accessible worlds, and the ordering source induces an ordering on it. This section is about a major dichotomy seen in the modal bases for modals in natural languages. Modal vocabularies often draw a distinction between so-called "epistemic" versus "root" modals. The terminology is well established in the linguistic literature, so I will continue to use it here, even though it's not clear what "root" is meant to refer to, and "epistemic" modals do not have any necessary connection to knowledge. In my older work on modality, I coined the term "circumstantial" modals for root modals, and this is still the term I prefer and use when circumstances in a wider sense are at stake. The term makes clear that with *can*, for example, the intended range of uses does not just include ability interpretations, but also so-called "metaphysical" modalities (Condoravdi 2002), which Abusch (forthcoming) showed to be cut from the same cloth as other cases of circumstantial modality. In the end, those terms are all likely to be problematic in one way or other, though, and it's ultimately the analysis that will tell us what the grammatically significant types of modality are. Established terms for different types of modalities pick out pretheoretical distinctions that are useful at the beginning of an investigation, but may not survive careful theorizing.

Epistemic and root modals differ syntactically. Epistemic modals occupy high positions in the hierarchy of verbal inflectional heads, root modals appear in lower positions. Both types of modals can have non-empty realistic modal bases. However, if they do, the facts relied on seem to be different in a way that has proven difficult to characterize in formal terms. Here are a few examples.

Root modals

(16) Sie wollte   schreien und konnte nicht, gewann   aber
     She wanted to scream   and could   not,   regained however
     endlich die   Herrschaft über ihre erlahmten Glieder.
     finally the   control   over her paralyzed limbs.

Genovev was so terrified that she was unable to move.[21]

(17) Der Jani-Hans schimpfte nie,   fluchen konnte er gar nicht.
      The Jani-Hans scolded   never, curse   could he at all not.

Jani-Hans had such a mild character that he just wasn't capable of getting angry.[22]

(18) Hier können die Tomaten gedeihen.
      Here can   the tomatoes prosper.

[21] Adapted from Graf (1978[1946]: 25).
[22] Adapted from Graf (1978[1946]: 32).

(19)   Wer nichts hat dem   kann man auch nichts   nehmen.[23]
      Who nothing has, from whom can   one   also   nothing take away.

Epistemic modals

(20)   Es kann nur einer   gewesen sein, der   sich im   Haus
      It can   only someone been have,   who REFL in the house
      auskennt hat.
      at home   was.

The Heimraths have been burgled and Girgl is trying to find out who might have been the thief. It must have been someone who was familiar with the house.[24]

(21)   Sie   hatten den Befehl, den jungen König zu suchen,   der   sich
      They had   order   the   young   king   to   look for, who REFL
      in einer   seiner Jagdhütten   aufhalten musste.
      in one of his   hunting huts stay   must.PAST

The young king has disappeared, and given the evidence available, he must be hiding in one of his hunting huts.[25]

(22) Soweit   wir wissen, muss es   für sie   nie   etwas   anderes
      As far as we   know,   must there for them never anything else
      gegeben haben als   Geborenwerden, Aufwachsen, unermüdliche Arbeit
      been   have   but being born,   growing up, tireless   work
      und Sterben.
      and dying.

Oskar Maria Graf draws this conclusion from the historical sources about the life of the Heimrath family some centuries ago.[26]

There is a subtle semantic difference between the two kinds of modals I grouped under the two headings. It is a difference in the kind of facts relied on. Root modals are typically future oriented and are used to talk about propensities and potentials of people, things, and spatio-temporal locations, given their current circumstances. Usually, circumstances permit or prevent events from happening. Only sometimes do they necessitate events: we have to die, cough, vomit, laugh, cry, or realize that we are lost.

To see the difference between root and epistemic modals with non-empty realistic modal bases more clearly, compare the (a)- and (b)-sentences in (23) and (24):

---

[23] Adapted from Graf (1978[1946]: 57).   [24] Adapted from Graf (1978[1946]: 66).
[25] Adapted from Graf (1978[1946]: 37).   [26] Adapted from Graf (1978[1946]: 12).

(23) a. Aus   dieser Kanne Milch kann die Kathl ein Pfund   Quark
        From this   can of milk   can   the Kathl one pound of cottage cheese
        machen.
        make.

     b. Es kann sein, dass die Kathl aus dieser Kanne Milch ein Pfund
        It may be   that the Kathl from this can of milk   one pound
        Quark   macht.
        cottage cheese makes.

(24) a. In dieser Gegend können Zwetschgenbäume wachsen.
        In this   area   can   plum trees   grow.

     b. Es kann sein, dass in dieser Gegend Zwetschgenbäume wachsen.
        It may be   that in this   area   plum trees   grow.

The modal *kann* ('can') in (23a) and (24a) can be a root or an epistemic
modal. For sentences (23b) and (24b), the epistemic interpretation is prominent. Given a circumstantial interpretation for the (a)-sentences and an
epistemic interpretation for the (b)-sentences, we can imagine situations
where I speak truly when uttering an (a)-sentence, but falsely when uttering
the corresponding (b)-sentence. Take (23): given the cottage cheese production methods and tools available to Kathl, it would be possible for her to
produce a pound of cottage cheese from the milk in the can. She has other
uses for the milk in the can, however, and never uses the whole can for the
production of cheese: a bit of the milk goes into her coffee, a bit into her
porridge, a bit goes to the cat, and whatever remains is used for her cheese.
The likelihood that Kathl will in fact produce a pound of cottage cheese from
the milk in the can might thus be close to zero.

When using a root modal, we neglect certain kinds of facts, even though
we might be aware of them. Suppose I am traveling in an exotic country and
discover that soil and climate are very much like that in my own country,
where plum trees prosper everywhere. In such a situation, an utterance of
(24a) in its circumstantial sense would probably be true. But (24b) might very
well be false, given that that country has had no contacts whatsoever with
Western civilization and the vegetation is altogether different from ours. The
available evidence rules out the possibility that plum trees grow in this area.

The kind of facts we take into account for root modality are a rather
slippery matter. This may give rise to misunderstandings and jokes.[27] I once
heard a philosopher say that one of the defining properties of a cup is that

---

[27] Horgan (1979) and Lewis (1979a) have more illustrations of this point.

you can pour things like coffee in it. A student objected to this in pointing out that—if this were true—a cup which has coffee in it already would not be a cup anymore.

When we talk to each other, we hardly ever make explicit in view of what circumstances something should be necessary or possible. We may give hints. Usually people understand. And they usually understand in pretty much the same way. Take (25):

(25)   Ich kann nicht Posaune   spielen
     I   can   not   trombone play.

Depending on the situation in which I utter (25), I may say rather different things. I may mean that I don't know how to play the trombone. I am sure that there is something in people's minds that becomes different when they start learning to play the trombone. A program is filled in. It is in view of that program that it is possible for me to play the trombone. Or suppose that I suffer from asthma. I can hardly breathe. In view of my physical condition I am not able to play the trombone, although I know how to do it. I may express this with (25). Or else imagine that I am traveling by sea. The ship sinks and so does my trombone. I manage to get to a lonely island and sadly mumble (25). I could play the trombone in view of my head and my lungs, but the trombone is out of reach. There are more conceivable types of situations covered by (25), but most of them bring in norms in addition to the facts. That is, most of them involve a non-empty ordering source. I'll discuss such cases in the following section.

A distinction between circumstances concerning the outside world, the body or the mind of a person plays a role in the semantic development of *können*. According to Deggau (1907), the Old High German equivalent of that modal was first used for intellectual capacities. Then, it could also express possibilities in view of outside circumstances. Only later was it used for talking about physical abilities. Kiefer (1983) shows that similar distinctions are made in Hungarian. In Hungarian, the verbal suffix *-hat/-het* expresses possibility. In its root reading, it can only be used for possibilities in view of outside circumstances. Taking up some of Kiefer's further observations, consider a phrase like *imstande sein* ('to be able'). I could say

(26)   Ich bin nicht imstande, Posaune   zu spielen.
     I   am not   able   trombone to play.

if I have asthma or weak nerves, or if I have no talent. I doubt whether I could say it in a situation where I haven't learnt how to play the trombone. And I could never say it on the island with my trombone lost at sea. The relevant circumstances for *imstande sein* are concerned with the strength of the body, character, or intellect. For *kann,* there is another restriction:

(27)   # Dieses Messer kann nicht schneiden.
          This   knife   can   not   cut.

(28)   # Dieser Hut kann den Kopf warmhalten.
          This   hat   can   the   head keep warm.

(29)   # Dieser Ofen kann nicht richtig   heizen.
          This   stove can   not   properly heat.

(27) to (29) sound funny. They suggest that the knife, the hat, or the stove are agents taking an active part in the cutting, the warming of the head, or the heating. To avoid this effect, we would have to say:

(27′)   Dieses Messer schneidet nicht.
          This   knife   cuts   not.

(28′)   Dieser Hut hält   den Kopf warm.
          This   hat keeps the head warm.

(29′)   Dieser Ofen heizt nicht richtig.
          This   stove heats not   properly.

One of the factors responsible for the deviance of (27) to (29) relates to agency: the knife is not an agent, but an instrument for cutting something. The hat is not an agent, but an instrument for warming the head. And the stove is not an agent, but an instrument for heating a room. Some machines, like music boxes, can do things all by themselves, thus functioning as agents. This seems to rescue (30):

(30)   Diese Spieluhr   kann "La Paloma" spielen.
          This music box can   "La Paloma" play.

In this section, I have examined realistic modal bases for the two major types of modals in natural languages: root (or circumstantial) versus epistemic modals. In both cases, realistic modal bases target relevant bodies of facts in the evaluation world and track them via counterpart relations in all accessible worlds. The kind of facts that are targeted by the two types of modals are different in kind, though: external or internal circumstances of people, things, or places that determine their possible futures contrast with evidence of things implying or suggesting the presence of other facts in the past, present, or future.

Formally, empty modal bases wind up as limiting cases of realistic ones. This is a welcome consequence. Natural languages have not come up with special vocabulary for logical and mathematical necessity and possibility. Root or epistemic modals are used in those cases, too, even if no non-trivial facts are involved. We can now hypothesize that both root and epistemic modals have realistic modal bases. If all modals are either root or epistemic, it follows that *all* modals have realistic modal bases. Potentially non-realistic conversational backgrounds must then function as ordering sources.

The distinction between root and epistemic modality is evident in the vocabulary of German. Verbs with inherent modality, modal adjectives ending in *-lich* and *-bar*, and phrases like *imstande sein* or *in der Lage sein* never express epistemic modality. Sentence adverbs like *wahrscheinlich* or *möglicherweise* and auxiliaries like *wird* or *dürfte* always express epistemic modality. The neutral auxiliaries *müssen* and *können* can express root or epistemic modality, depending on their syntactic position.

If root and epistemic modals occupy different positions in the hierarchy of verbal inflectional heads, we may wonder whether the subtle semantic differences between the two types of modals can be derived from their syntactic differences. Valentine Hacquard's work (Hacquard 2006, 2010) points to a positive answer. Hacquard observes that during semantic composition, different regions of a verb's extended projection manipulate different kinds of semantic objects from which modal bases can be systematically projected. Argument structure is built in the lower regions of extended verbal projections, for example, and, consequently, modals in those regions can target the potentials and propensities of events, event participants and event locations. In higher regions, inflectional heads like tense shift the perspective to the speech event and the speaker. This is why, according to Hacquard, the possibilities of modals appearing in higher regions are keyed to the epistemic possibilities of speakers. While the last conclusion does not seem to be correct, Hacquard's general idea to derive the core differences between root and epistemic modals from their different syntactic positions is a major step towards explaining a distinction that has long resisted analysis.

2.7 Approaching norms and ideals with root modals

Root modals have realistic modal bases that interact with normative ordering sources to produce deontic, bouletic, teleological, or propensity interpretations. As with epistemic modals, ordering sources for root modals induce orderings on the set of accessible worlds that allow us to define suitable notions of necessity, possibility, and comparative possibility. Some root modals tolerate a wide range of ordering sources. Others are submitted to tighter restrictions.

Können and dürfen

(31) Du kannst doch nicht nur Häuser bauen oder Semmeln backen und wenn
     You can   not only houses build or rolls   bake and when
     du dann gestorben bist, ist alles   aus,   alles.   weggewischt.
     you then dead   are is everything finished, everything wiped out.

Shortly before his death, old Graf realizes that according to some conception of an ideal life, you should do more than just care for your property or do your daily work.[28]

(32) Sagen kannst gewiss   nicht, dass ich dir einmal schlecht geraten hab'.
     Say   can you certainly not   that I you once   bad advice given have.

Jani Hans always advised the Heimrath widow well. Given this fact, it goes against ideals of truthfulness and trust that she say anything to the contrary.[29]

(33) Dieses Brot kann man ja   direkt   seiner Majestät empfehlen.
     This   bread can one indeed straight away to his Majesty recommend.

This bread is good. If you recommend something good to him, the King will be pleased. If you recommend something bad to him, however, the King will hate you. Given these facts, it is compatible with a desirable future where the King loves you that you recommend this bread to him.[30]

(34) Kann ich jetzt gehen?
      Can I   now leave?

Imagine a student who says (34) to his teacher. The teacher is the source of law and order for him. What she wants is ordered and nothing is ordered unless she wants it. The boy wants to know whether it is compatible with his teacher's orders that he leaves. In this case, *kann* is deontic. For *darf*, a deontic ordering source is common, but not obligatory. Suppose two burglars are trying to enter a farmhouse and whisper to each other:

(35) Jetzt dürfen wir keinen Lärm machen.
      Now   may   we no   noise make.

It is not that they are not allowed to make a noise. They can't make a noise in view of their goal to burgle the farmers without getting caught. *Kann* and

---

[28] Adapted from Graf (1978[1946]: 114).   [29] Adapted from Graf (1978[1946]: 60).
[30] Adapted from Graf (1978[1946]: 94).

darf have similar meanings. Both express possibility. But there are differences. *Darf* requires an ideal according to which possibilities are assessed. *Kann* is more neutral. With *kann*, possibilities may depend on brute facts alone—that is, the ordering source may be empty. *Darf* doesn't admit ordering sources related to normalcy standards. Suppose I have a horrible headache and say with a deep sigh:

(36)   Ich kann das nicht aushalten.
       I   can this not bear.

This use of *kann* involves standards concerning normal tolerance thresholds for pain. I couldn't convey the same meaning by uttering

(37)   Ich darf das nicht aushalten.
       I   may this not   bear.

Kann may have difficulties with bouletic ordering sources. Imagine that tomorrow is the coronation of the King and I say:

(38)   Morgen   darf es nicht regnen.
       Tomorrow may it not   rain.

What I say here is roughly that according to what we all want, it shouldn't rain tomorrow. I couldn't get this interpretation by uttering:

(39)   Morgen   kann es nicht regnen.
       Tomorrow can it not   rain.

I conclude that there are restrictions for *kann* and *darf* that concern the admissible ordering sources.

Müssen and sollen

(40)   Wegen der Lola Montez hat er dem   Thron entsagen müssen.
       Because of Lola Montez has he the.DAT throne abdicate must.INF

Ludwig I of Bavaria loved Lola Montez. People became angry. Revolution broke out. Respecting the public interest he had to resign.[31]

(41)   Es muss mir   gehören, es muss.
       It must to me belong,   it must.

Kastenjakl is desperate to buy a piece of land from the Heimraths. His own wishes dictate that it must belong to him.[32]

---

[31] Adapted from Graf (1978[1946]: 39).
[32] Adapted from Graf (1978[1946]: 78).

(42) Lump muss man sein, nur als Lump zwingt   man die lumpige Welt.
     Crook must one be,   only as crook conquers one the crooky world.

Lenz presents his goal in life in the second part of the sentence. Given the facts of the actual world, you must be a crook if you want to conquer the world.[33]

(43) Arbeiten haben wir bis jetzt   müssen, arbeiten werden
      Work   have we up to now must.INF, work   will
      wir auch weiter   müssen.
      we also in future must.INF.

The Heimraths are peasants. Given their social status, they have to work if they are aspiring to a decent and honest life where they aren't beggars or burglars.[34]

    Like *kann, muss* accepts a wide range of ordering sources. The ordering source may be empty, too. This is suggested by sentences like:

(44) Er musste   husten.
      He must.PAST cough.

Like *darf, soll* requires a non-empty ordering source.

(45) Ein Richard Wagner Festspielhaus sollte   nach den
      A   Richard Wagner festival hall   shall.PAST after the
      Entwürfen des   Architekten Semper gebaut werden.
      designs   of the architect   Semper built be.

According to the plans of King Ludwig II of Bavaria, a Richard Wagner festival hall was to be built after the designs of the architect Semper.[35]

(46) Ich bitt' euch gar schön, der hochwürdige Herr Pfarrer soll kommen.
      I   ask you very nicely, the reverend   Sir   priest shall come.

Gauzner Michl is dying. He wants a priest to come and see him.[36] In Luther's translation, God uses *sollen* a lot when he talks to Moses.

(47) Sechs Tage soltu   erbeiten und alle deine Werck thun.
      Six   days shalt thou labor   and all thy   work do.

---

[33] Adapted from Graf (1978[1946]: 82).
[34] Adapted from Graf (1978[1946]: 57).
[35] Adapted from Graf (1978[1946]: 41).
[36] Adapted from Graf (1978[1946]: 103).

According to what God wants, it is necessary that you work six days a week. In some societies, what God wants is commanded. In other societies, what God wants is good and recommended, but not commanded. If I lived in a society of the first kind, I would most naturally say:

(48)   Ich muss sechs Tage arbeiten und alle meine Werke tun.
        I   must six   days work   and all my   work do.

If I lived in a society of the second kind, however, I would prefer to say:

(49)   Ich soll sechs Tage arbeiten und alle meine Werke tun.
        I   shall six   days work   and all my   work do.
        I am supposed to work for six days and to do all my work.

Sollen might express the weakened kind of necessity that comes with a non-empty ordering source, as proposed in the original paper. But it could also be a degree modal covering the upper end of a scale induced by an ordering source corresponding to what is good, planned, or recommended, or by what someone wants, plans, or recommends.[37] Actually, it is not just what *anyone* wants, plans, or recommends. The one who does so cannot be identical with the individual referred to by the subject of the sentence in which *sollen* occurs, for example. I can't say

(50)   Ich soll ein Bäcker werden.
        I   shall a   baker become.
        I am supposed to become a baker.

if it is mine but no one else's wish that I become a baker. Compare this with Gunnar Bech's characterization in Bech (1949): "*sollen*...bezeichnet einen nicht dem Subjekt innewohnenden Willen," "*sollen* refers to a will which is not inherent in the subject." Since in a passive sentence like (51), *er* is not the "logical" subject, (51) is not a counterexample to Bech's principle:

(51)   Er soll in Ruhe gelassen werden.
        He shall in peace left   be.

I could use (51) for expressing that it is according to his own wishes that he shouldn't be bothered. *Muss* is neutral with respect to who wants me to become a baker.

---

[37] The assumption that *sollen* might be an upper-end degree modal has interesting consequences that deserve to be explored in a separate investigation—in particular because of the intimate connection between *sollen*-type modals and imperatives. We would expect absence of a dual and apparently variable modal strength, for example. The extant literature on *sollen*-type modals and imperatives looks promising for a degree modal analysis.

(52)   Ich muss ein Bäcker werden.
        I   must a   baker become.

(52) can be used if I, myself, or someone else wants me to become a baker.
   The suffixes *-bar* and *-lich* allow all kinds of ordering sources, depending on the adjective they are attached to.

-bar and -lich

(53)   Dieses Eintrittsbillet   ist nicht übertragbar.
        This   admission ticket is not   transferable.

According to the regulations, it is not possible to give this ticket to anyone else.

(54)   Diese Tasse ist zerbrechlich.
        This cup   is fragile.

(54) has a realistic modal base and an empty ordering source. It is in view of certain properties inherent in the cup that it is possible for it to break.

(55)   Dieser Vorschlag ist annehmbar.
        This   proposal is acceptable.

Given our common goals, it is possible to accept this proposal.

(56)   Diese Lage   ist unerträglich.
        This situation is intolerable.

Every night, Marie-Louise's living room becomes the meeting place for all the cats in the neighborhood. This is intolerable in view of normal standards concerning property, noise, and smell. We may add a phrase like *for Marie-Louise* to indicate that the standards involved are more subjective.

(57)   Für Marie-Louise ist diese Lage unerträglich.
        For Marie-Louise is this situation intolerable.

Ordering sources permit the grading of possibilities:

(58)   Ich kann eher   Bäcker als   Stellmacher werden.
        I   can rather baker than cartwright   become.
        'It is more possible for me to become a baker than a cartwright.'

Maxl was wounded during the war against the Prussians. Given this, becoming a baker is a better possibility for him than becoming a cartwright: becoming a baker would require less effort for him, and he would therefore also do a better job as a baker.

Kann eher. . . . als expresses comparative possibility. Comparative possibility was the main motivation for introducing a distinction between modal bases and ordering sources in 2.4. We saw that for epistemic modals, the interaction between stereotypical ordering sources and modal bases projected from pieces of evidence produces comparative and quantitative notions of epistemic probability. It seems that for root modals, the interaction between stereotypical ordering sources and modal bases projected from the current circumstances of individuals and spatio-temporal locations produces comparative and quantitative notions of propensity—sometimes referred to as "aleatory probability." To illustrate, a fair coin has the propensity to land heads 50% of times when it is tossed in a fair setting. The coin has that propensity even if it is never tossed—it's one of its inherent properties. Hacking (1975) quotes a passage by Richard von Mises, which uses various comparative forms of the German adjective *möglich* ('possible') to illustrate the difference between epistemic and aleatory probability:[38]

Ordinary language recognizes different degrees of possibility or realizability. An event may be called possible or impossible, but it can also be called quite possible or barely possible (*schwer oder leicht möglich*) according to the amount of effort that must be expended to bring it about. It is only 'barely possible' to write longhand at 40 words per minute; impossible at 120. Nevertheless it is 'quite possible' to do this using a typewriter [. . .] In this sense we call two events equally possible if the same effort is required to produce each of them. This is what Jacques Bernoulli, a forerunner of Laplace, calls *quod pari facilitate mihi obtingeri possit* [. . .] But this is not what Laplace's definition means. We may call an event 'more possible' [*eher möglich*] than another when we wish to express our conjecture about whatever can be expected to happen. There can be no doubt that equipossibility as used in the classical definition of probability is to be understood in this sense, as denoting equally warranted conjectures [1951, p. 78].

Hacking explains that "according to Mises the epistemic concept of probability corresponds to an epistemic concept of possibility, while the aleatory concept of probability corresponds to a concept of physical possibility."[39] The two major interpretations of probability thus seem to be intimately linked to the fundamental difference between root and epistemic modality.

---

[38] Quoted from Hacking (1975: 123–4).
[39] Hacking (1975: 124).

In the following section, I will discuss practical inferences, which provide an additional argument in favor of separating realistic and normative conversational backgrounds.

2.8   Practical reasoning

Capturing the semantics of modals via two interacting conversational backgrounds has interesting consequences for what has been called "practical inference."[40] A practical inference may have the following form:

I want to become mayor.
I will become mayor only if I go to the pub.

Therefore I should go to the pub.

Spelling out hidden assumptions:

All I want is to become mayor.
The relevant circumstances are such that I will become mayor only if I go to the pub.

Therefore, considering the relevant circumstances and what I want, I should go to the pub.

In this section, I will tentatively assume that *should* is a necessity modal, rather than an upper-end degree modal—an assumption that will ultimately have to be submitted to further scrutiny. The phrase *the relevant circumstances* in the second premise of the inference above contributes a modal base f that maps a world w to the set of propositions that correspond to the relevant circumstances in w. *What I want* contributes an ordering source g that maps a possible world w to the set of propositions that correspond to what I want in w. Let's assume that $f(w)$ contains just one proposition in our example: the proposition that I will become mayor only if I go to the pub. Assume furthermore that $g(w)$ only contains the proposition that I will become mayor. The union of $f(w)$ and $g(w)$ is consistent, then. It follows that the proposition that I go to the pub is a necessity in w with respect to f and g iff $f(w) \cup g(w)$ implies that I do so. Since the implication holds, the inference comes out valid.

---

[40] Anscombe (1957), von Wright (1963, 1972).

Let us now look at a slightly more complicated example:

All I want is two things, namely avoid going to the pub and become mayor. The relevant circumstances are such that I will become mayor only if I don't avoid going to the pub.

Therefore, considering the relevant circumstances and what I want,

Conclusion one: I should go to the pub.
Conclusion two: I should avoid going to the pub.
Conclusion three: I could avoid going to the pub and still become mayor.
Conclusion four: I could go to the pub.
Conclusion five: I could avoid going to the pub.

This is the horrible story of someone who wants something but rejects the necessary means leading to the fulfillment of her desires. Which conclusion can we draw in such a case? The first three conclusions are out, but the last two are fine. Our current analysis predicts this. Suppose *should*, *the relevant circumstances*, and *what I want* are interpreted as in the previous example and *could* expresses possibility. This time round, $g(w)$ contains two propositions: that I will become mayor and that I avoid going to the pub. If $\cap f(w)$ is the set of worlds accessible from w, then:

(a) For all worlds $v \in \cap f(w)$:
     If I avoid going to the pub in v, I won't become mayor in v.

Given the definition of possibility, it follows right away that conclusion three is false. Wishes cannot override facts. Consider now the ordering source $g(w)$. It induces a three-cell partition of $\cap f(w)$ as follows:

- A is the set of all worlds in $\cap f(w)$ where I go to the pub and become mayor
- B is the set of all worlds in $\cap f(w)$ where I avoid going to the pub and won't become mayor
- C is the set of all worlds in $\cap f(w)$ where I go to the pub, but still won't become mayor.

The reader can verify that all of the following statements are true:

(b) A, B, and C are not empty, they are pairwise disjoint and $A \cup B \cup C = \cap f(w)$.
(c) If $v \in A$ and $z \in B$, then neither $v \leq_{g(w)} z$ nor $z \leq_{g(w)} v$.
(d) For all v and $z \in A$: $v \leq_{g(w)} z$.

(e) For all v and $z \in B$: $v \leq_{g(w)} z$.
(f) If $z \in C$ and $v \in A \cup B$, then $v \leq_{g(w)} z$, but not $z \leq_{g(w)} v$.

All worlds in A are worlds where I go to the pub, and for none of those worlds is there any world where I avoid going to the pub that is at least as close to what I want. This makes the proposition that I go to the pub a possibility. Consequently, conclusion two is predicted to be false and conclusion four is predicted to be true. All worlds in B are worlds where I avoid going to the pub, and for none of those worlds is there any world where I do go to the pub that is at least as close to what I want. This makes the proposition that I avoid going to the pub a possibility. Consequently, conclusion one is predicted to be false and conclusion five is predicted to be true. Separating modal bases and ordering sources allows us to make the correct predictions in practical inferences, then.

The separation of modal bases and ordering sources also leads to an insightful analysis of conditional modality. In Kratzer (1978, 1979), I was not able to offer a general recipe for how *if*-clauses modify modals. I had to give meaning rules for each modal separately. In so doing, I missed a generalization about how *if*-clauses restrict modals of various strengths and flavors. In the following section, I will present a sketch of a theory of conditional modality as a first step towards a general account of conditionals.

2.9 Conditionals

In Kratzer (1978, 1979), I argued that many conditionals involve modals in an explicit or implicit way. The logical forms of such conditionals conform to the following rough schema, where an adjoined *if*-clause modifies a sentence that has a modal sitting in its left periphery:

(If . . . . . .), (necessarily . . . . . .)
(If . . . . . .), (possibly . . . . . .)
(If . . . . . .), (probably . . . . . .)
etc.

The matrix clauses of such conditional constructions are overtly or covertly modalized sentences of the kind we have been discussing. The job of *if*-clauses in modalized conditionals is simple: they restrict the modal base of the associated modal in the matrix clause. In a first approximation, this proposal can be spelled out as follows:

Conditional modality

Suppose u is an utterance of a sentence of the form $(if\ \alpha)\ \beta$, where u_1 is the part of u where the *if*-clause is uttered, u_2 is the part of u where β is uttered, and the proposition expressed by α is p. We have then:

(i) u_1 requires one, and only one, modal base and one, and only one, ordering source to be felicitous[41]

(ii) if f is the modal base and g the ordering source for u_1, then f^+ is the modal base and g the ordering source for u_2, where for any world w, $f^+(w) = f(w) \cup \{p\}$.

There are various possibilities for fleshing out the informal characterization of conditional modality above, and more research is needed to see which possibility is right. Much depends on how exactly conversational backgrounds enter into the interpretation of sentences with modals. Are they arguments of modals that might be syntactically represented? Or are they contextual or evaluation parameters without syntactic expression? As we have seen, there are also reasons to believe that modal bases might only be represented indirectly in grammar via suitable modal anchors. To have at least a preliminary definition to hold on to, here is a slightly more formalized characterization of conditional modality. Modal base dependencies might ultimately have to be derived from anchor dependencies, but this potential inaccuracy does no harm for our current purposes. *If*-clauses do target modal bases in one way or other, if not directly, then at least indirectly:

Conditional modality (alternative definition, still not the last word)

For any conversational backgrounds f and g:

$$[[if\varrho\ \alpha\ \beta]]^{f,g} = [[\beta]]^{f^+,g}, \text{where for all } w \in W, f^+(w) = f(w) \cup \{[[\alpha]]^{f,g}\}.$$

Different kinds of conditionals emerge from different settings for the parameters f and g. In what follows, consider utterances of sentences realizing the schema *(if α), (necessarily γ)* and suppose that p and q are the propositions expressed by α and γ respectively and that *necessarily* expresses necessity as defined in 2.4. Material implication emerges as the special case where the modal base is totally realistic and the ordering source is empty:

Material implication

A material implication is characterized by a totally realistic modal base f and an empty ordering source g. Sketch of proof:

---

[41] Instead of the uniqueness condition, a solution along the lines of Lewis (1979a) or Pinkal (1977, 1979) would be preferable here as well. There is quite a bit of vagueness surrounding conditionals.

Case one: Suppose p is true in w. Then $\cap f^+(w) = \{w\}$. But then q is a necessity in w with respect to f^+ and g iff q is true in w.

Case two: Suppose p is false in w. Then $\cap f^+(w) = \emptyset$. But then q is trivially a necessity in w with respect to f^+ and g.

Strict implication

A strict implication is characterized by an empty modal base f and an empty ordering source g.

Sketch of proof: since $g(w)$ is empty, we have $u \leq_{g(w)} v$ for all worlds u and v in $\cap f^+(w)$. Since $f^+(w) = f(w) \cup \{p\} = \{p\}$, q is a necessity in w with respect to f^+ and g iff q is true in all worlds of $\cap \{p\}$. But that means that p logically implies q.

Counterfactuals

A counterfactual is characterized by an empty modal base f and a totally realistic ordering source g.

David Lewis (personal communication[42]) showed that the above analysis of counterfactuals is equivalent to the one in Kratzer (1981a; reprinted here as chapter 3). Here is the idea behind the proposed account of counterfactuals: all possible worlds where the antecedent p is true are ordered with respect to their being more or less near to what is actually the case in the world under consideration. What is actually the case is a vague concept. There are many ways of uniquely characterizing a world. Put formally, there are many functions g such that $\cap g(w) = \{w\}$ for a given world w. The differences between them cannot possibly make a difference when they are used as modal bases, but they become important when they function as ordering sources. To illustrate, consider conversational backgrounds g_1 and g_2 such that $g_1(w) = \{r, s\}$ and $g_2(w) = \{r \cap s\}$. Even though $\cap g_1(w) = \cap g_2(w)$, $g_1(w)$, and $g_2(w)$ can induce different orderings. Take two worlds u and v such that r is true and s is false in u, and r and s are both false in v. Then $v \leq_{g_2(w)} u$, but not $v \leq_{g_1(w)} u$. Since realistic contexts are unlikely to pick out unique ordering sources for counterfactuals, counterfactuals are predicted to be inherently vague. Since counterfactuals *are* inherently vague, this is the right result (see chapter 3 or Kratzer (1981a) for more discussion). No such vagueness is expected for material implications, where totally realistic conversational backgrounds function as modal bases.

As a last example, I will briefly discuss *deontic conditionals*, which have non-empty ordering sources like counterfactuals. Imagine my uttering the following sentences:

---

[42] Now Lewis (1981).

(59) Jedem   Menschen muss Gerechtigkeit widerfahren.
     To every person   must justice   be given.

(60) Wenn jemand   ungerecht behandelt wurde, muss das Unrecht
     If   someone unjustly   treated   was,   must the injustice
     gesühnt   werden.
     amended for get.

(61) Wenn jemand   ungerecht behandelt wurde, muss das Unrecht
     If   someone unjustly   treated   was,   must the injustice
     belohnt   werden.
     rewarded be.

Traditional approaches to conditionals would have to analyze (60) and (61) as modalized material implications and assign them the logical form *necessarily* $(\alpha \rightarrow \beta)$. This leads to trouble.[43] Suppose for convenience that we also follow tradition in relativizing modals to a mere accessibility relation. The proposition expressed by (59) would now be true (in the actual world) iff there is no injustice in any morally accessible world. The proposition expressed by (60) would be true iff any injustice there may be is amended for in all morally accessible worlds. And the proposition expressed by (61) would be true iff any injustice there may be is rewarded in all morally accessible worlds. The problem is that, supposing that the proposition expressed by (59) is true, the propositions expressed by (60) and (61) come out vacuously true. If there is no injustice in any morally accessible world, anything you like is true in morally accessible worlds where there is injustice. The proposed analysis of conditionals avoids this problem. Simplifying somehow, assume that the modal base f is empty and the ordering source g corresponds to what is morally good. The proposition expressed by (59) is now true (in the actual world) iff there is no injustice in any world that comes closest to what is morally good. The proposition expressed by (60) is true iff whatever injustice there is is amended for in all worlds with injustice that come closest to what is morally good. And the proposition expressed by (61) is true iff whatever injustice there is is rewarded in all worlds with injustice that come closest to what is morally good. On this analysis, it is possible for the first two propositions to be true, and the third one to be false. For us, a world where injustice is amended for is not good, since there is no injustice in a good world. But it is still closer to what is good than any world where injustice is

---

[43] Hansson (1969), van Fraassen (1972), Lewis (1973a) have detailed discussions of the problem.

rewarded. These truth conditions are in essence those that David Lewis derives in Lewis (1973a).

Whether an analysis of conditionals is correct is often assessed by examining its predictions for inference patterns like "transitivity," "strengthening the antecedent," or "contraposition."[44] The analysis I am proposing predicts that the three inference patterns can't be expected to be valid for all those types of conditionals that involve a non-empty ordering source. In the literature, the failure of these inference patterns is usually discussed in connection with deontic conditionals, probability conditionals and counterfactuals. If we analyze these conditionals in the way suggested here, their specific behavior in inferences is an automatic consequence of the analysis.

2.10 Conclusion

This chapter has tried to elucidate what a speaker has to know to master the semantics of modal constructions in her language. Most importantly, she needs to make the right distinctions between modals by keeping track of three parameters: modal base, ordering source, and modal force. To monitor settings for the three parameters, she needs to pay attention to the lexical properties of individual modals, the syntactic structures they appear in, and the discourse context. She might also have to rely on general cognitive mechanisms for projecting modal bases from suitable modal anchors made available in various places along the verbal projection spine. Modal bases and ordering sources are complicated formal objects and she needs to know how to manipulate them in computing the denotations of complex modal constructions, including degree constructions and conditionals. Finally, she has to come to terms with the fact that realistic utterance contexts rarely provide unique modal bases or ordering sources for modal constructions. She needs to be able to manage a high degree of context-dependency and vagueness, then.

Acknowledgments

I am very much indebted to the late David Lewis who informed me about his work on ordering semantics before publication. Lewis's work on ordering semantics has since been published as Lewis (1981). The research for the original version of this chapter was carried out as part of my collaboration

---

[44] See for example Lewis (1973a), Kratzer (1978, 1979).

with a DFG-project on modals in Düsseldorf. I'd like to thank Gisela Brünner, Angelika Redder, and Dieter Wunderlich for discussions, hospitality, and patience. I am also grateful for conversations with Manfred Bierwisch, Gerald Gazdar, and Ewald Lang. I thank Amy Rose Deal for help with the preparation of the manuscript of the current version of the chapter, and Lisa Matthewson, Aynat Rubinstein, Katrin Schulz, and Valentine Hacquard for comments. Special thanks to Barry Schein for telling me what the original version of this paper was about.

INTRODUCING CHAPTER 3

At the end of *What 'Must' and 'Can' Must and Can Mean*, a challenge is raised for theories of conflict resolution within a premise semantics. The way conflicts are resolved in a premise semantics depends on the way the premises are divided up and lumped together. Are there deep and non-trivial principles guiding this process that might be worth exploring? This question has set the agenda for much of my work in premise semantics. In his 1981 paper on ordering semantics, David Lewis described the task then ahead of me as follows:

> We must be selective in the choice of premises... By judicious selection, we can accomplish the same sort of discrimination as would result from unequal treatment of premises. As Kratzer explains..., the outcome depends on the way we lump items of information together in single premises or divide them between several premises. Lumped items stand or fall together, divided items can be given up one at a time. Hence if an item is lumped into several premises, that makes it comparatively hard to give up; whereas if it is confined to a premise of its own, it can be given up without effect on anything else. This lumping and dividing turns out to be surprisingly powerful as a method for discriminating among worlds - so much so that... premise semantics can do anything that ordering semantics can. Formally, there is nothing to choose. Intuitively, the question is whether the same premises that it would seem natural to select are the ones that lump and divide properly; on that question I shall venture no opinion.

(1981: 220–1)

What I embarked on, then, was no longer a purely logical enterprise. As Lewis made clear, there is now the empirical question "whether the same premises that it would seem natural to select are the ones that lump and divide properly." In *Partition and Revision*, the truth of a counterfactual depends on a set of premises that represent the facts of the world of evaluation. Counterfactual assumptions conflict with the facts, and the conflict is resolved by the very same mechanism of making the best of an inconsistent set that was invoked in chapter 1. *Partition and Revision* explores the hypothesis that variability in the way the facts of a world "hang together" might yield a correct and explanatory characterization of the vagueness and indeterminacy of counterfactuals. The project is continued in much more depth and detail in *An Investigation of the Lumps of Thought* (chapter 5), which shifts the focus of investigation to finding non-trivial constraints for constructing premise sets for counterfactuals.

The original version of *Partition and Revision* appeared in the *Journal of Philosophical Logic* 10 (1981), 201–16 and is reprinted here with many stylistic changes.

Chapter 3

Partition and Revision: The Semantics of Counterfactuals

3.1 A straightforward analysis seems to fail

What is for me the most intuitive analysis of counterfactuals goes as follows: the truth of counterfactuals depends on everything that is the case in the world of evaluation: in assessing them, we have to consider all possible ways of adding as many facts to the antecedent as consistency permits. If the consequent follows from every such possibility, the whole counterfactual is true.

Here is a way to express the idea in possible worlds semantics, where, as before, propositions are subsets of W, a proposition p is true in w iff w is a member of p, and the notions of consistency, logical compatibility, and consequence are defined as usual. Suppose I utter a sentence of the form:

(1)   If it were the case that α, then it would be the case that β,

where q and r are the propositions expressed by α and β respectively. We need to specify how the proposition p expressed by the utterance of the whole sentence depends on q and r. Let f be the function from W that assigns to every world the set of all those propositions that "are the case" in it. Then p is the set of all worlds w of W that meet the following condition:

The Analysis

If $A_w(q)$ is the set of all consistent subsets of $f(w) \cup \{q\}$ that contain q, then every set in $A_w(q)$ has a superset X in $A_w(q)$ such that $\cap X \subseteq r$.[1]

If we don't have to worry about the existence of maximal sets, there is a simpler way to express the same condition:

---

[1] This treatment of counterfactuals is based on my treatment of inconsistencies in Kratzer (1977). A German predecessor of that paper ("Relative Modalität") was distributed in 1975 as a working paper of the Konstanz Cooperative Research Center 99 (SFB 99). Frank Veltman (1976) presents a formally analogous analysis of counterfactuals which relies on beliefs and not on facts, however.

A simplified version of the Analysis

The proposition *r* follows from every maximal set in $A_w(q)$. (A set is maximal in *B* iff it has no proper superset in *B*.)

Surprisingly, this analysis produces the following, blatantly wrong, truth-conditions:

The Critical Truth-Conditions

   (i) if *q* is true, then *p* is true iff *r* is true
   (ii) if *q* is false, then *p* is true iff *r* follows from *q* (i.e., $q \subseteq r$).

The reader may be curious to see how this result is obtained. The proof is as follows:[2]

The Critical Argument

We assume—and this seems natural enough—that "what is the case" in *w* is to be identified with the set of propositions true in *w*. Suppose *q* is true in *w*. This means that $q \in f(w)$. Thus $f(w)$ is a superset of every subset of $f(w) \cup \{q\} = f(w)$, and $r \in f(w)$ iff $\cap f(w) \subseteq r$. (In fact, $\cap f(w) = \{w\}$.) So if *q* is true in *w*, then *p* is true in *w* iff *r* is true in *w*. Now suppose *q* is false in *w*, and let w^* be an arbitrary world in *q*. Then $\{w^*\} = \cap\{\neg q \cup \{w^*\}, q\}$, so $\{\neg q \cup \{w^*\}, q\}$ is consistent and $\{\neg q \cup \{w^*\}, q\} \subseteq f(w) \cup \{q\}$. Thus $\{\neg q \cup \{w^*\}, q\} \in A_w(q)$ and hence if $w \in p$ then $\cap\{\neg q \cup \{w^*\}, q\} \subseteq r$. This means that $w^* \in r$, supposing that $w \in p$. Since w^* was an arbitrary world in *q*, we have $q \subseteq r$. On the other hand, if $q \subseteq r$, then $p = W$, and so in particular $w \in p$.

I have run into a dilemma: I first presented an analysis of counterfactuals that I think is very plausible, and then I presented an argument that seems to show that the same analysis has rather implausible consequences. It's not that both clauses of the Critical Truth-Conditions are implausible. Clause (i), at least, is what we want. A counterfactual whose antecedent happens to be true should be true iff its consequent is true as well. What we don't want is clause (ii). Suppose I utter a sentence like:

(2)   If I were sleeping right now, I wouldn't be writing.

No doubt, what I just said is true. At the moment, I am not sleeping. But if I were, it wouldn't follow from logic alone that I wasn't writing. I see two possibilities for avoiding the dilemma: I can give up the analysis or check the argument again. I prefer the second option.

---

[2] I am indebted to David Lewis for the last part.

3.2 Escaping through atomism

There is nothing to be done about the formal parts of the Critical Argument. Perhaps, though, something can be done about its crucial assumption. What is the case in a world could be taken to be something other than the set of all propositions true in that world. In fact, the logical atomists did just that. For Wittgenstein, the world is characterized by its *atomic* facts: "the world is everything which is the case" (*Tractatus*, 1) and "what is the case—the fact—is the existence of atomic facts" (*Tractatus*, 2). Taking an atomistic view of what is the case would undercut the last part of the proof. If it is an atomic fact that I am tired, it is not an atomic fact that I am tired or toads are able to drive cars, although the latter proposition follows from the former. It is these "disjunctive" facts that are deadly for our analysis. They may suddenly play an important role if we dare make the counterfactual assumption that I am not tired. The two propositions that I am not tired and that I am tired or toads are able to drive cars would then form a consistent set that logically implies that toads are able to drive cars. Wittgenstein's view of what is the case would save our analysis. But can we adopt such a view, and what are atomic facts? Furthermore, is a world determined by its atomic facts, and do atomic facts play a crucial part in determining the truth of counterfactuals? These questions take us to John Pollock's account of subjunctive reasoning.[3]

Formally, Pollock's analysis is similar to mine,[4] but in this paper I want to concentrate on its intuitive motivation. Pollock defends atomic propositions (*"simple propositions"*), but not on metaphysical grounds. He thinks that the only way you could justify this notion is to take it as basically epistemo-logical: a simple proposition is one whose truth can be known non-induct-ively without first coming to know the truth of some proposition or propositions that entail it. Pollock doesn't consider simple propositions to be the only ones responsible for the truth or falsity of counterfactuals. Internal negations of simple propositions have to be considered, as well as laws of nature (*"strong subjunctive generalizations"*) and actual necessities (*"weak subjunctive generalizations"*). The laws of gravity are examples of strong subjunctive generalizations. That anyone drinking from a particular bottle (hidden in Roderick Chisholm's closet and accidentally containing rat poison) would die is an example of a weak subjunctive generalization. If subjunctive generalizations are used for an analysis of counterfactuals there is the danger of circularity. Aren't those generalizations counterfactuals

---

[3] Pollock (1976).   [4] See Lewis (1981).

themselves? For Pollock they are not, and he gives them an independent analysis.[5] He is thus free to use them for the counterfactual enterprise.

Let me summarize the discussion so far. The truth of a counterfactual depends on what is the case in the world of evaluation. But not all propositions that are actually true can be taken into account. We have to make a choice. Pollock proposes a refined version of atomism. His justification is epistemological and thus not open to the kind of criticism put forward against Wittgenstein. Furthermore, Pollock's atomism is not as exclusive as Wittgenstein's: he grants a place to certain kinds of complex propositions. I propose to mold Pollock's suggestions into the format of the truth-conditions I presented above. Pollock's actual proposals are more complicated than my presentation of them is going to be. For example, I shall neglect the important issue of temporal priorities. I believe that those simplifications do not affect my point.

One more time, imagine an utterance of a sentence of the form (1), where p, q, and r are the propositions expressed by the whole sentence, the antecedent, and the consequent respectively. Let f_1 be the function from W that assigns to every world the set of all its true strong subjunctive generalizations. Let f_2 be the function from W that assigns to every world the set of all its true weak subjunctive generalizations. Finally, let f_3 be the function from W that assigns to every world the set of all its true simple propositions and negations of simple propositions. Then p is true in precisely those worlds w of W that satisfy the following condition:

A Pollock-like analysis

Let $A_w^1(q)$ be the set of all consistent subsets of $f_1(w) \cup \{q\}$ that contain q, let $A_w^2(q)$ be the set of all consistent subsets of $f_1(w) \cup f_2(w) \cup \{q\}$ that are extensions of a maximal set in $A_w^1(q)$, and let $A_w^3(q)$ be the set of all consistent subsets of $f_1(w) \cup f_2(w) \cup f_3(w) \cup \{q\}$ that are extensions of a maximal set in $A_w^2(q)$. Then for every maximal set X in $A_w^3(q)$, $\cap X \subseteq r$.

We will need Pollock-like truth-conditions for "might"-counterfactuals as well. These are obtained by replacing the last clause of the "would"- condition by: "then for some maximal set X in $A_w^3(q)$, $\cap X \cap r \neq \emptyset$."

It would be straightforward, though cumbersome, to accommodate these two definitions to the more general case, where we don't assume the existence of maximal sets. For our present purposes, the simpler version will do. Note that the definition ensures that in counterfactual reasoning, laws of nature have priority over actual necessities and actual necessities have priority over simple facts.

---

[5] Pollock (1976).

Although the Critical Argument does not apply to this analysis, there are other objections against it. One is that we lost clause (i) of the Critical Truth-Conditions unless we stipulate that a world is uniquely characterized by all its true simple propositions, negations of simple propositions, and subjunctive generalizations. Another objection is more serious. There are examples that show that Pollock's partitioning of the world can't be the one underlying counterfactual reasoning in general.

3.3 Counterexamples and amendments

Consider the following examples:

Restaurant

Hans and Babette spend the evening together. They go to a restaurant called "Dutchman's Delight," sit down, order, eat, and talk. Suppose now, counter-factually, that Babette had gone to a bistro called "Frenchman's Horror" instead. Where would Hans have gone? (I have to add that Hans rather likes this bistro.)

Bush walk

Regina and I go on a walk in the bush. We have to pass a hanging bridge. I pass first. Regina is waiting. I am in the middle of the bridge. Suppose now, counterfactually, that I had .passed a bit faster and had just left the bridge. Where would Regina be? Would she still be waiting?

Dancing School

I am taking dancing lessons at Wander's dancing school. Last Saturday, there were five men to dance with: John, James, Jack, Joseph, and Jeremy. I danced with the latter three only. Suppose now, counterfactually, that I had danced with at least four of the men. With whom might I have danced?

I will comment on each example separately.

Re Restaurant

I think that—given the circumstances—Hans would have gone to the bistro, too, if Babette had gone there. If this counterfactual is true, it is so mainly in virtue of the fact that Hans and Babette spend the evening together. Spending the evening together is no law of nature, nor an actual necessity, nor a simple fact. It involves simpler facts:

Hans picks Babette up. Hans takes the bus number five at five o'clock. Babette takes the bus number five at five o'clock. Babette sits next to Hans in the bus. Hans talks to Babette. Babette talks to Hans. And so on. Probably, those facts are still not simple facts. That Hans picks Babette up involves in turn simpler facts like: Hans enters Babette's house. Hans knocks at the door. And so on. However small these details may be, they will be listed by f_3.

The counterfactual assumption that Babette had gone to a different restaurant doesn't conflict with our laws of nature or actual necessities. So the conflict arises only in connection with f_3. There will now be several ways of achieving consistency. If we let Hans continue on his way to "Dutchman's Delight," he has to stop talking to Babette, for example. And if we let him continue talking to Babette, he has to go with her. But clearly a Pollock-like analysis wouldn't give priority to the second possibility.

Perhaps we can repair the analysis. Instead of having three kinds of facts, we might need four. Let f_1 and f_2 be as before. Let f_3 be responsible for facts like the one that Hans and Babette spend the (entire) evening together. And let f_4 be as f_3 above. The definitions have to be changed accordingly. They would now imply that Hans would have gone to the bistro, too, if Babette had gone there. But then, how many kinds of facts will we end up with? And how complicated is our system of priorities going to be?

Re Bush walk

I think that Regina might have started passing over the bridge if I had just left the bridge, so it is not true that she would still be waiting. She might be, but she wouldn't necessarily be. The supposition that I had just left the bridge affects many actual simple facts, but there seems to be no logical reason to remove the fact that Regina is waiting at the beginning of the bridge. There is no law of nature or actual necessity either which would prevent her from doing so. So it is quite likely that Regina's waiting turns out to be what Nicholas Rescher called an "innocent bystander"[6]—a proposition which (in terms of our definitions) is contained in every maximal set of $A_w{}^3(q)$. Since Regina's waiting is incompatible with her having started passing over the bridge, a Pollock-like analysis would require that it would have to be false that she might have started passing already, if only I had passed a bit faster. Yet this conflicts with our intuitions.

If we want to repair the analysis, we have to get rid of the fact that Regina is waiting at the beginning of the bridge. In the previous example, we had to get rid of certain facts, too, such as the simple facts connected with the fact that Hans went to "Dutchman's Delight." We were able to get rid of those unwelcome facts by giving priority to the more general fact that Hans and Babette

---

[6] Rescher (1973).

spent the entire evening together. A similar move is not possible here. The difference is this: in the Hans-and-Babette example, a Pollock-like analysis has the effect of making true a "might"-counterfactual only, whereas it is the corresponding "would"-counterfactual that should be true. We give priority to the possibility that Hans spends the evening with Babette. In the bridge example, the situation is reversed: a Pollock-like analysis has the effect of making a "would"-counterfactual true, whereas it is the corresponding "might"-counterfactual only that should be true. We don't give priority to either Regina's waiting or her passing; both possibilities are equally legitimate.

The conclusion seems to be that, sometimes, there are simple facts that cannot enter into the assessment of a counterfactual. Does this mean that we have to drop some of those facts? If we did so, we would be in danger of losing clause (i) of the Critical Truth-Conditions once and for all, for we couldn't be sure that the remaining facts would still provide a unique characterization of the world under consideration. We have to compensate for the facts we drop and again the admission of more complex facts will help us out.

Instead of thinking of Regina's waiting and my passing in terms of two separate facts, say p and q, we may consider them to be one fact $p \cap q$ (or parts of a single fact involving even more conjuncts). If those two facts are lumped together, they stand or fall together. If we make the counterfactual assumption that I am not on the bridge anymore, Regina's waiting will be removed together with my passing. Since the whole lump of propositions is incompatible with the counterfactual assumption, it doesn't have a chance of becoming a member of any set in $A_w{}^3(q)$.

It may be helpful to have a short illustration of how an analysis of counterfactuals in terms of maximal consistent sets is responsive to the way propositions are lumped together. Let p, q, and r be any propositions such that $\{p, \neg q, r\}$ is consistent and p doesn't follow from $\{\neg q, r\}$. Consider now the two inconsistent sets $\{p, q, r, \neg q\}$ and $\{p \cap q, r, \neg q\}$. The first set contains p and q as members. However, neither proposition is a member of the second set, which contains the conjunction (that is, the intersection) of the two propositions without containing the separate conjuncts. For both sets, let us now examine the sets of all consistent subsets that contain $\neg q$.

$$A = \{\{\neg q\}, \{p, \neg q\}, \{r, \neg q\}, \{p, r, \neg q\}\}$$
$$B = \{\{\neg q\}, \{r, \neg q\}\}$$

The proposition p follows from the only maximal set in A, but it doesn't follow from the only maximal set in B. Thus, lumping p and q together makes it possible for us to get rid of p along with q.

Re Dancing School

Pollock would predict that if I had danced with at least four of the men, I might have danced with Jeremy, Joseph, Jack, and James, or else with Jeremy, Joseph, Jack, and John. Those are the two possibilities permitted by his analysis: we have to keep the three men I actually danced with, and we can't add more than one extra man. Our reasoning is not as rigid as that, however; it seems that I might have danced with all five of the men or with any combination of four. To account for this without risk of losing clause (i) of the Critical Truth-Conditions, we must take recourse to lumped propositions again: my dancing with Jeremy, Joseph, and Jack, as well as my not dancing with James and John, should be parts of a single fact. If we assume that I had danced with at least four of the men, this lump of facts will be removed as a whole.

The three examples showed that Pollock's tripartition is not a partition of facts that underlies counterfactual reasoning in general. Two amendments seem necessary: more types of complex facts have to be admitted, and the system of priorities mentioned in the truth-conditions has to be extended. We saw that priorities can't always be used for "knocking out" propositions. Sometimes, we need other mechanisms for doing so. Thus lumped facts entered the picture. At this stage, it might be good to reconsider the reasons that may motivate us to load our truth-conditions with a weird system of priorities. Let's go back to Hans and Babette, then: Hans would have gone to the bistro, too, if Babette had gone there. I took this counterfactual to be true in the situation depicted above and I responded as if this judgment forced us to accept the amendments (i) and (ii).

We are not really committed to (ii), however. We might argue that the presence of the more general fact that Hans and Babette spent the evening together has the effect of lumping together other facts: it would then be one fact, for example, that Hans and Babette have dinner at "Dutchman's Delight." On such a view, we wouldn't have to extend our system of priorities anymore. If we make the counterfactual assumption that Babette has dinner somewhere else, Hans's activities are removed along with hers. As a consequence, there wouldn't be any propositions left that could be competitors for the fact that Hans and Babette spend the evening together.

A similar line of reasoning applies to the original Pollock-like truth-conditions. They stipulate that, in counterfactual reasoning, laws of nature have priority over actual necessities and actual necessities have priority over simple facts. Here too, the evidence originally motivating the introduction of priorities can be interpreted in a different way.

Suppose, for instance, that there is a mirror next door. At the moment, I am not looking into it. But suppose I did. Would I see my face reflected or wouldn't I? I am sure I would. The laws of optics wouldn't change, and there wouldn't be miraculous strokes of fate destroying the mirror or making me blind. What has to give way is the fact that I don't see my face reflected right now. Why is it that fact that has to be given up? We may seek an answer in terms of priorities. But we might just as well seek an answer in terms of lumping. We would then assume that my not looking into the mirror and my not seeing my face reflected are facts that are lumped together (along with other facts).

Examples like the last one suggest that priorities are most likely to be superfluous: the phenomena to be accounted for can be explained by lumping as well. And lumping is a device we need anyway. If all this is true, we can accept the analysis at the beginning of this chapter. However, when returning there, we are now directly confronted with the problem of giving an account of the notion, "what is the case."

3.4 Back to the original analysis

So far, a clear-cut notion of "what is the case" hasn't emerged from our deliberations. A vague notion, however, can be stated: what is the case in a world is a set of propositions that characterizes it uniquely. Call such a set of propositions a *partition* of the respective world. A *partition function* is then a function that assigns to every world a partition of it. Formally, a partition function is a function f on W that assigns to every w in W a set of propositions such that $\cap f(w) = \{w\}$. Examples of partition functions are the function that assigns to every world the set of all its true propositions and the function that assigns to every world w the set $\{\{w\}\}$. The notion of a "fact" would then have to be relativized to a partition function: a proposition p is a *fact* of a world w with respect to a partition function f iff p is a member of $f(w)$.

Our analysis of counterfactuals now has to be relativized to a partition function as well. Which proposition is expressed by an utterance of a sentence of the form (one) will then not only depend on the propositions expressed by the constituent sentences, but also on a partition function contributed by the context of conversation. The function f I earlier described as "the function that assigns to every world 'what is the case' in it" will then be a parameter and not a constant: different contexts fix the parameter in different ways. In theory, there are many possible partition functions. But in practice, their range is restricted by our modes of cognition. The human mind doesn't split up the world in arbitrary ways. A further narrowing down of possibilities comes from the context of conversation. Some contexts impose a particular view of the world: atomistic, holistic, Pollockistic perhaps. Usually, these restrictions are not sufficient to determine a unique partition function for a particular context of conversation. This is a source of vagueness in conditionals.

Counterfactuals are *context-dependent*, since their interpretation depends on a parameter that has to be fixed by the utterance situation. Counterfactuals are also *vague*, since this parameter is seldom fixed in a determinate way. There are context-dependent expressions that are less vague than counterfactuals. Take for example the word "I." A normal utterance of "I" refers to the speaker. There is hardly ever any vagueness about who the speaker is. Or consider "this" and "that" when used to refer to individuals. We mostly fix the individuals we want to refer to in an unambiguous way. Pointing may help. We succeed because our standards for splitting up the world into individuals are rather rigid. There is comparatively little room for vagueness. Things are different with "here" and "now." A typical utterance of "here" refers to some indeterminate area around the speaker.[7] A typical utterance of "now" refers to some indeterminate interval around the utterance time. Typically it remains open which area or which interval this is exactly. Our everyday standards for splitting up space into places or times into intervals are variable and hazy. And so are—I believe—our everyday standards for splitting up the world into facts.

If I am right in assuming that there is an intimate connection between partition functions and counterfactuals, we should expect the variability and indeterminacy of the partition function to determine the variability and vagueness of counterfactuals. On the other hand, the *in*variable properties of counterfactuals should be determined by the invariable properties of the partition function and the invariable role it plays in the analysis. What we know about counterfactuals supports both expectations.

The first expectation

The analysis I have proposed makes the interpretation of counterfactuals depend on a parameter f. The two functions I mentioned as examples for partition functions represent two extreme ways of fixing this parameter. In

[7] Klein (1982).

both cases, the analysis predicts that a counterfactual reduces to material implication if its antecedent is true, and to strict implication if its antecedent is false (in the evaluation world). The Critical Argument established this for the function that assigns to every world the set of all its true propositions. We will now prove it for the function f that assigns to every world w of W the set $\{\{w\}\}$.

Hegel's Counterfactual

Suppose that a sentence of the form (1) is uttered in a situation that fixes the parameter f so that $f(w)=\{\{w\}\}$ for all w in W. Let p, q, and r be the propositions expressed by the utterance of the whole sentence, the antecedent, and the consequent respectively.

(i) Assume that q is true in a world w of W. Then $\{\{q\}, \{q, \{w\}\}\}$ is the set of all consistent subsets of $f(w) \cup \{q\}$ that contain q and $\{q, \{w\}\}$ is the only maximal set in this set. Now r follows from $\{q, \{w\}\}$ iff r is true in w. This means that if q is true in w, then p is true in w iff r is true in w as well.

(ii) Assume that q is false in w. If q is the empty set, then p is true trivially and r follows from q. If q is not the empty set, then the set of all consistent subsets of $f(w) \cup \{q\}$ is simply $\{\{q\}\}$ and $\{q\}$ is the only maximal set in this set. This means that if q is false in w, then p is true in w iff r follows from q.

The partition function underlying Hegel's Counterfactual corresponds to a holistic view of the world: all facts hang together. Our analysis predicts that a holistic view of the world should reduce counterfactuals to strict implications if their antecedents are false in the evaluation world. But do counterfactuals really oscillate so as to include strict implication as the limiting case? I think they do. If we adopt a skeptical strategy in a conversation, we can push every counterfactual with false antecedent towards strict implication. We just have to insist again and again that—after all—everything is connected to everything else in our world. Here is an example of such a conversation:

A holist's argument

Hans: If I had left five minutes earlier, I would have caught the train.

Anna: Not necessarily. You might have got run over by a car.

Hans: But there weren't any cars around at that time. I saw it from the window.

Anna: But if you had left earlier, someone else might have left earlier, too. He might have taken his car and might have run you over. What would have caused *you* to leave five minutes earlier, might have caused *him* to leave five minutes earlier, too.

By lumping together fact after fact, Anna will succeed in destroying every counterfactual that Hans might think of, with the exception of those counterfactuals where the proposition expressed by the consequent follows from the one expressed by the antecedent.

In making a counterfactual assumption, we make a kind of revision to the actual world. The extent of this revision depends on the underlying partition. If everything is linked to everything else, the world is a whole. If you change a bit of it, the rest may change as well.

Examples like the conversation between Anna and Hans support our first expectation: the range of variability of counterfactuals corresponds to the range of variability of the partition function. We still need support for our second expectation.

The second expectation

There are certain principles for counterfactual reasoning that hold independently of a particular utterance situation and on which everyone seems to agree. One of those principles is expressed in clause (i) of the Critical Truth-Conditions. It says that a counterfactual with true antecedent should be true iff its consequent is true. While brooding over amendments in the preceding section, we always kept in mind that we should never lose this principle. And indeed, we have saved it. This can be seen by going back to part 2 of the Critical Argument. The only property of the function f that is needed for this part of the argument is the property of being a partition function.

Examples of other commonly held principles that are validated by our semantics, are the following:[8]

> If α were the case, then β would be the case.
> If α were the case, then γ would be the case.
> ———————————————————————————
> If α were the case, then β and γ would be the case.
>
> If α were the case, then β would be the case.
> If α were the case, then γ would be the case.
> ———————————————————————————
> If α and β were the case, then γ would be the case.

As usual for counterfactuals, the inference patterns of strengthening the antecedent, transitivity, and contraposition are not validated.

John Burgess (1981) gave axiomatizations and completeness proofs for a number of conditional logics. Burgess's proofs are based on ordering frames

---

[8] We have to assume, of course, that the partition function contributed by the context of conversation stays the same during the inference.

as discussed in Lewis (1981). That those proofs include a completeness proof for the semantics of counterfactuals presented here follows from Lewis's equivalence proofs in the same paper. The invariable properties of the partition function and the role it plays in our analysis are thus strong enough for characterizing a plausible logic of counterfactuals.

3.5 Conclusion

An analysis that seemed to fail is viable after all. It is viable if we let it depend on a partition function to be provided by the context of conversation. The analysis deliberately leaves certain traits of the partition function open. This should be so. Specifying those traits, as Pollock does, leads to wrong predictions. Leaving them open seems to give counterfactuals just the right amount of variability and vagueness.

Acknowledgments

I want to thank Max and Mary Cresswell for discussions and hospitality in January and February 1979. I am also indebted to the Max Planck Gesellschaft for a travel grant to New Zealand.

A previous version of this paper was read at the 1979 Bielefeld conference on theories of meaning and language use sponsored by the Deutsche Forschungsgemeinschaft. I profited from written or oral comments by Jonathan Bennett, Ulrich Blau, Franz von Kutschera, David Lewis, Wolfgang Spohn, Richard Thomason, Frank Veltman, and Thomas Ede Zimmermann. I am also grateful to Lorraine Tyler for checking my English for the original publication, and to Aynat Rubinstein for preparing the manuscript for the current re-edition.

INTRODUCING CHAPTER 4

My earliest properly published work on conditionals is the third part of Kratzer (1978), which I submitted as my dissertation. My first English paper on conditionals is Kratzer (1979), which introduced some of the ideas in Kratzer (1978) to an English-speaking readership. In both works, I extended the restrictor view of *if*-clauses that David Lewis (1975) had proposed for conditionals in the direct scope of adverbs of quantification to conditionals appearing with modals. The properties of both indicative and subjunctive conditionals could then be derived from the properties of the participating operators. One of the puzzles I set out to solve in my dissertation was why, in spite of more than 2000 years of research on conditionals, no consensus on what they mean and how they should be analyzed had emerged. The answer I came up with was that two potentially hidden parameters are involved in the interpretation of conditionals. *If*-clauses restrict quantificational operators, but the operators can be covert, and hence may go unnoticed. To complicate matters further, the operators overtly or covertly restricted by *if*-clauses may depend on contextually provided domain restrictions—a second source of indeterminacy. The reason why such a wide range of interpretations has been proposed in the literature on simple indicative conditionals could then be that particular settings for potentially hidden parameters were mistaken for the general case.

The original version of chapter 4 appeared in Anne M. Farley, Peter Farley, and Karl Eric McCollough (eds.), *Papers from the Parasession on Pragmatics and Grammatical Theory*, Chicago: Chicago Linguistics Society (1986), 115–35. The paper was reprinted as Chapter 30 in Arnim v. Stechow and Dieter Wunderlich (eds.), *Handbuch Semantik/Handbook Semantics*, Berlin and New York: de Gruyter (1991), 651–6.

Chapter 4

Conditionals

4.1 Grice

In his William James lectures[1], Paul Grice defends an analysis of indicative conditionals in terms of material implication. The observation that sometimes non-truth-functional factors seem to enter the interpretation of indicative conditionals is explained by invoking conversational implicatures adding to the meaning proper of the construction. Consider (1):

(1) If my hen has laid eggs today, then the Cologne Cathedral will collapse tomorrow morning.[2]

On a Gricean account, (1) is interpreted as material implication. My utterance of it, however, *implicates* that there is some non-accidental connection between my hen laying eggs and a possible collapse of the Cologne Cathedral. That is, what I ultimately convey to my audience is some stricter form of implication. Roughly, this implicature comes about in the following way: suppose I just happened to know that my hen didn't lay eggs today or that the Cologne Cathedral would collapse tomorrow. On a material implication analysis of conditionals, my utterance would be true, but misleading. I could, and indeed should, have said (2) or (3), which would have led to a stronger claim.

(2) My hen hasn't laid eggs today.

(3) The Cologne Cathedral will collapse tomorrow.

The dilemma we are facing is that, under a material implication analysis of conditionals, (1) is true just in case one of (2) or (3) is true. Yet if I had known that one of (2) or (3) was true, I shouldn't have said (1) to begin with. Why, then, *did* I say (1)? The most plausible explanation would be that I had evidence for a non-accidental connection that guaranteed the truth of the consequent of (1) should the antecedent turn out to be true. Trusting that you

---

[1] Lecture IV, now published in Grice (1989. 58–85).
[2] The sentence is not *quite* Frege's sentence in Frege (1923).

would be able to figure out why I said what I did, and that you would realize that I was counting on your figuring out why I said what I did, I conveyed to you that I considered the antecedent and the consequent of (1) to be non-accidentally connected.

A Gricean analysis of indicative conditionals is appealing in that, unlike so many other accounts replacing a material implication analysis, it is able to explain why material implication accounts have cropped up again and again in the history of logic and mathematics. A material implication interpretation would be *the* interpretation of indicative conditionals once we abstract away from principles guiding cooperative social interaction. It would be an interpretation accessible to all of us, not an artificial construct created for the sole use by an eccentric group of academics. Learning logic would consist in dropping a few rules for cooperative social interaction.

4.2 Gibbard's proof

In *Two Recent Theories of Conditionals*, Allan Gibbard (Gibbard 1981) proves that any conditional operator $\Rightarrow$ satisfying (i) and the two additional rather obvious principles (ii) and (iii) reduces to material implication.

(i) $p \Rightarrow (q \Rightarrow r)$ and $(p \,\&\, q) \Rightarrow r$ are logically equivalent.
(ii) $p \Rightarrow q$ logically implies the corresponding material conditional. That is, $p \Rightarrow q$ is false whenever p is true and q is false.
(iii) If p logically implies q, then $p \Rightarrow q$ is a logical truth.

Here is a sketch of Gibbard's proof: since condition (ii) states that $p \Rightarrow q$ logically implies $p \to q$, all we have to show is that $p \to q$ logically implies $p \Rightarrow q$, where the simple arrow stands for material implication and the double arrow stands for any connective satisfying conditions (i) to (iii). Consider now $(*)$:

$$(*) \quad (p \to q) \Rightarrow (p \Rightarrow q)$$

Given (i), $(*)$ is logically equivalent to $(**)$:

$$(**) \quad ((p \to q) \,\&\, p) \Rightarrow q.$$

According to (iii), $(**)$ is a logical truth, and that means that $(*)$ is a logical truth as well. But $(*)$ logically implies $(***)$ according to (ii), and hence $(***)$, too, is a logical truth.

$$(***) \quad (p \to q) \to (p \Rightarrow q)$$

But then $p \rightarrow q$ logically implies $p \Rightarrow q$. QED.

How plausible are the three conditions (i) to (iii)? Do they all hold for bare indicative conditionals in English? Conditions (ii) and (iii) are generally accepted. Condition (i) is less obvious, but seems to be satisfied as well. The (a) and (b) cases of (4) to (6) feel pairwise equivalent:[3]

(4)   a. If you are back before eight then if the roast is ready we will have dinner together.

   b. If you are back before eight and the roast is ready we will have dinner together.

(5)   a. If you drink one more can of beer then if I drink one more can of beer then we'll be completely out of beer.

   b. If you drink one more can of beer and I drink one more can of beer then we'll be completely out of beer.

(6)   a. If you drink one more beer then if I drink two more whiskies then if you give one more leer at my wife then if I give one more leer at your wife then if you smoke another cigarette then if I get hit in the face by one more beer then if I sit down on two more pretzels then I'm leaving.

   b. If you drink one more beer and I drink two more whiskies and you give one more leer at my wife and I give one more leer at your wife and you smoke another cigarette and I get hit in the face by one more beer and I sit down on two more pretzels then I'm leaving.

Gibbard's proof, then, seems to exclude any sort of stricter implication as a candidate for the interpretation of bare indicative conditionals in English. It lends further support to a material implication analysis in the spirit of Grice.

4.3 The decline of material implication

The two preceding sections built a strong case in favor of a material implication interpretation of indicative conditionals. This case cannot withstand closer scrutiny, however. The recent history of semantics has seen the steady decline of the material conditional. There was a time, for example, when even sentences like

(7)   All porches have screens.

---

[3] (5a) and (6a) are from Culicover (1970: 367).

were formalized with the help of material implication:

(8) $\forall x$ (x is a porch $\rightarrow$ x has screens)

These times are gone. Formalizations like (8) disappeared for reasons of generality. Realizing that

(9)   Some porches have screens.

cannot be formalized as

(10) $\exists x$ (x is a porch $\rightarrow$ x has screens)

was not yet fatal. But attempts to formalize sentences like

(11)   Most porches have screens.

made it clear that material conditionals had no role to play in the formalization of sentences with quantifiers. Another two-place connective—conjunction—is successful with (9), but then again is a complete failure with (11). Paying close attention to quantifiers like *most* led to the theory of generalized quantifiers within "interpretational" frameworks and to the theory of restrictive quantification in the "representational" tradition.[4] On the latter approach, we have representations as in (12):

(12)   (most x: x is a porch)   (x has screens)
        quantifier   restriction   nuclear scope

In (12), the clause *x is a porch* is interpreted as restricting the domain of the quantifier *most*. (12) is true iff most individuals satisfying the restriction *x is a porch* also satisfy *x has screens*, the part of the construction that is often referred to as its "nuclear scope" (Heim 1982).

A more direct attack on the material conditional came from adverbial quantifiers scoping over indicative conditionals. In *Adverbs of Quantification*, David Lewis (1975) examines sentences of the following kind:

(13)   Sometimes
        Always
        Usually   } if a man buys a horse, he pays cash for it.
        Never

There is some discussion in Lewis's article about what kind of things adverbs like *sometimes*, *always*, and *usually* or *most of the time* quantify over. For convenience, let us assume that they are quantifiers over events, as assumed

---

[4] Lewis (1972), Barwise and Cooper (1981), Cushing (1976), McCawley (1981), among many others.

in Rothstein (1995), for example. Admittedly, this proposal does not fit with Lewis's views, who takes adverbial quantifiers to be unselective binders—a proposal adopted in Heim (1982). Nothing hinges on this divergence for the current discussion, though. If adverbs of quantification were sentential operators, and indicative conditionals were formalized in the traditional way, we would be led to bipartite logical representations in the format displayed in (14):

(14)   For some event e ⎱   (e is an event where a man buys a horse)
       For all events e ⎰   → (e is part of an event where the man in
       For most events e ⎰   e pays cash for the horse in e).
       For no event e   ⎰

For the same reasons that material conditionals cannot *generally* be part of the formalization of sentences with nominal quantifiers, material conditionals cannot *generally* be part of the formalization of sentences with adverbial quantifiers. In the way of illustration suppose the logical form of (15a) were (15b):

(15)   a. Most of the time, if a man buys a horse, he pays cash for it.

       b. For most events e ((e is an event where a man buys a horse) → (e is
          part of an event where the man in e pays cash for the horse in e)).

If formalized as (15b), (15a) should be true on a scenario where, say, out of a million events of some kind or other, 2000 are events where a man buys a horse, and, out of those, 1990 are sales that are settled by check. (15a) is intuitively false on such a scenario, since most of the horse sales are not settled by cash. (15b) comes out true, however, since most of the one million events that make up the domain of quantification are not events where a man buys a horse to begin with.

   The problem can be solved by adopting restricted quantification structures for adverbial quantifiers, too.

(16)   (Most e: e is an event where a man buys a horse) (e is part of an event
       where the man in e pays cash for the horse in e).

(16) has the same kind of tripartite logical form as (12) above. It consists of a quantifier, a restriction, and a nuclear scope. (16) is true just in case most events that satisfy the quantifier restriction also satisfy the nuclear scope. What originated as an *if*-clause in surface structure ended up as a quantifier restriction at logical form. On such an account, there is no such thing as a

two-place *if...then* operator in the logical representations of the sentences in (13). The function of *if*-clauses is invariably to restrict the domain of the adverb. We have to concede, then, that there are indicative conditionals that cannot be analyzed as material conditionals.

4.4 Probability conditionals

In his lectures on logic and conversation, Paul Grice discusses an example that he dubs "Grice's Paradox."[5] It goes as follows. Yog and Zog play chess according to normal rules, but with the special conditions that Yog has white 9 out of 10 times and that there are no draws. Up to now, there have been a hundred games. When Yog had white, he won 80 out of 90. And when he had black, he lost 10 out of 10. Suppose Yog and Zog played one of the hundred games last night and we don't yet know what its outcome was. In such a situation, we might say (17) or (18).

(17)   If Yog had white, there is a probability of 8/9 that he won.

(18)   If Yog lost, there is a probability of 1/2 that he had black.

Both statements would be true on Grice's scenario. If we stick to a material implication analysis of conditionals, the options for possible logical forms for (17) or (18) are (19) or (20).

(19)   A $\rightarrow$ x-probably B

(20)   x-probably (A $\rightarrow$ B)

(19) can be dismissed right away. A material conditional of the form (19) is true if A is false. But Yog's having black wouldn't be sufficient to make (17) true, and Yog's winning wouldn't be sufficient for the truth of (18). (20) needs to be inspected further. Before thinking about the expected truth-conditions, let us check whether syntactic structures that surface as (17) or (18) might go through a stage that looks more like (20) in the course of their syntactic derivation. There is a structural discrepancy between (17) and (18) on the one hand and (20). If the meanings of (17) or (18) are to be computed off structures like (20), where the probability operator takes scope over the conditional, there needs to be a derivational connection between the two types of structures.

The syntactic properties of conditionals have been elucidated by Geis (1970, 1985), Iatridou (1991), von Fintel (1994), Bhatt and Pancheva (2006),

---

[5] William James Lectures, lecture IV; now published in Grice (1989: 78).

and Haegeman (2010), among others. Syntactically, *if*-clauses are adverbial clauses that, like other adverbial clauses, can appear in different positions, as illustrated in (21):

(21)   a. If Yog lost, there is a 50% chance that he played black.
        b. There is a 50% chance that, if Yog lost, he played black.
        c. There is a 50% chance that Yog lost if he played black.

The existence of syntactic variation of the kind seen in (21) invites the conjecture that some of the variants are related via movement. If (21a) were derived from (21b) via movement of the *if*-clause to the left periphery of the sentence, the *if*-clause could be interpreted while still being in the lower position, or else could be reconstructed into that position for purposes of interpretation. Even for (21a), then, the structure receiving a semantic interpretation could be (21b), and hence a structure conforming to the schema in (20). For the sake of the argument, let us temporarily assume that some such story is correct and see what happens with Grice's example. When submitted to semantic interpretation, (17) would look as in (22):

(22)   There is probability of 8/9 that (if Yog had white (he won)).

If *if* is given the interpretation in (23), the embedded conditional in (22) comes out as a material conditional, as intended.

(23) $[[if]] = \lambda p \lambda q \lambda w \, (p(w) \rightarrow q(w))$

(24) and (25) could thus be thought of as convenient schemata capturing the logical essence of the stages of (17) and (18) where semantic interpretation takes place.

(24)   8/9-probably (Yog had white $\rightarrow$ Yog won)

(25)   1/2-probably (Yog lost $\rightarrow$ Yog had black)

And here is Grice's paradox: since in chess not having black is having white, and, if there are no draws, not losing is winning, the two embedded material conditionals in (24) and (25) are contrapositions of each other. But then they are logically equivalent and couldn't have different probabilities.

To see how we might get out of the paradox, let's slowly go through the reasoning that convinced us that (17) and (18) are true on Grice's story.

Why (17) is judged true

We are assuming that there were a total of 100 games. The *if*-clause tells us that we only need to consider those of the 100 games where Yog had white.

We are now left with 90 games. Out of those, Yog won 80. Those games are 8/9 of the games we are considering, and this is why (17) is true.

Why (18) is judged true

As before, we are assuming that there were a total of 100 games. This time round, the *if*-clause instructs us to only consider those games where Yog lost. There are 20 such games. Out of those, Yog had black in 10 cases. Those 10 games are half of the games we are considering, and this is why (18) is true.

This is, of course, how conditional probabilities are standardly computed. But that observation alone does not solve our puzzle. We are confronted with the task to explain *why* conditionals and probability operators interact in this apparently exceptional way. The dilemma brought out by Grice's paradox is exacerbated by the fact that Lewis (1976) showed that the problem isn't just the material conditional. There is no way of interpreting any two-place connective $\Rightarrow$ so that, *quite generally*, structures like (26) below can be interpreted as saying that the conditional probability of B given A is x.[6]

(26)   x-probably (A $\Rightarrow$ B)

What should we do? The answer I want to suggest will not come as a surprise by now. In (17) and (18), too, the role of *if*-clauses is to provide domain restrictions for quantificational operators. The schematic logical forms for (17) and (18) would then resemble those of the quantified sentences discussed earlier:

(27)   (8/9 probably: Yog had white in g) (Yog won g)

(28)   (1/2-probably: Yog lost g) (Yog had black in g)

(27) is true iff the ratio of games satisfying the nuclear scope to the games satisfying the restriction is 8/9. (28) is true iff that ratio is 1/2. (27) and (28) are no longer based on the assumption that there is any such thing as a two-place conditional operator carried by *if... then*, as traditionally assumed. (17) and (18) have logical structures where the only role of the *if*-clause is to restrict the probability operator. With logical forms like (27) and (28), Grice's paradox disappears. The threat of Lewis (1976) is diverted as well: the reason why the probabilities of conditional propositions can't seem to match the corresponding conditional probabilities is that, in a sense, there *are* no conditional propositions that are embedded under probability operators.

If we are serious about the syntax/semantics interface, our job is not done, however. We still have to show how plausible syntactic structures can provide

---

[6] See Égré and Cozic (2010) for a most recent discussion of the dilemma.

the right input for a semantic interpretation component that derives truth-conditions for conditionals in a fully compositional and general way for all cases where *if*-clauses restrict operators of any kind. To make headway on such a task, we would need a good grasp of the semantics of all the operators involved. Semantically, conditionals are no longer much of a topic in their own right, then. We can only truly understand them in connection with the operators they restrict.

At the end of chapter 2, we saw that *if*-clauses can restrict modal operators of various flavors and strengths by changing their modal bases. It seems that they can do so without operating over modals directly. This is reflected in the meaning assignment (29) from Kratzer (1981b), which was reproduced in chapter 2. According to (29), *if*-clauses affect a modal base parameter that subsequent modals depend on:

Conditional modality

(29)   For any conversational backgrounds f and g:

$$[[if\ \alpha\ \beta)]]^{f,g} = [[\beta]]^{f^*,g}, \text{ where for all } w \in W, f^*(w)$$

$$= f(w) \cup \{[[\alpha]]^{f,g}\}.$$

(29) cannot be the last word on the impact of *if*-clauses on modals, though. More plausible accounts have to allow for *if*-clauses to restrict modals in long stretches of subsequent discourse, as in (30).

(30)   If a wolf entered the house, he must have eaten grandma, since she was bedridden. He might have eaten the girl with the red cap, too. In fact, that's rather likely. The poor little thing wouldn't have been able to defend herself.

In (30), the *if*-clause restricts four modal expressions in a row: *must* in its own clause, *might* in the second clause, *rather likely* in the third clause, and *would* in the fourth clause. This suggests that natural languages have overt or non-overt anaphoric mechanisms that allow modal expressions to pick up possibilities introduced in preceding discourse. The nature of those mechanisms has been a matter of debate (Roberts 1987, 1989; Geurts 1995; Frank 1996; Stone 1999; Kratzer, forthcoming) and is an issue that I am not trying to resolve here. An overt anaphoric device related to *if*-clauses is the pronoun *then*, which seems to represent the modal domain in conditional configurations like (31) (von Fintel 1994; Schlenker 2004).

(31)   If a wolf entered the house, *then* he must have eaten grandma, since she was bedridden.

If *if*-clauses can restrict modals at a distance, and if conditional probabilities are special cases of conditional modalities, we reach the conclusion that among the variants (21a) to (21c) from above, it is actually (21a) that should be submitted to semantic interpretation.

(21) a. If Yog lost ((then) (there is a 50% chance that he had black))

There is no need to "restore" the *if*-clause in (21a) to a position within the scope of the probability operator for purposes of interpretation. In fact, there are strong semantic reasons *not* to do so, as we have seen. On the other hand, Bhatt and Pancheva (2006) suggest that binding facts might sometimes force reconstruction of an *if*-clause. The data they present in support of this suggestion all involve pronouns with a logophoric flavor, though, as in (32a). Logophoric pronouns are known to have non-standard binding properties. Once logophoricity is controlled for, binding facts, too, speak against the reconstruction of left-peripheral *if*-clauses. This is shown by the ungrammaticality of (32b):

(32) a. If pictures of himself appear on the Internet, there is a good chance that John will get upset.

      b. *If pictures of himself appear on the Internet, there is a good chance that John won the election.

According to (29), the *if*-clause in (21a) resets the domain of worlds that are relevant for the probability operator in the main clause so that only worlds where Yog lost are being considered. In line with the analysis of epistemic probability operators in chapter 2, we now need to find a suitable probability measure P that assigns 1 to the set A of all worlds where Yog lost, 0 to any proposition that is incompatible with A, and moreover preserves the original relation of comparative possibility (determined by the ordering source for the probability operator) for all propositions that are subsets of A.

   To see how the right result for Grice's Paradox could come out of the analysis of epistemic modality in chapter 2, let us simplify his example a little to avoid number explosion. Assume that there were just ten games between Yog and Zog on ten consecutive days, and the last one took place last night. Yog had white in nine of the ten games, and he lost twice: the one time he had black and once when he had white. Assume furthermore that all of this information comes from a 100% reliable report, which functions as "evidence of things" feeding a realistic modal base. All accessible worlds have (counterparts of) those ten games, then, on their respective days. In each accessible world, (a counterpart of) Yog plays white nine of ten times and loses the one time he plays black, and once when he has white. Since the report was silent about when Yog or Zog played white or black, and which games they won or lost, the accessible worlds differ accordingly. The worlds differ in countless other respects, too, of course, but we are only interested in who won or lost and who played white or black in those ten games. We therefore need to disregard all other differences and group together all accessible worlds that answer the questions we care about in the same way. This amounts to partitioning the set of accessible worlds into equivalence classes of worlds that agree on who the winner or loser of each of the ten games was and who played which color. We can assemble a base set of possibilities W to work with by picking an arbitrary representative from each cell in the partition. W has as many members as there are ways of partitioning the set of ten games into three cells A, B, and C, so that both A and B have one member, and C has eight: A is the slot for the one game where Yog plays black, B is the slot for the one game where Yog plays white and loses, and C is the slot for the remaining 8 games, which are the games where Yog plays white and wins.

Possibilities for Yog's Games

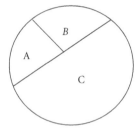

There are 90 ways of assigning pairs of distinct games from the pool of ten games to slots A and B: each of the ten games can fill slot A, and being there, can co-appear with nine different games in slot B. The remaining games must always go into slot C. The set W has 90 members, then.

There is nothing in Grice's story suggesting that the 90 members of W should be ranked with respect to each other. The ordering source is empty in this particular case, then, and all members of W are "equipossible": each of the 90 worlds in W has probability 1/90. This gives us a suitable probability measure P that assigns 1/90 to each singleton subset of W. Assignments to the other subsets of W follow from the additivity of P: for disjoint sets S and S', $P(S \cup S') = P(S) + P(S')$.

We can now pose the crucial question: what is the probability that Yog lost last night's game? The question boils down to asking how many worlds there are in W where Yog lost last night's game. The answer is 18, and that means that the probability that Yog lost last night's game is $18/90 = 1/5 = 20\%$. To compute the truth-conditions for (33), we follow our familiar recipe:

(33)   (If Yog lost last night's game (there is a 50% chance that he played black))

Under the impact of the *if*-clause, the accessible worlds are restricted to the set W' of worlds from W where Yog lost last night's game. Since W' has 18 members, the probability of each world in W' is reset to $1/18$, and that leads to a new probability measure P' that assigns $1/18$ to all singleton subsets of W' and 0 to all propositions that are incompatible with W'. Out of the 18 worlds of W' there are 9 where the lost game is the one where he played black. The probability that Yog had black in last night's game under the assumption that he lost it is thus $9/18 = 1/2 = 50\%$.

In Grice's example, we are given frequencies for certain properties to occur within a group of 100 games, and we are drawing conclusions about the likelihood for a particular one of the 100 games to have one of those properties. The analysis of epistemic probability in chapter 2 provides the correct account for such cases. There was one new piece I had to add to the analysis, however. The modal base all by itself does not yet give us a suitable set of worlds for a suitable probability measure. We have to make sure that the measure is only sensitive to variation of the kind we are interested in. I therefore had to invoke a particular partition of the set of accessible worlds. I took that partition to be a reflection of what is often called "question under discussion" or "discourse topic." Discourse topics construed as questions play an important role in semantics and pragmatics, quite independently of epistemic probability (von Fintel 1994; Roberts 1996; Büring 1997; Beaver and Clark 2008). The idea of discourse topics inducing partitions on sets of accessible worlds is not new either: it comes from Groenendijk and Stokhof's seminal work (Groenendijk and Stokhof 1984), and was taken up in Simons (2000), and, most recently, in Yalcin (2008).

4.5 Epistemic conditionals

The picture that has been emerging in the previous sections is that *if*-clauses are restrictive devices for certain types of operators, including adverbs of quantification, modals, and probability operators. There are, however, also "bare" conditionals like (1), which do not have any overt operator that the *if*-clause could restrict. In Kratzer (1978, 1979, 1981b) I argued that we should consider bare conditionals as implicitly modalized. Simplifying slightly, we can think of modal operators as quantifiers whose domains are sets of possible worlds or situations. *If*-clauses can restrict those domains further. The logical form for (34a), for example, would be (34b), where *MUST* is an unpronounced modal:

(34) a. If the lights in his study are on, Roger is home.
      b. (*MUST*: the lights in his study are on) (Roger is home)

(34) is true iff Roger is home in all accessible worlds where the lights in his study are on. The modal in (34) seems to be of the epistemic variety[7] with a realistic modal base characterizing a salient piece of factual evidence. In the limiting case, the evidence might be *all* of reality, and, consequently, the modal domain shrinks to a singleton set containing the utterance world as its only member. Bare epistemic conditionals like (34) reduce to material implication under those conditions.

A speaker can felicitously use a modal that is relativized to all of reality without actually knowing all of reality. You do not have to be omniscient to assert a material conditional. More generally, speakers can make claims whose truth or falsehood depends on particular pieces of evidence without knowing what that evidence consists of. Suppose we are confronted with a locked cabinet we know to contain the relevant factual evidence about the murder of Much-Girgl. We have no clue about what that evidence is, but for the sheer fun of it, start placing bets on who might have killed Girgl, given the evidence in the cabinet. Used in such a context, the modals in (35) and (36) are interpreted as being relativized to the evidence in the cabinet even if that evidence is not known to the speaker or to any other discourse participant.

(35) Kastenjakl must have done it.

(36) Gauzner-Michl might have done it.

I would like to emphasize that if there is a non-overt modal in bare conditionals, it is not expected to have exactly the same meaning as its overt counterpart. There is a difference in meaning between (34a) and (37):

(37) If the lights in his study are on, Roger must be home.

---

[7] Epistemic interpretations are the backbone of data semantics: Veltman (1976, 1984, 1985), Landman (1986). Data semantics emphasized the important connection between epistemic modality and bare indicative conditionals.

By using epistemic *must* in sentences like (37), speakers indicate that they are relying on a particular, non-trivial, piece of evidence. The use of *must* in (37) may point to a psychological condition that prompts Roger to turn all lights off whenever he leaves his house. Overt *must* shows the characteristic constraints of so-called "indirect evidentials" (Westmoreland 1998; Drubig 2001; von Fintel and Gillies 2010). It cannot be used felicitously for claims based on direct perceptual or experiential evidence, for example.

(38)   a. # Your nose must be dripping. I can see it.
       b.   You must have a cold. Your nose is dripping.

(39)   a. # I must have a terrible headache. I feel lousy.
       b.   The baby must have a terrible headache. He is screaming and pressing his hands against his temples.

In contrast to (37), I can use (34a) felicitously when all I am doing is bet on the corresponding conditional without relying on any particular piece of evidence at all. In such situations, *MUST* in (34b) is most plausibly understood as relativized to all of reality, and, consequently, the conditional I bet on is a material conditional.

One of the results of chapter 1 was that conversational backgrounds need to be functions from circumstances of evaluation, and that means that one and the same conversational background might yield different premise sets depending on what those circumstances are. We saw that it is essential that conversational backgrounds be such functions, rather than just premise sets. If they were just premise sets, modal statements would not be contingent, and we would run into serious trouble with embedded modals. It is now time to ask what circumstances of evaluation are. Up to now, I have been assuming that they are just possible worlds, but that was a convenient simplification. They should be functions from pairs of worlds and spatio-temporal locations, or, alternatively, functions from partial worlds or situations.[8] To see why, think about the law, for example. What the law is may be different at different times or in different parts of the world. The law today is different from the law a hundred years ago, and the law in America is different from that in Australia.

---

[8] The importance of situations of evaluation (Austinian topic situations) in natural language semantics has been emphasized for many years by François Recanati, most recently in Recanati (2007). See also Kratzer (2007) for an overview of the role of situations in natural language semantics. Within a Lewisian ontology, any individual or situation is part of a unique world. If we don't want to make this assumption, we could construe situations of evaluation as centered worlds, and hence as pairs consisting of a world and an individual, situation, or spatio-temporal location. This move is made in Egan, Hawthorne, and Weatherson (2005).

If circumstances of evaluation for conversational backgrounds are no longer whole worlds, but can be smaller entities like situations or spatio-temporal locations, modal claims are expected to be context dependent. Typically, the context of use would be expected to tell us what the circumstances of evaluation for a modal are. However, since contexts are rarely specific enough to live up to such expectations, modal claims often end up being underdetermined and vague. This makes it possible for discourse participants to shift modal boundaries in the course of a conversation. Here is an illustration.[9] You and I, standing next to each other and looking in the same direction so that our visual fields are roughly the same, are watching a man who is approaching. At first, we can only see the bare outlines of the man. Given our evidence, the man may be Fred. A few seconds later, the situation has become clearer. The man cannot possibly be Fred. In light of the new evidence, it must be Martin. While we were watching the man, the dialogue in (40) might have taken place:

(40)   Me (when the man was in the distance):   The man might be Fred.
       You (when the man was closer):   No, it must be Martin.

There is a way of understanding the dialogue in (40) where we were both right: What I said was true if *might* was relativized to the initial evidence we had. In your response, you re-evaluated what I said under the impact of the later evidence, and my very words wound up as saying something false. This justified your *no*.

Crucially, our exchange could have taken place without even the slightest change in modal base. If conversational backgrounds are functions from situations or spatio-temporal locations to premise sets, premise sets representing the available evidence can change as time goes by. One and the same conversational background can thus represent changes in premise sets.

Our dialogue might have been the same if we had observed the man from different vantage points. From where I was, the available evidence was compatible with the man being Fred. From where you were, the available evidence ruled out that possibility. As before, the modal base seems to have remained the same. All that changed were the circumstances of evaluation.

In the example of the approaching man, I made my initial claim based on the evidence I had. That's the best any speaker can be expected to do. Since my evidence was compatible with Fred's approaching, I was justified in asserting what I did. There was no—or very little—indeterminacy about

---

[9] I expanded the discussion of this example in Kratzer (1986) in response to von Fintel and Gillies (2010).

the assertability conditions, then. But wasn't there still something a little less subjective that I put on the common table? Wasn't there still a claim I committed myself to for the assertion game we were playing with each other? I think there was, but for that claim, the situation of evaluation might have been genuinely underspecified. That gave you the opportunity to jump right in on both occasions and reinterpret what I said by silently drawing attention to different situations of evaluation. On the first scenario, the new evidence we both had led to your *no*. On the second scenario, any super-situation of the situation you had access to would have been suitable to justify your *no*. Since you had access to a situation that provided evidence ruling out Fred as the man who was approaching, any of its supersituations provided evidence ruling out that possibility, too. Your evidence trumped mine, then, regardless of what it might have been.

Lewis (1979a) has more examples illustrating how modal underspecification allows addressees to shift modal boundaries in ways unintended by the speaker. Here is one:

Suppose I am talking with some elected official about the ways he might deal with an embarrassment. So far, we have been ignoring those possibilities that would be political suicide for him. He says: "You see, I must either destroy the evidence or else claim that I did it to stop Communism. What else can I do?" I rudely reply: "There is one other possibility – you can put the public interest first for once!"

Lewis (1979a: 354).

Capturing modal underspecification was the central force driving the analyses in Kratzer (1977, 1978, 1981b), where modal claims were said to depend on contextual parameters that actual contexts are unlikely to provide unique values for.[10] The role model was the analysis of counterfactuals in Lewis (1973a). By letting the truth of counterfactuals depend on a rarely resolved contextual parameter, Lewis intended to capture the particular type of vagueness they exhibit.

In statements with unmodified epistemic modals, truth-conditions and assertability conditions can come apart. It may happen that, for one and the same modal statement, truth-conditions are inherently vague, while assertability conditions are relatively sharp. For assertability conditions, speaker's evidence is what counts, but that's not necessarily so for truth-conditions.

---

[10] Von Fintel and Gillies (forthcoming) also acknowledge the possibly irreducible indeterminacy for epistemic *might*, but account for it in a slightly different way. They propose that utterances of epistemic modals may put "clouds" of propositions with particular properties into play. On the current approach, the indeterminacy of modals follows from the indeterminacy of circumstances of evaluation—a general source of indeterminacy for any kind of claim.

This is shown by the surprising contrast between the dialogues in (41) and (42):

(41)   Harriet: I am innocent. I didn't kill Philip.
        Judge: But I still have evidence suggesting that you might have.

(42)   Harriet: I am innocent. I didn't kill Philip.
        # Judge: But you still might have.

There is something slightly odd about the judge's response in (42). His reply seems unresponsive to what Harriet just said. If *might*-claims were relativized to the speaker's evidence by default, (42) should be as appropriate as (41), contrary to fact. The kinematics of discourse, then, brings out a clear distinction between the truth-conditions of *might*-claims submitted to the assertion game and the evidence speakers need to have to be justified to make such claims.

   If bare conditionals are implicitly modalized, we expect them to show the same dependence on situations of evaluation that we see with modals. That's precisely what we find, as illustrated by a famous example by Allan Gibbard (Gibbard 1981: 231).

Sly Pete and Mr. Stone are playing poker on a Mississippi riverboat. It is now up to Pete to call or fold. My henchman Zack sees Stone's hand, which is quite good, and signals its content to Pete. My henchman Jack sees both hands, and sees that Pete's hand is rather low, so that Stone's is the winning hand. At this point, the room is cleared. A few minutes later, Zack slips me a note which says "If Pete called, he won," and Jack slips me a note which says "If Pete called, he lost."

To exploit Gibbard's story more directly for our discussion, imagine that Zack's and Jack's notes had, in fact, said (43) and (44) respectively.

(43)   Pete might have called, and if he did, he won.

(44)   Pete might have called, but if he did, he lost.

(43) and (44) are not compatible with each other. This rules out a material implication analysis for the conditionals in (43) and (44), which would predict the two sentences to be compatible. The conditionals in the second conjuncts of (43) and (44) are technically bare, but they talk about the same possibilities as the preceding *might*. They are implicitly modalized, then. If the unpronounced modal is *MUST*, the logical forms for (43) and (44) look as follows:

(45)   *Might* (Pete called) & (*MUST*: Pete called) (Pete won)

(46)   *Might* (Pete called) & (*MUST*: Pete called) (Pete lost)

(45) says that there is an accessible world where Pete called, and he won in all accessible worlds where he did. (46) says that there is an accessible world where Pete called, and he lost in all accessible worlds where he did. If the set of accessible worlds stays the same, the two statements are not compatible with each other. Our initial intuitions about (43) and (44) are thus accounted for. There is still a big puzzle remaining, though. There is also the intuition that both Zack and Jack were right. How could that be? How could the two henchmen make logically incompatible statements, given that, as Gibbard tells us, neither one made any mistakes in reaching their conclusions?

Zack knows that Pete knew Stone's hand. He can thus appropriately assert "If Pete called, he won." Jack knows that Pete held the losing hand, and thus can appropriately assert "If Pete called, he lost." From this, we can see that neither is asserting anything false. For one sincerely asserts something false only when one is mistaken about something germane. In this case, neither Zack nor Jack has any relevant false beliefs.[11]

On Gibbard's story, both (47) and (48) are true:

(47)   a. Given the evidence available where Zack was, Pete might have called, and given that same evidence, Pete won if he called.

b. (*May*: the evidence that was available where Zack was holds) (Pete called) & (*MUST*: the evidence that was available where Zack was holds & Pete called) (Pete won).

(48)   a. Given the evidence available where Jack was, Pete might have called, and given that same evidence, Pete lost if he called.

b. (*May*: the evidence that was available where Jack was holds) (Pete called) & (*MUST*: the evidence that was available where Jack was holds & Pete called) (Pete lost).

Zack's and Jack's claims were both justified, then. (47) and (48) were obtained from the logical forms (45) and (46) by filling in Zack's and Jack's subjective circumstances of evaluation. No particular circumstances of evaluation were given in Zack's and Jack's notes, so the claims made by their notes might have remained genuinely underdetermined. The impression of incompatibility could still be accounted for by recourse to supervaluations, the standard way of dealing with unresolved vagueness (van Fraassen 1969; Kamp 1975): no

---

[11] Gibbard (1981: 231).

matter how you set the situation of evaluation in (45) and (46), as long as it is set uniformly for all four occurrences of modals, the two statements come out as logically incompatible with each other.

Unspecified or underspecified situations of evaluation rarely lead to a breakdown of communication. Discourse participants can extract the information they are after under the presumption that assertability conditions are satisfied. Even if Zack's and Jack's notes themselves provide no information about the circumstances of evaluation, Zack and Jack can be confident that their boss will get the information he requested. Under the presumption that the two henchmen were justified in asserting what they did, the boss can work with the truth of (47) and (48). Presuming furthermore that they both relied on factual evidence, he can infer that Pete did not call: if the assumption that Pete called plus a true set of propositions A logically implies that Pete won, and the assumption that Pete called plus a true set of propositions B logically implies that Pete didn't win, then Pete can't have called.

I conclude that there are bare conditionals that are modalized via *MUST*, and hence are epistemic conditionals. The assumption allows us to reconcile the fact that (43) and (44) are incompatible with each other with the fact that Zack and Jack made no mistake in reporting what they did. It also explains why Zack and Jack's boss was able to deduce that Pete folded. The proposed account draws an essential distinction between truth-conditions and assertability conditions for conditionals. In contrast to Adams (1965, 1970), Gibbard (1981), and Edgington (1986, 1995), our account maintains that bare conditionals are the kinds of things that can in principle have truth-conditions. Being implicitly modalized, their truth-conditions depend on a premise set determined by the current circumstances of evaluation for the modal's modal base. It is a general property of circumstances of evaluation that they can remain un- or underspecified. We saw that even if the truth-conditions for a conditional assertion can remain underdetermined, the corresponding assertability conditions don't have to be. The presumption of cooperativeness allows us to rely on the assertability conditions, rather than the truth-conditions, to convey the information we want to convey and obtain the information we are seeking. Supervaluations account for the fact that there can still be a logic of conditionals. In fact, since different settings for situations of evaluation determine different accessibility relations, we *expect* there to be different logics for conditionals—all equally legitimate. The material interpretation appears as a limiting case.

4.6 Gibbard's proof reconsidered: silent operators

I have argued that bare conditionals are implicitly modalized. But doesn't Gibbard's proof show that that couldn't be the case in any interesting way? That proof seemed to demonstrate that natural language conditionals could not receive any other interpretation but material implication. Note, however, that one assumption slipped into that whole argument that is no longer obvious: Gibbard assumes that *if... then* in English corresponds to a two-place propositional operator. We saw that the logical forms for natural language conditionals have a very different structure: there simply is no two-place conditional connective. *If*-clauses restrict operators.

The critical configurations to scrutinize are those with stacked *if*-clauses. If the claim that conditionals are modalized merely amounted to positing a stricter version of a two-place conditional operator, as defined in (49), the logical structure of (50a) could be represented as (50b), which, given (49), amounts to the nested tripartite operator structure (50c):

(49) $p \Rightarrow q =_{\text{def}} (MUST: p) \, q$

(50)   a. If you are back before eight, then, if the roast is ready, we will have dinner together.

   b. (You are back before eight $\Rightarrow$ (the roast is ready $\Rightarrow$ we will have dinner together))

   c. (*MUST*: you are back before eight) ((*MUST*: the roast is ready) (we will have dinner together))

(50c) has two occurrences of *MUST*, one embedded within the scope of the other. On the restrictor view of *if*-clauses, when two or more stacked *if*-clauses in a row appear in an English sentence, they are most naturally analyzed as successively restricting one and the same operator, just as stacked relative clauses are most naturally analyzed as successively restricting one and the same noun. Neglecting *then*, the syntactic structure of (50a) is (51a). (51a) can be submitted to semantic interpretation as is. Two applications of the interpretation rule (29) guarantee that the resulting truth-conditions correspond to those for the simple, unnested, tripartite operator structure in (51b).

(51)   a. (If you are back before eight (if the roast is ready (*MUST* (we will have dinner together))))

   b. (*MUST*: you are back before eight & the roast is ready) (we will have dinner together)

Gibbard's proof, then, does not threaten the analysis of conditionals proposed here.

The history of the conditional is the story of a syntactic mistake. There is no two-place *if...then* connective in the logical forms for natural languages. *If*-clauses are devices for restricting the domains of operators. Bare indicative conditionals have unpronounced modal operators. Epistemic *MUST* is one option. Work by Farkas and Sugioka (1983) and the papers in Carlson and Pelletier (1995) suggest that silent generic operators are another possibility. Kadmon (1987) coined the fitting terms "one-case" and "multi-case" conditionals for the two types of conditionals. (52) is modeled after one of Kadmon's one-case conditionals[12]:

(52)   If a man walked in and decided to stay, Sally was pleased.

(53) is one of her multi-case conditionals:[13]

(53)   If a semanticist hears of a good job, she applies for it.

(52) is an epistemic conditional on the current proposal; (53) would be a generic conditional. In both cases, *if*-clauses restrict operators that remain silent.

If *if*-clauses can restrict silent operators, we should find cases where a given *if*-clause fails to restrict a subsequent overt modal. Example (54) from Zvolenszky (2002; see also Frank 1997) is an illustration:

(54)   If Britney Spears drinks Coke in public, she must drink Coke in public.

The only way to understand (54) is that if Britney Spears drinks Coke in public, then she is under the obligation to drink Coke in public. On the current approach, we can get this reading if the *if*-clause in (54) restricts a silent modal, rather than the overt modal *must*. If the silent modal is *MUST*, the syntactic structure of (54) would be (55):

(55)   (If Britney Spears drinks Coke in public (*MUST* (she must drink Coke in public))).

(55) delivers the correct interpretation: the deontic modal is interpreted within the scope of an epistemic modal. Without any particular contextual restrictions, we might interpret the conditional as a material conditional, then.

The puzzle to solve is why the doubly modalized interpretation is the only interpretation we perceive for (54). As Zvolenszky observes, if (54) wasn't

----

[12] Kadmon (1987: 229).   [13] Kadmon (1987: 234).

doubly modalized, it would only have a tautological interpretation. To see this, suppose *must* is a deontic modal with some realistic modal base *f*, and *p* is the proposition that Britney Spears drinks Coke in public. Without the double modalization, (54) would then be predicted to be true in a world *w* just in case *p* is true in all worlds of $\cap(f(w) \cup \{p\})$ that are best in view of what Britney's obligations are in *w*. But *p* is trivially true in those worlds.

Maybe we do not readily perceive trivial interpretations if non-trivial interpretations are simultaneously available. I am not sure whether an explanation along those lines is viable for Zvolenszky's puzzle, though. I do not have problems perceiving a trivial interpretation for (56), for example, even though a non-trivial interpretation is simultaneously available.

(56)   I could not possibly work more than I do.

The question why (54) only has a doubly modalized interpretation is thus still open. I believe that the answer is likely to come from a better understanding of other cases where *if*-clauses cannot restrict overt modals. It seems that *if*-clauses can't ever restrict ability modals, for example:[14]

(57)   a. If I was taller, I could reach the ceiling.
       b. If he has a kitchen, he can cook.

(57a) seems to say that if I was taller, I would have the ability to reach the ceiling, not that if I was taller I might reach the ceiling. And (57b) seems to convey that if he has a kitchen, he has the opportunity to cook, not that if he has a kitchen, he might cook. Non-overt modals are obligatory for (57a) and (57b), too, then, and future research has to tell us why that is so.

4.7 Conditional propositions after all?

I have argued that, contrary to appearance, quantificational operators, including adverbs of quantification, probability operators, and other modal operators, do not operate over "conditional propositions." The persistent belief that there could be such "conditional propositions" is based on a simple syntactic mistake. *If*-clauses need to be parsed as adverbial modifiers that restrict operators that might be silent and a distance away. This is what we might call "the restrictor view" of *if*-clauses.

---

[14] I owe this observation to Rainer Bäuerle and Urs Egli; personal communication from the early eighties.

The restrictor view of *if*-clauses has recently been challenged by von Fintel (2003, 2007), Huitink (2008), and Rothschild (2009). The apparent counter-examples look like (58):

(58)   If a wolf entered the house, he might have eaten the little girl with the red cap. In fact, that's rather likely.

The second sentence of (58) says that it's rather likely that, if a wolf entered the house, he ate the little girl with the red cap. But then the pronoun *that* seems to have picked up a conditional proposition from previous discourse. Doesn't this show that probability operators can operate over conditional propositions? Not so. We already saw that *if*-clauses can restrict modals at a distance. The *if*-clause in (58) should thus be able to restrict *rather likely* at a distance. If it does, the correct interpretation results under the assumption that the antecedent for *that* is just the consequent of the conditional, rather than the whole conditional. There are two distinct discourse anaphoric links in *that's rather likely* in (58), then: one pointing back to the antecedent of the preceding conditional, and the other one pointing back to the consequent. That we have to allow for this possibility independently, is shown by our earlier example (30):

(30)   If a wolf entered the house, he must have eaten grandma, since she was bedridden. He might have eaten the girl with the red cap, too. In fact, that's rather likely. The poor little thing wouldn't have been able to defend herself.

The third clause in (30) has an interpretation that says that it is rather likely that, if a wolf entered the house, he ate the little girl with the red cap. But then *rather likely* is restricted by the *if*-clause in the first sentence, and *that* refers to the proposition in the scope of *might* in the second sentence. No conditional proposition is picked up. If the *if*-clause can restrict *rather likely* at a distance in (30), there is no reason to think that it shouldn't be able to do so in (58) as well. The case against embedded "conditional propositions" still stands, then.

INTRODUCING CHAPTER 5

Partition and Revision (chapter 3) presented a premise semantics for counter-factuals that attributes their vagueness to the many ways the facts of a world hang together—form "lumps," that is. *An Investigation of the Lumps of Thought* is an investigation of lumping relations and their role in explaining puzzling pieces of counterfactual reasoning.

Lumping relations require a semantics based on partial possible worlds or situations. A situation semantics opens up new possibilities for the analysis of counterfactuals and has also led to progress in other areas of semantics, but it does so at a price: we need to rethink much of what we learned in our beginning semantics classes. There are now many possible denotations for even the most basic logical words. Are there guidelines that help us pick the right ones? If there are several denotations for a given word, all equally plausible, do we find the expected ambiguities? About a third of the chapter wrestles with those questions before a framework is in place that lets us move on to counterfactual reasoning.

Apart from many stylistic changes, some cuts, countless clarifications, and a few minor corrections, the plot of the original *Lumps of Thought* has remained the same, with one big exception: as a late reply to early criticism by Irene Heim, the passage on Goodman's Puzzle (section 5.5.2) has been completely rewritten, and there is now a new account of non-accidental generalizations and their place in counterfactual reasoning. The account says that lawlike generalizations determine confirming propositions that correspond to Jean Nicod's confirmation sets (Nicod 1924) and play a key role in the construction of premise sets: the engine assembling premise sets for counterfactuals is biased towards premise sets that imply confirming propositions for the lawlike generalizations they contain. If this is right, a non-trivial constraint guides the construction of premise sets for counter-factuals. The constraint helps us explain semantic conundrums like Good-man's Puzzle. That there should be such a constraint in the first place suggests that premise sets, rather than similarity relations between worlds, are the right kinds of theoretical objects for stating generalizations about counter-factual reasoning.

Many examples (some new, some old) support the new approach to Goodman's Puzzle, including classics like Tichý's hat example and Lewis's barometer example, as well as Veltman's more recent example about the three sisters who have to share a single bed. There is also a surprising new prediction. If, as Nicod said, logically equivalent generalizations can have different confirmation sets, we predict that the very way a relevant generalization is phrased should be able to affect our judgments about the truth-conditions of counterfactuals. It does. In our situation-based premise semantics we can say how and why.

An Investigation of the Lumps of Thought originally appeared in *Linguistics & Philosophy* 12 (1989), 607–53.

Chapter 5

An Investigation of the Lumps of Thought[1]

5.1 What lumps of thought are

Imagine the following situation: one evening in 1905, Paula painted a still life with apples and bananas. She spent most of the evening painting and left the easel only to make herself a cup of tea, eat a piece of bread, discard a banana, or look for an apple displaying a particular shade of red. Against the background of this situation, consider the following two dialogues that might have taken place the following day:

Dialogue with a pedant

Pedant: What did you do yesterday evening?

Paula: The only thing I did yesterday evening was paint this still life over there.

Pedant: This cannot be true. You must have done something else like eat, drink, look out of the window.

Paula: Yes, strictly speaking, I did other things besides paint this still life. I made myself a cup of tea, ate a piece of bread, discarded a banana, and went to the kitchen to look for an apple.

[1] Research for this chapter was supported by NSF grant BNS 87-19999 to Emmon Bach, Angelika Kratzer, and Barbara Partee. Different parts of the work reported here were presented in talks at the University of Massachusetts at Amherst in February and August 1985, at Yale University in January 1986, at the University of Texas at Austin in April 1987, at the 6th Amsterdam colloquium in April 1987 (in absentia), at MIT in April 1988, and at CSLI in Stanford in September 1988. I thank the audiences of these talks for their reactions. I also thank Ed Gettier for his efforts to find counterexamples, and Irene Heim for actually finding some. I thank Emmon Bach and Barbara Partee for discussions while co-teaching a course on events, and Elisabeth Selkirk for inspiring the proposed focus-sensitive semantics for negation. Barbara Partee, Irene Heim, Fred Landman, Steve Berman, Nirit Kadmon, Karina Wilkinson, Alice ter Meulen, Max Cresswell, Jon Barwise, John Bigelow, Gennaro Chierchia, Peter Staudacher, Arnim von Stechow, and Roger Schwarzschild all read some early version of the paper and gave much appreciated feedback. Two anonymous reviewers for *Linguistics and Philosophy* helped shape the 1989 version, Barry Schein helped shape the current version, and Aynat Rubinstein helped prepare the manuscript for the new edition. The paper owes an obvious debt to the work of David Lewis.

Dialogue with a lunatic

Lunatic: What did you do yesterday evening?

Paula: The only thing I did yesterday evening was paint this still life over there.

Lunatic: This is not true. You also painted these apples and you also painted these bananas. Hence painting this still life was not the only thing you did yesterday evening.

In both dialogues, Paula exaggerated in claiming that painting a still life was the only thing she had done that evening. She had done other things, and the pedant correctly noticed this. Being a captive of his unfortunate character, he could not help insisting on the truth, and that is really all we can blame him for.

The lunatic case is very different. I don't think that Paula has to accept that person's criticism. She didn't paint apples and bananas apart from painting a still life. Painting apples and painting bananas was part of her painting a still life, like my arms and legs are part of me. Wherever I go, my arms and legs will come along. Is it true, then, that I can never be alone? I think not. Somehow, when I talk about myself, my parts have no independent existence; their presence doesn't count. Likewise, on that memorable evening, a very special relationship between three propositions was established: it was true that Paula painted a still life. And it was also true that she painted apples and that she painted bananas. But once we consider the first proposition a fact of this world (at the time in question), we are no longer entitled to consider the latter two propositions as separate facts. If you count the entities in this room and you count me as one of them, you'd better forget about my ears. And if you count the facts of our world and you count Paula's painting a still life as one of them, you'd better overlook her painting apples. Quite generally, whenever we start counting, we have to make sure that the entities in our domain are truly distinct.[2] Consider the following example (inspired by Carlson (1977 [1980]: 212–14), which illustrates the lunatic's fallacy in a different domain.

Noah's ark

How many kinds of animals did Noah take into the ark? He took a pair of dogs. That's one kind. He also took a pair of cats. That's another kind. Hence

---

[2] I used the story of the pedant and the lunatic as lead-ins for a situation semantics because it seemed to me that the use of *only* in phrases like *the only thing I did* or the use of *also* in phrases like *you also did* point to a notion of distinctness that needs to be stated at the level of particular situations or events. The issue has since been investigated in depth by Shai Cohen (Cohen 2009), who reached a different conclusion.

he took at least two kinds of animals. He also took a pair of doves. Now we have three kinds. He also took mammals. That's certainly a kind we haven't had before. That makes four kinds of animals. And he took birds, which gives us five kinds . . .

We often think of the facts of a world as the propositions that are true in it. And we construe propositions as sets of possible worlds. The proposition that Paula painted a still life is the set of possible worlds where Paula painted a still life; the proposition that Paula painted apples is the set of possible worlds where she painted apples. Both of those propositions happen to be true in our world. In our world, the two propositions are even more closely related, though: they are not distinct facts of our world. There is an aspect of the actual world that makes the proposition that Paula painted a still life true. And that very same aspect also makes the proposition that she painted apples true. It will be useful to have a technical term for the relationship we are after. Let us say that the proposition that Paula painted a still life *lumps* the proposition that she painted apples in the actual world.[3]

Like many interesting semantic relationships, the lumping relation is affected by vagueness. Imagine that my neighbor's house burned down. His kitchen burned down as part of it. The proposition that his house burned down, then, lumps the proposition that his kitchen burned down in the actual world. My neighbor's barn was destroyed by the same fire. Was the barn part of the house? Does the proposition that his house burned down lump the proposition that his barn burned down in the actual world? We may or may not able to settle on an answer to this question. We don't have to. There will be clear cases, and there will be other cases that are not so clear. If the lumping relation plays a role in the semantics of certain constructions, we expect its vagueness to contribute to the vagueness of those constructions in a systematic and predictable way.

Traditional possible worlds semantics construes propositions as sets of possible worlds. Within this framework, it is not obvious how we can formally capture the lumping relation. It seems, then, that we may be missing something in possible worlds semantics. We may be missing something, but it may not be very important. Or is it? The following sections will show that, paying close attention to the lumping relation, we can gain new insights into the labyrinth of counterfactual reasoning, an area that has puzzled semanticists for a long time.

---

[3] A proposition lumps another proposition in a world *w* in virtue of certain part-whole relationships holding between situations of *w*. The two propositions themselves don't stand in a part-whole relationship.

5.2 How lumps of thought can be characterized in terms of situations

We are faced with the following task: we want to characterize the special relationship holding—in our world, on some evening in 1905—between the proposition that Paula painted a still life and the two propositions that she painted apples and that she painted bananas. Obviously, this relationship is not logical implication. Paula's painting a still life doesn't logically imply her painting apples and bananas. Material implication isn't a better candidate. In the actual world, at the time we are looking at, Paula's painting a still life materially implies her making herself a cup of tea, for example. Assuming that our scenario is true, both of those propositions were true at the time. But the proposition that Paula is making herself a cup of tea is not part of the "lump of facts" whose properties we are trying to capture.

We saw that the proposition that Paula painted a still life and the proposition that she painted apples do not have distinct truth-makers in our world: whatever aspect of our world makes the first true also makes the second true. On the other hand, not every aspect of our world that makes the proposition that Paula painted a still life true is also an aspect of our world that makes any of the following propositions true: that Paula made herself a cup of tea, that she ate a piece of bread, that she discarded a banana, that she went to the kitchen. It seems, then, that we might be able to characterize the lumping relation within a semantic framework where aspects or parts of possible worlds can make propositions true. If propositions are sets of partial possible worlds—situations—we can characterize the lumping relation via the notion of truth in a possible situation.

Suppose we are given a set of possible worlds. I will simplify and largely consider worlds without much of a history—slices of worlds; worlds at a time. Along with the worlds, we are given their parts—their situations. Since worlds are parts of themselves, they are also situations—maximal situations. The lumping relation can now be defined as follows:

Lumping

A proposition p lumps a proposition q in a world w iff (i) and (ii) both hold:

  (i) p is true in w.
  (ii) Whenever a situation s is part of w and p is true in s, then q is true in s as well.[4]

---

[4] Condition (ii) corresponds to Yablo's notion of "local implication," which he uses for a preliminary definition of truth-making (Yablo 2006). I have linked truth-making to the notion of "exemplification" in Kratzer (1990, 1998a, 2002, 2007); also chapter 6 of this collection. Barry Schein explores a related notion ("rendering") in chapters 9 and 10 of Schein (1993).

The definition assumes that propositions can be true not only in whole worlds, but also in parts thereof—in situations. This assumption is not popular in possible worlds semantics (in spite of Kripke (1965)), but acquired momentum with Barwise and Perry (1983), Veltman (1985), and Landman (1986). The idea is simple enough, but is not easy to execute. There is the danger of losing classical two-valued logic, and there are insecurities concerning negation and quantification. While being indebted to my predecessors, my proposals differ from theirs in significant detail. The motivation for those deviations comes from a close look at natural language semantics, and—quite surprisingly—from an in-depth investigation of counterfactual reasoning.

5.3 A semantics based on situations

5.3.1 *A metaphysics for situations*

What are situations? For the proposition that I am hungry now to be true in a situation, the situation has to contain me or a temporal slice of me. It also has to contain something that supports the truth of the proposition that I am hungry now. For the proposition that I am tired now to be true in a situation, the situation must again contain me or a time slice of me. And it must contain something that supports the truth of the proposition that I am tired now. If neither proposition lumps the other in the actual world, a situation must be able to contain me and whatever it is about me that makes it true that I am hungry now, without containing whatever it is about me that makes it true that I am tired now.

We need a way of distinguishing between an individual *per se* and those aspects of the world that make it true that the individual has properties like being hungry or tired. A distinction of precisely this kind is made in theories of universals.[5] David Armstrong, for example, distinguishes two types of particulars, called "thick" and "thin." Thin particulars are also referred to as "bare" in the literature. Thick particulars are particulars together with the universals they instantiate. Thin particulars are whatever is left when we mereologically subtract the universals a particular instantiates.[6] A state of affairs, according to Armstrong, is a thin particular instantiating a monadic universal, or two or more thin particulars instantiating a polyadic universal. Bringing Armstrong's states of affairs together with Lewis's view on possibilia

---

[5] Armstrong (1978: vol. 1). See also Lewis (1986: section 1.5) and Sider (2006).

[6] If thin (or bare) particulars seem hard to swallow, I recommend Sider (2006), who concludes: "There, I have that off my chest! The complaint about 'bare particulars' is mostly confusion."

(Lewis 1986), we can make one more move and distinguish states of affairs that are world mates from those that are not. States of affairs are world mates just in case their particulars are, and still following Lewis (1986), we can say that particulars are world mates just in case they stand in spatio-temporal relations to each other. Given such a metaphysical set-up, possible situations can now be taken to be mereologically composed of states of affairs that are world mates.

When quantifying over situations, we don't quantify over just any kind of situations, though. Like quantification over individuals, quantification over situation is restricted, and the restrictions typically exclude arbitrary sums. Arbitrary sums made up of cabbages and eggplants from an Arcimboldo painting and apples and oranges from a Cézanne aren't still lifes. They are not in the extension of "still life," that is, and hence don't count when still lifes are quantified over. Most predicates of natural languages have nicely individuated, spatio-temporally connected entities in their extensions. But there is lexical and contextual variability. Suppose I have a hundred each of forks, knives, and spoons.[7] That makes a hundred place sets assuming that a place set consists of a knife, a fork, and a spoon. It does not matter how my silverware is currently arranged: some pieces might be in the drawer, some in the dishwasher, some on the table. What's in the extension of "place set," then? Or consider Chris, who has five pairs of pants and five dress shirts that can be worn in all combinations.[8] Chris has twenty-five different outfits, then. But why can't he share them with his twenty-four friends when they all go dancing together? How many outfits does Chris *really* have? What's in the extension of "outfit"? And while we are at it, imagine that I have a construction kit for still lifes. There are I don't know how many still lifes in this box...[9]

We are now prepared to return to the question we started out with: if I am hungry and tired right now, does this mean that my being hungry right now and my being tired right now are one and the same situation? There may or may not be a universal corresponding to the property of being hungry. If so, there is a state of affairs, and hence a situation, consisting of the current time slice of my thin self and that universal. If there is also a universal corresponding to the property of being tired, there must be a state of affairs, and hence a

---

[7] I owe this example to Stephen Yablo; personal communication.

[8] This is a puzzle that I gave to my undergraduate students as an extra credit bonus question after discussing principles of counting in connection with Gennaro Chierchia's work (see now e.g. Chierchia 2010). One of the students must have been so desperate, or fascinated, that (s)he posted the puzzle anonymously on the internet, where it was discovered by Manfred Krifka (Krifka 2009).

[9] Krifka 2009 has more examples of this kind: tangram puzzles, crane construction sets, etc.

situation, consisting of the current time slice of my thin self and that universal. The two states of affairs contain the same time slice of the same thin particular. But they contain different universals, and hence are different. If there aren't universals corresponding to the properties of being hungry and being tired, a different story needs to be told. Maybe my being hungry and my being tired can each be factored into several states of affairs. Maybe...It does not matter how the story goes. My being hungry and my being tired now have a chance to come out as distinct facts. What matters is that a situation doesn't have to contain thick particulars—particulars with all the universals they instantiate. Thin particulars may do.

5.3.2 *Ingredients for a situation semantics*

Here are the crucial features of the situation semantics I will rely on:

S The set of possible situations (including the set of thick particulars).

A The set of possible thin particulars.

$\leq$ A partial ordering on $S \cup A$ such that at least the following conditions are satisfied:

   (i) For no $s \in S$ is there an $a \in A$ such that $s \leq a$.

   (ii) For all $s \in S \cup A$ there is a unique $s' \in S$ such that $s \leq s'$ and for all $s'' \in S$: if $s' \leq s''$, then $s'' = s'$.

$P(S)$ The power set of S; the set of propositions.

W The set of maximal elements with respect to $\leq$; the set of possible worlds. For all $s \in S$, w_s is the world of s: the maximal element s is related to by $\leq$.

Intuitively, $\leq$ is a part-relation restricted to world mates. No possible situation is part of a thin particular. Every possible thin particular or situation is related to a unique maximal element: its world. If individuals are related to a unique world, you and me, for example, cannot exist in other possible worlds. Other individuals very much like us may represent us there (our counterparts), but we are not there ourselves. Lewis (1986) presents a detailed defense of the serviceability of these views; see also D. K. Lewis (1968) and (1973a).

5.3.3 *The logical properties and relations*

The situation semantics outlined above makes it possible to define classical and non-classical versions of the basic semantic properties and relations. We might consider a non-classical notion of validity in terms of truth in all possible situations, for example, or else stick to the classical notion in terms of truth in all possible worlds. The following definitions capture the classical notions.

Truth

A proposition $p \in P(S)$ is *true* in a situation $s \in S$ iff $s \in p$.

Validity

A proposition $p \in P(S)$ is *valid* iff $p \cap W = W$.

Consistency

A set of propositions $A \subseteq P(S)$ is *consistent* iff there is a $w \in W$ such that $w \in \cap A$.

Compatibility

A proposition $p \in P(S)$ is *compatible* with a set of propositions $A \subseteq P(S)$ iff $A \cup \{p\}$ is consistent.

Logical Consequence

A proposition $p \in P(S)$ *follows* from a set of propositions $A \subseteq P(S)$ iff for all $w \in W$: if $w \in \cap A$, then $w \in p$.

Logical Equivalence

Two propositions p and $q \in P(S)$ are *logically equivalent* iff $p \cap W = q \cap W$.

The notions of "validity," "consistency," "compatibility," "logical consequence," and "logical equivalence" depend only on the possible worlds part of propositions. This insures that the semantics is classical.

Here is the "official" definition of the lumping relation:

Lumping

For all propositions p and $q \in P(S)$ and all $w \in W$: p *lumps* q in w iff (i) and (ii):
    (i) $w \in p$.
    (ii) For all $s \in S$, if $s \leq w$ and $s \in p$, then $s \in q$.

5.3.4 *Persistence*

If propositions are sets of possible situations and situations stand in part-whole relations, we might find empirically significant constraints on propositions that depend on part-whole relations. Suppose a proposition p is true in a situation s. Does p remain true in all situations that have s as a part?

If so, *p* is persistent in the terminology of Barwise and Perry, or T-stable in the terminology of Veltman and Landman. (I am neglecting matters of time. I am not talking about persistence through time. The situations we are considering all have the same temporal location.) If you establish that a proposition is true in the limited part of the world accessible to you, can you conclude that that proposition is also true in the whole world you live in? You can, if the proposition at stake is persistent. Persistence, then, is a very desirable property of propositions. Are all propositions expressed by utterances in natural languages persistent? Not obviously so.

Consider the proposition *p* that is true in a situation *s* iff whenever there is a tree in *s*, *s* is part of a situation where the tree in *s* is laden with wonderful apples. Now look at this orchard over there. All its trees are laden with wonderful apples. Obviously, *p* is true in the part of our world that has just my orchard in it with all its apple trees. What about situations that have my orchard as a part: Amherst with all its trees, Hampshire County, Massachusetts, the United States, the Planet Earth? In those situations *p* is false. The proposition *p* is thus an example of a proposition that is not persistent. Are propositions like *p* ever expressed by utterances of natural languages?

There is no straightforward answer. Let us return to my orchard. A man from Boston wants to buy it. He wonders whether all its trees are apple trees. I inform him: "Yes, and every tree is laden with wonderful apples." In asserting

(1)   Every tree is laden with wonderful apples.

I didn't make a claim about every tree in the world. The context of my utterance made clear that I only claimed every tree in my orchard to be laden with wonderful apples. How can we account for the limitations of my assertion? We might say that in uttering (1), I did indeed express the proposition *p*, but I only claimed *p* to be true in a very limited part of our world. This is the view expressed by Barwise and Perry about parallel examples with definite descriptions. They accounted for implicit quantifier restrictions by taking the proposition expressed by my utterance of (1) to be *p*. As a result, they were committed to the view that not all propositions expressed by utterances of natural languages are persistent.

There is an alternative, however. The limitations observed when I uttered (1) could also be part of the very proposition expressed. One way[10] of implementing this idea would be to assume that quantifiers like "every," "most," "all," and so forth depend for their interpretation on a restricting

---

[10] See Kratzer (2007, forthcoming) for another possibility.

property that can be provided by the context of use.[11] The proposition expressed by an utterance of sentence (1) could then vary with the restricting property provided by the utterance situation. Depending on the situation, it may be the proposition that every tree in the whole world is laden with wonderful apples, or that every tree in my orchard is laden with wonderful apples, or that every tree in your orchard is laden with wonderful apples, or that every tree as far away as Mindelheim is laden with wonderful apples, and so forth. On this approach, we are not committed to the view that my actual utterance of (1) expressed a non-persistent proposition. The proposition expressed would have been the same if I had uttered the following sentence:

(2)   Every tree in my orchard is laden with wonderful apples.

Allowing for implicit quantifier restrictions makes it possible to hold on to a principle stating that all propositions expressed by utterances in natural languages are persistent, and this is what I will tentatively assume here: propositions expressed by utterances in natural languages obey what I will call the "Persistence Constraint." The Persistence Constraint has interesting empirical consequences. It sometimes forces us to posit sentence meanings and Logical Forms that have independent justifications in different areas of semantics. Here is the formal definition of persistence:

Persistence

A proposition $p \in \mathrm{P}(S)$ is persistent iff for all s and $s' \in S$: whenever $s \leq s'$ and $s \in p$, then $s' \in p$.

I will neglect most matters of context-dependency in this chapter. I will usually pretend that sentence meanings are simply propositions, rather than functions assigning propositions to utterance contexts as suggested in Stalnaker (1970), Cresswell (1973), Kaplan (1978), Kratzer (1978), or Lewis (1980), among others.

5.3.5 *Sentence denotations*

This section provides illustrations for sentence meanings within a situation semantics. In view of the discussion of counterfactual reasoning later on, the emphasis is on the interpretation of quantifiers and the logical connectives. Following Chomsky (1981), semantic interpretation is assumed to take place at a level of Logical Form, where quantifiers have been raised out of their

---

[11] That quantifiers can be restricted by the utterance context was clearly seen by George Boole (1854), who coined the term "universe of discourse."

surface positions to form restricted quantifier structures of the sort discussed in Cushing (1976) and McCawley (1981), and many others since.

In the definitions to follow, α and β are variables for sentences. For any sentence α, $[[α]]^g$ is the proposition expressed by α under variable assignment g. As is common in semantics, I will sometimes take the liberty to construe propositions as characteristic functions of sets of possible situations, rather than as sets of possible situations. Here are examples of meaning definitions for atomic sentences:

(D1) *Atomic sentences*

For any variable assignment g:

$[[x \text{ is sleeping}]]^g = λs\ g(x)$ is sleeping in s.

$[[Paula \text{ is sleeping}]]^g = λs\ ∃a[a$ is a counterpart of Paula in w_s & a is sleeping in s].

Variables range over thin particulars—elements of the domain A. Likewise, names denote thin particulars. For it to be true that Paula is sleeping in a situation we require her (thin self or her counterpart's thin self) to be part of that situation. Verbs behave differently with respect to such "physical presence" requirements. That I am talking to you can only be true in a situation that has us as parts. That I am longing for a piece of bread can be true in a situation that doesn't contain any bread.

With complex sentences, we need to start paying attention to the Persistence Constraint. The Persistence Constraint doesn't affect the semantics for conjunction, disjunction, and existential quantification, though. The definitions familiar from possible worlds semantics work for situation semantics as well.

(D2) *Conjunction*

$[[α \text{ and } β]]^g = λs[\ [[α]]^g(s)$ & $[[β]]^g(s)]$.

(D3) *Disjunction*

$[[α \text{ or } β]]^g = λs[\ [[α]]^g(s) ∨ [[β]]^g(s)]$.

(D4) *Existential quantification*

$[[Some\ x: α)β]]^g = λs∃g'\ [g' ∼_x g$ & $[[α]]^{g'}(s)$ & $[[β]]^{g'}(s)\ ]$.[12]

Conjunction, disjunction, and existential quantification all preserve persistence: if $[[α]]^g$ and $[[β]]^g$ are persistent, so are $[[α \text{ and } β]]^g$, $[[α \text{ or } β]]^g$, and $[[(some\ x: α)β]]^g$.

---

[12] Convention: "$g' ∼_x g$" stands for "g' is an x-alternative of g."

Universal quantification requires special treatment in a situation seman-tics. If we want to produce persistent propositions, we cannot adopt the familiar truth conditions in (D5).

(D5) *Non-persistent universal quantification*

$[[(\textit{For all } x\text{: } \alpha)\beta]]^g = \lambda s \forall g'[[g' \sim_x g \,\&\, [[\alpha]]^{g'}(s)] \rightarrow [[\beta]]^{g'}(s) \,]$.

If we interpreted sentence (1) (via its logical form (1'))

(1)   Every tree is laden with wonderful apples.
(1')   (For all x: x is a tree) x is laden with wonderful apples.

as definition (D5) tells us to, it would express the proposition p we encoun-tered in section 5.3.3. We saw that p is not persistent. While ruling out definitions like (D5), the Persistence Constraint still allows many other conceivable definitions, including those in (D6) to (D8).

(D6) *Radical universal quantification*

$[[(\textit{For all } x\text{: } \alpha)\beta]]^g =$
$\lambda s[s \in W \,\&\, \forall g'[[g' \sim_x g \,\&\, [[\alpha]]^{g'}(s)] \rightarrow [[\beta]]^{g'}(s) \,]]$.

(D7) *Non-accidental universal quantification*

$[[(\textit{For all } x\text{: } \alpha)\beta]]^g =$
$\lambda s \,\forall g'[[g' \sim_x g \,\&\, [[\alpha]]^{g'}(w_s)] \rightarrow [[\beta]]^{g'}(w_s)]$.

(D8) *Accidental universal quantification*

$[[(\textit{For all } x\text{: } \alpha)\beta]]^g =$
$\lambda s \forall g'[[g' \sim_x g \,\&\, [[\alpha]]^{g'}(w_s)] \rightarrow [\,[[\alpha]]^{g'}(s)] \,\&\, [[\beta]]^{g'}(s) \,]]$.

Definitions (D5) to (D8) assign four different propositions to a given uni-versally quantified sentence. The four propositions are true in the same possible worlds, but not in the same possible situations. They are logically equivalent, but not identical. They differ as to how their truth is "distributed" over the situations of a world. We already saw that (D5) doesn't assign persistent propositions to universally quantified sentences. (D6) assigns propositions that are persistent, but can only be true in worlds. Such pro-positions are very strong lumpers. If they are true in a world, they lump every other true proposition in that world. Propositions of this kind don't seem to be viable candidates as denotations for universally quantified sentences: suppose p is the proposition that every tree is laden with wonderful apples, q is the proposition that I bought three cords of wood, and both p and q are true in our world. Intuitively, there are no part-whole relationships between the two facts described by p and q. There is thus no lumping relation between *p* and *q* in our world, and that rules out (D6), which predicts such a relationship.

According to (D7), universal quantification preserves persistence as desired, but it creates propositions that are true in all or none of the situations of a world, and are thus very poor lumpers. This interpretation is a conceivable interpretation for non-accidental generalizations (see section 5.5.1, but also section 5.5.2), but is undesirable in our case, as shown by the following example: suppose that being a friend of exaggerations as much as of apple trees, I foolishly claim that the only thing that is the case in our world at this time of the year is that every tree in my orchard is laden with wonderful apples. And here comes the lunatic again. Pointing to one of the trees he counters: "That's not true, it is also the case that *this* tree here is laden with wonderful apples." This is the kind of remark we have come to expect from him, and the characteristic oddity of his reasoning is an indication that the proposition expressed by (3) (as uttered by him)

(3)   This tree here is laden with wonderful apples.

is lumped by the proposition expressed by (2) (as uttered by me) in our world.

(2)   Every tree in my orchard is laden with wonderful apples.

(2′)   (For all x: x is a tree and x is in my orchard) x is laden with wonderful apples.

(D7) does not account for this intuition. According to (D7), the proposition expressed by (2) can be true in actual situations that don't contain the lunatic's tree as a part. Hence the proposition (D7) assigns to (2) does not lump the proposition expressed by (3) in the actual world.

(D8) produces propositions with the desired lumping properties in all worlds where the universal generalization is non-vacuously true. According to (D8), the proposition expressed by (2) can be true in a situation *s* only if *s* contains all individuals that satisfy the quantifier restriction in the world of *s*. Quite generally, on the accidental interpretation, the proposition expressed by an utterance of a universally quantified sentence can be true in a situation *s* only if all the individuals satisfying its restrictive clause in the world of *s* satisfy both its restrictive and its matrix clause in *s*. If the propositions expressed by (2) and (3) are both true in a world, then, we correctly predict that the first lumps the second in that world.

There is still a problem with (D8), though. It implies that if an accidental universal proposition is vacuously true in a world *w*, it is true in all situations of *w*, and hence lumped by all true propositions in *w*. This is the lumping behavior of non-accidental generalizations (see section 5.5.1). If lumping behavior matters for counterfactual reasoning, as I will argue in section 5.4, we need to repair the problem and rewrite (D8) so that accidental universal propositions that are vacuously true in a world *w* lump all true propositions in *w*, and are thus unviable as additional premises in counterfactual reasoning. They would always trigger a clash with a false antecedent.

(D8) *Accidental universal quantification (revised)*

$[[(For\ all\ x{:}\ \alpha)\beta]]^g =$
$\lambda s[[\neg\,\exists g'[g' \sim_x g\ \&\ [[\alpha]]^{g'}(w_s)] \rightarrow s \in W]\ \&\ \forall g'[[g' \sim_x g\ \&\ [[\alpha]]^{g'}(w_s)] \rightarrow$
$[\,[[\alpha]]^{g'}(s)\ \&\ [[\beta]]^{g'}(s)\,]]].$

Similar considerations lead to meaning assignments for other quantifiers. Take "exactly two." "Exactly two" also presents a potential persistence problem (unlike "at least two"). Here is a proposal for a persistent interpretation:

(D9) *exactly two (Accidental interpretation)*

$[[(exactly\ two\ x{:}\ \alpha)\beta]]^g =$
$\lambda s\,\exists g'\,\exists g''[[g' \sim_x g\ \&\ g'' \sim_x g\ \&\ g' \neq g''\ \&\ [[\alpha]]^{g'}(s)]\ \&\ [[\beta]]^{g'}(s)\ \&\ [[\alpha]]^{g''}(s)$
$\&\ [[\beta]]^{g''}(s)]\ \&\ \forall g'''[[g''' \sim_x g\ \&\ [[\alpha]]^{g'''}(w_s)\ \&\ [[\beta]]^{g'''}(w_s)] \rightarrow [g''' = g'$
$\vee\ g'''{=}g'']]].$

According to (D9), sentence (4) with logical form (4′)

(4)   Exactly two trees in my yard have bird nests in them.

(4′)   (Exactly two x: x is a tree in my yard) x has bird nests in x.

expresses a proposition that can be true in a situation *s* only if whenever an individual satisfies both the restrictive and matrix clause in the world of *s* it satisfies both the restrictive and matrix clause in *s*. The proposition assigned to (4) (via 4′) is persistent and has the desired lumping properties: in our world, the fact that this tree here (I am pointing at a tree in my yard) has bird nests in it is part of the fact that exactly two trees in my yard have bird nests in them.

Possible meaning definitions for conjunction, disjunction, and various sorts of quantifiers are now in place. In traditional frameworks, the propositions a semantic theory assigns to a sentence derive their empirical justification from their predictive power concerning truth in a world, logical consequence, and so forth. We have seen that in a situation semantics, an additional criterion of adequacy comes into play: we now also have to predict the correct lumping properties of propositions. I have been using lunatic stories to help sharpen intuitions about the lumping relation. Those stories are of limited use however. The investigation of counterfactual reasoning is a much more serious and interesting domain for exploring lumping relations.

5.4 Counterfactual reasoning

5.4.1 *Some facts about counterfactuals*

Counterfactuals come in different varieties. Here are two examples:

(5)   If Mr. Brown read a newspaper, he would read the Morning Union.

(6)   If Mr. Brown read a newspaper, he might read the Morning Union.

(5) expresses a "would"-counterfactual, (6) a "might"-counterfactual. Finding the right truth-conditions for counterfactuals has been one of the most hotly debated questions in semantics and the philosophy of science. Most scholars agree that the truth of a counterfactual in a world depends, in some way or other, on what is the case in that world. What makes the semantics of counterfactual sentences so difficult is that not all facts have equal weight: some are important, others are altogether irrelevant.

There are two approaches to this problem. Philosophers like Goodman (1947) actually took it upon themselves to at least try to say what kind of factual premises are taken into account in the evaluation of a counterfactual. The idea was that after adding those premises to the antecedent of the counterfactual, the consequent should follow logically from the resulting set. Goodman eventually reached the conclusion that the additional premises aren't specifiable in a non-circular way.

An alternative view was advanced by Stalnaker (1968) and Lewis (1973a), who carefully avoided any precise characterization of the additional premises needed for a particular piece of counterfactual reasoning. Stalnaker and Lewis both stress the vagueness of counterfactuals. Their goal was to develop a theory of counterfactuals that correctly predicts their pervasive indeterminacy and vagueness. Both Stalnaker's and Lewis's analyses are built around the inherently vague concept of similarity. To see an illustration, take (7).

(7)   If I were looking into a mirror, I would see a face with brown eyes.

According to Lewis, the counterfactual expressed by (7) is true in a world w just in case there is a world w' such that, in w', I am looking into a mirror and see a face with brown eyes, and w' is closer to the actual world than any world where I am looking into a mirror and don't see a face with brown eyes. "Might"-counterfactuals are interpreted as duals of the corresponding "would"-counterfactuals. The "might"-counterfactual corresponding to (7), for example, is true in a world w iff the counterfactual expressed by (7') is false in w.

(7′)   If I were looking into a mirror, I would not see a face with brown eyes.

A semantics for counterfactuals along those lines may look innocent, but assuming certain properties of the similarity relation, it made it possible to formally characterize an interesting body of valid counterfactual reasoning. This is a success. It is, however, not yet a complete success.

Imagine the following scenario.[13] Last year, a zebra escaped from the Hamburg zoo. The escape was made possible by a forgetful keeper who forgot to close the door of a compound containing zebras, giraffes, and gazelles. A zebra felt like escaping and took off. The other animals preferred to stay in captivity. Suppose now counterfactually that some other animal had escaped instead. Would it be another zebra? Not necessarily. I think it might have been a giraffe or a gazelle. Yet if the similarity theory of counterfactuals were correct, we would expect that, everything else being equal, similarity with the animal that actually escaped should play a role in evaluating this particular piece of counterfactual reasoning. Given that all animals in the compound had an equal chance of escaping, the most similar worlds to our world in which a different animal escaped are likely to be worlds in which another zebra escaped. That is, on the similarity approach, the counterfactual expressed by (8) should be false in our world.

(8)   If a different animal had escaped instead, it might have been a gazelle.

Intuitively, however, I wouldn't make a false claim if I uttered (8), given the circumstances I described. The fact that overall similarity with the animal that actually escaped is irrelevant in this case suggests that the similarity involved in counterfactual reasoning is not our everyday notion of similarity. It has to be a special kind of similarity. In fact, that's how Lewis reacted to counterexamples of this sort (Lewis 1979b). Lewis and Stalnaker characterize the special kind of similarity relevant for counterfactuals in very general terms. There is nothing in their approach that would actually explain why it is that in our example, similarity with the actual zebra that escaped is not a concern. I want to emphasize that it is not that the similarity theory says anything false about examples like the zebra example. It doesn't say enough. It stays vague where our intuitions are relatively sharp. We should aim for a theory of counterfactuals that predicts vagueness for precisely the cases where our intuitions are vague, and makes sharp predictions for precisely the cases where our intuitions are sharp.

---

[13]   The zebra example incorporates some very helpful suggestions from an anonymous reviewer.

5.4.2 *Truth-conditions for counterfactuals*

There is an intuitive and appealing way of thinking about the truthconditions for counterfactuals. It is an analysis that, in my heart of hearts, I have always believed to be correct (see Kratzer 1978, 1981a). Taken at face value, however, that analysis turns out to be so obviously wrong that it doesn't seem to merit any serious attention. The analysis is this:

"Would"-counterfactuals

A "would"-counterfactual is true in a world *w* iff every way of adding propositions that are true in *w* to the antecedent while preserving consistency reaches a point where the resulting set of propositions logically implies the consequent.

"Might"-counterfactuals

A "might"-counterfactual is true in a world *w* iff not every way of adding propositions that are true in *w* to the antecedent while preserving consistency reaches a point where adding the consequent results in an inconsistent set.

In a context where situations play such a prominent role, it may be surprising that I specified the truth-conditions for counterfactuals only for worlds. Shouldn't we say something about their truth in situations? I think we should indeed, but all we should say is that counterfactuals can only be true in situations that are worlds. This seems to be the most general way of insuring that we will not run into problems with the Persistence Constraint.

Plausible as it may seem, the analysis I just sketched doesn't look viable. Here are some counterexamples:

The first counterexample

Suppose that in the actual world, Paula is buying a pound of apples. Besides that, nothing special is going on. The Atlantic Ocean isn't drying up, for example, nor is the moon falling down. The following propositions are then all true in our world:[14]

(9) a. Paula is buying a pound of apples.
  b. The Atlantic Ocean isn't drying up.
  c. The moon isn't falling down.
  d. Paula is buying a pound of apples or the Atlantic Ocean is drying up.
  e. Paula is buying a pound of apples or the moon is falling down.

---

[14] The "or" in (9d) and (9e) is to be understood as the truth-functional inclusive "or" familiar from propositional logic. English "or" can also have a generic reading (see section 5.5).

Given those facts, our analysis of "might"-counterfactuals predicts that the counterfactuals expressed by (10a) and (10b) should both be true in our world:

(10)   a. If Paula weren't buying a pound of apples, the Atlantic Ocean might be drying up.
          b. If Paula weren't buying a pound of apples, the moon might be falling down.

That Paula isn't buying a pound of apples is logically compatible with (9d). The consequent of the counterfactual expressed by (10a) follows from the antecedent in conjunction with (9d). We can now add any propositions whatsoever to those two propositions: the consequent of the counterfactual will always follow from the resulting set. There is thus a way of adding true propositions to the antecedent of our counterfactual while preserving consistency that never reaches a point where adding the consequent would lead to inconsistency. Very similar considerations apply to the counterfactual expressed by (10b). (9e) is compatible with its antecedent. Its consequent follows from the antecedent in conjunction with (9e) and from every superset containing those two propositions. The two counterfactuals are thus wrongly predicted to be true in our world.

The second counterexample[15]

Imagine the following situation: Paula and Otto are the only people in this room. They are both painters. They have a good friend, Clara, who is a sculptor. The following propositions are thus true:

(11)   a. Paula is in this room.
          b. Otto is in this room.
          c. There are exactly two people in this room.
          d. All people in this room are painters.

Given the premises in (11), our analysis predicts the counterfactual expressed by (12) to be true:

(12)   If Clara were in this room, too, she might be a painter.

That Clara is in this room is logically compatible with (11d), and the consequent of the counterfactual expressed by (12) follows from the antecedent in conjunction with (11d). We predict, then, that the counterfactual expressed by (12) is true. This is not a welcome result, since the mere act of

---

[15] The example is inspired by Goodman (1947): all the coins in my pocket are silver.

entering a room all filled with painters has no effect on your becoming a painter yourself.

5.4.3 *We forgot about lumps*

In constructing the two counterexamples to an obviously plausible analysis, I made, I think, a mistake. I forgot that propositions never come alone. In trying to consistently add true propositions to the antecedents of the various counterfactuals, I forgot that whenever we add a proposition, it will bring along all propositions lumped by it in the evaluation world. With this perspective in mind, let us start over.

The first counterexample re-examined

Here are all relevant propositions:

(9) a. Paula is buying a pound of apples.
   b. The Atlantic Ocean isn't drying up.
   c. The moon isn't falling down.
   d. Paula is buying a pound of apples or the Atlantic Ocean is drying up.
   e. Paula is buying a pound of apples or the moon is falling down.

(10) a. If Paula weren't buying a pound of apples, the Atlantic Ocean might be drying up.
   b. If Paula weren't buying a pound of apples, the moon might be falling down.

I argued that, according to our analysis, the counterfactual expressed by (10a) had to be true in our world, since we can consistently add (9d) to its antecedent, and the consequent follows from the resulting set and all its supersets. But once we add (9d) to the antecedent, it brings along (9a). In our world, where the Atlantic Ocean isn't drying up, every situation where Paula is buying a pound of apples or the Atlantic Ocean is drying up is a situation where Paula is buying a pound of apples. Hence (9a) is lumped by (9d) in our world. (9a), however, is not compatible with the antecedent of the counterfactual in (10a). Seen in this way, we cannot consistently add (9d) to the antecedent of our counterfactual. The same line of reasoning applies to the counterfactual in (10b). If reformulated so as to conform to the lumping requirement, our analysis no longer implies that implausible counterfactuals like those expressed by (10a) and (10b) are true in our world.

The second counterexample re-examined

Recall the relevant propositions:

(11)   a. Paula is in this room.
       b. Otto is in this room.
       c. There are exactly two people in this room.
       d. All people in this room are painters.

(12)   If Clara were in this room, too, she might be a painter.

I mistakenly thought that our analysis predicts that the counterfactual expressed by (12) should be true in our world, since we can consistently add (11d) to its antecedent, and the consequent follows from the resulting set and all of its supersets. But as soon as we add (11d), it brings along other propositions. Since (11d) is an accidental universal generalization, it can only be true in an actual situation s if Paula and Otto are in this room in s. But then s must be a situation where (11a) and (11b) are true. Hence (11d) lumps (11a) and (11b) in our world. (11d) also lumps (11c). (11a), (11b), and (11c) are thus all lumped by (11d). But adding all of those propositions to the antecedent of our counterfactual leads to inconsistency.

Taking the idea of lumping seriously enabled us to discard two representative counterexamples to our analysis. Let us now see how our analysis handles the zebra example.

The zebra example re-examined

Recall the story: a zebra escaped from the Hamburg zoo (call it "John"). The escape was caused by a negligent keeper who forgot to close the door of the compound housing zebras, giraffes, and gazelles. We supposed counterfactually that some other animal had escaped instead and, in ruminating about what sort of animal it might have been, we wondered why similarity with the original zebra didn't play a role here. On the present approach, we have an explanation: if the actual properties of the zebra mattered, it would be because of the following propositions:

(13)   a. A zebra escaped.
       b. A striped animal escaped.
       c. A black and white animal escaped.
       d. A male animal escaped.
          . . . .

Given lumping, none of the propositions in (13) can be consistently added to the antecedent of a conditional of the form: "If the animal that escaped had not been John. . . ." In our world (at the time considered), every situation where a zebra escaped is a situation where John escaped. Every situation where a striped animal escaped is again a situation where John escaped and so forth, for all the properties of John. Hence in our world, the proposition that John escaped is lumped by (13a) to (13d).

In drawing conclusions from our counterfactual assumption, similarity with the actual zebra doesn't play a role. Other sorts of similarities with the actual world do matter, though. If a different animal had escaped instead of John, there would still be the forgetful keeper (call him "Carl") who left the door open. There would still be the night house for kiwis and owls. There would still be the cages for lions and tigers. And there would still be the monkey rock. The proposed analysis predicts this. Take the proposition "Carl left the door to the compound housing zebras, giraffes, and gazelles open." This proposition doesn't lump the proposition "John escaped from the Hamburg zoo" in our world. Nor does it seem to lump any other dangerous proposition. The propositions "there is a night house for kiwis and owls in the Hamburg zoo," "there are cages for lions and tigers in the Hamburg zoo," or "there is a monkey rock in the Hamburg zoo" are likewise innocent lumpers. We can safely add them to the antecedent of our counterfactual. No inconsistency will arise.

The examples we looked at suggest that our original analysis of counterfactuals might be tenable after all if it is enriched by lumping. Note that counterfactuals themselves can never be added consistently to the antecedent of a counterfactual, except when the antecedent happens to be true. To preserve persistence, I have been assuming that counterfactuals can only be true in situations that are worlds. Consequently, a true counterfactual lumps all true propositions in any given world. Using a true counterfactual in the evaluation of a counterfactual with a false antecedent, then, always leads to inconsistency.

5.4.4 *The formal definitions*

We now have a first idea of how a simple analysis of counterfactuals plus a lumping mechanism can account for some non-trivial pieces of counterfactual reasoning. Our analysis says that the truth of a counterfactual depends on a set of propositions representing the facts of the world of evaluation. Call that set of facts the "Base Set." Base Sets have to obey some constraints. Not all true propositions qualify. Which propositions do is an empirical question. For concreteness, I will mention a few potential constraints, but the issue is far from settled, and proposals are tentative.[16] In one way or other, propositions

---

[16] Kratzer (1990, 2002, re-edited as chapter 6 of this collection) and Kratzer (2005) already explore a different path: propositional facts that are not lawlike generalizations are projected directly from situations. The hope is that such projections might give us cognitively viable propositions that do not only have the right level of specificity, but are also lumped in the right way. It would also be reasonable to expect such projections to be constrained by general principles of category projection (see e.g. the survey in Murphy 2002).

in Base Sets have to be "cognitively viable." Cognitively viable propositions should correspond to natural categories; they shouldn't carve up logical space in "gruesome" ways (Goodman 1955). Depending on context, they should also have a certain grain; they cannot draw too fine distinctions (Yalcin 2008; Chemla (in press); also chapter 6). A plausible necessary condition for a cognitively viable proposition is that it should be possible for an actual human to believe it. This excludes too specific propositions—most notably singleton propositions. For a singleton proposition {w} to be believed by a person, the person's set of doxastic alternatives would have to be a subset of {w}. Setting aside the trivial case where there are no doxastic alternatives, it follows that the person would have to be omniscient in a rather strong sense. Her beliefs would have to be so specific that they would have to be able to distinguish the actual world from all other worlds—including its perfect duplicates. This, I take, is impossible for any human to do.

Non-persistent propositions are candidates for exclusion from Base Sets, too, and so are pairs of distinct logically equivalent propositions. More generally, Base Sets should be required to be non-redundant in a certain sense:

Redundancy

A set of propositions is redundant if it contains propositions p and q such that $p \neq q$ and $p \cap W \subseteq q \cap W$.

In the particular sense defined above, a non-redundant set of propositions can't contain both a proposition and its (proper) logical consequences. It couldn't contain both the proposition $p \cap q$ and the propositions p or q, for example, since $p \cap q$ logically implies both p and q. Requiring Base Sets to be non-redundant accounts for the intuition that when describing the world, we should lump and split consistently.

To preserve the good results of the analysis in chapter 3, we should also require Base Sets to characterize worlds completely. This requirement now needs to be weakened a bit, though. We have to respect whatever grain is set by cognitive viability: Base Sets are descriptions of worlds that are as complete as cognitive viability allows. Assembling all constraints into a tentative proposal yields the following:

Admissible Base Sets for counterfactuals

For any world w, an admissible Base Set is a subset F_w of $P(S)$ satisfying conditions (i) to (v):

   (i) Truth: $w \in \cap F_w$.
   (ii) Persistence: All $p \in F_w$ are persistent.
   (iii) Cognitive Viability: All $p \in F_w$ are cognitively viable.

(iv) Non-Redundancy: F_w is not redundant.

(v) Completeness: $\cap F_w$ contains all and only worlds that are indistinguishable from w, given the grain set by Cognitive Viability.

Pairing an admissible Base Set F_w and a proposition p, we can define a set $F_{w,p}$ of premise sets that the truth conditions for counterfactuals crucially rely on.

The Crucial Set

For any world w, admissible Base Set F_w, and proposition p, $F_{w,p}$ is the set of all subsets A of $F_w \cup \{p\}$ satisfying the following conditions:

(i) A is consistent

(ii) $p \in$ A

(iii) A is closed under lumping in w: for all $q \in$ A and $r \in F_w$: if q lumps r in w, then $r \in$ A.

The last two definitions give the by now familiar truth conditions for "would"- and "might"-counterfactuals.

"Would"-counterfactuals

Given a world w and an admissible Base Set F_w, a "would"-counterfactual with antecedent p and consequent q is true in w iff for every set in $F_{w,p}$ there is a superset in $F_{w,p}$ that logically implies q.

"Might"-counterfactuals

Given a world w and an admissible Base Set F_w, a "might"-counterfactual with antecedent p and consequent q is true in w iff there is a set in $F_{w,p}$ such that q is compatible with all its supersets in $F_{w,p}$.

The proposal that is now on the table says that counterfactuals do not have absolute truth-conditions. Their truth depends on a contextual parameter providing a Base Set representing what is the case in the world of evaluation. Not all true propositions qualify. I have tentatively listed a few constraints. Among those, cognitive viability is the big unknown. Cognitive viability is not a matter of a few hastily formulated definitions, though. Whether particular groupings of possible situations are or aren't cognitively viable is a question about human category formation that needs to be answered empirically.

Like the account of chapter 3, the current account allows many Base Sets for any given world. Facts can be lumped together in various ways, and there are choices between logically equivalent propositions that have to be made, depending on their status as accidental versus non-accidental generalizations, for example. While particular types of contexts might privilege certain Base Sets over others, there is bound to be a great deal of indeterminacy that remains. This is good. We have learned from Lewis and Stalnaker that we should aim for an analysis that captures the range of indeterminacy and vagueness that actual counterfactuals come with. The slight disagreement I am having with Lewis and Stalnaker is about what kind of account predicts that range most accurately and insightfully.

As we have seen, in a situation semantics, there are many distinct propositions that are true in the same possible worlds, but differ with respect to truth in possible situations. This needs getting used to. We need to pay attention to both truth-conditions and lumping conditions. To take a simple example, the sets $\{w \in W\!: w \in p \text{ or } \neg\, w \in p\}$ and $\{s \in S\!: s \in p \text{ or } \neg\, s \in p\}$ are distinct, but logically equivalent, propositions. The first set is W, the set of all possible worlds; the second set is S, the set of all possible situations. Looking at the lumping properties of the two propositions brings out dramatic differences that can acquire empirical momentum in counterfactual reasoning on our account. In any given world, the proposition W lumps every true proposition in that world—it is a strong lumper that is hard to lump. In contrast, in any given world, the proposition S only lumps propositions that are true in all situations of that world—it is a poor lumper that is easy to lump.

The following two sections will show how lumping differences can account for the different roles of accidental and non-accidental generalizations in counterfactual reasoning. Accidental generalizations are stronger lumpers than non-accidental ones. The clearest cases of non-accidental generalizations are the logical tautologies, of course. Logical tautologies should thus be represented as the poorest possible lumpers. It follows that if one of the two tautologies W and S appears in any premise set for counterfactuals at all, it would have to be the poor lumper S, rather than the strong lumper W.[17] Logical tautologies don't run the show in premise sets for counterfactuals. They do not contribute to representing the facts of a world. They have no empirical bite; can do neither good nor harm.

---

[17] Kanazawa, Kaufmann, and Peters (2005) overlook this essential point in deriving their "triviality results." Their proofs miss the mark since they rely on premises that were already explicitly excluded in the original 1989 version of this chapter. Like section 5.5 of the current chapter, section 5 of the original paper argued that non-accidental generalizations should be taken to be true in all or none of the situations of a world. Since logical tautologies are non-accidental generalizations *par excellence*, Kanazawa et al. made a mistake by putting W, rather than S, in some of the critical premise sets they consider. W is an extremely strong lumper that will wreak havoc in any premise set for counterfactuals. That's the kind of phenomenon that lumping semantics is all about. The second, related, mistake in Kanazawa et al. is to not use the non-accidental interpretation of disjunction in section 5.1 of Kratzer (1989) for interpreting $\phi \vee \neg\, \phi$. Being a tautology, $\phi \vee \neg\, \phi$ is another obvious case of a non-accidental generalization, and hence needs to be assigned the poor lumper S as its denotation.

5.5 Representing non-accidental generalizations

5.5.1 *Non-accidental generalizations: a first proposal*

The examples of counterfactual reasoning discussed so far illustrate the lumping properties of propositions expressed by quantified sentences and disjunctions. But those constructions are subtly ambiguous. They also have interpretations where they express non-accidental generalizations. Consider the counterfactuals in (14a) to (14c):

(14)   a. If the Queen hadn't opened the New Zealand Parliament last year, the Governor-General would have done so.

   b. If this (we are sitting in an Italian restaurant) were a Chinese restaurant, fortune cookies would be served with the check.

   c. If this man (I am pointing at a picture of the current king of Spain) didn't rule Spain, someone else would.

I think all three counterfactuals are true in the actual world. Their truth is primarily supported by the truth of the generalizations in (15a) to (15c) respectively:

(15)   a. In New Zealand, either the Queen or the Governor-General opens Parliament.

   b. In all Chinese restaurants, fortune cookies are served with the check.

   c. A king rules Spain.

(15a) is a disjunction, (15b) is a universally quantified sentence, and (15c) has an existential quantifier. If we interpret those sentences as proposed in section 5.3 (definitions (D3), (D8), and (D4)), we are in trouble.

First, take the New Zealand case and the interpretation of disjunction in (D3). We are looking at the "last year"-slice of our world history. Since the Queen opened Parliament in New Zealand last year, every part where (15a) is true is a part where the Queen opened Parliament. But that the Queen opened Parliament is incompatible with the antecedent of the counterfactual in (14a). Consequently, (15a) can never support the truth of that counterfactual.

The Chinese restaurant counterfactual (14b) doesn't fare much better, if we endorse the accidental interpretation for universal quantification in (D8). On that interpretation, every actual situation where (15b) is true is a situation where fortune cookies are served in whatever actual Chinese restaurants there are. Suppose there are exactly three of them: Amherst Chinese, Panda East, and China Dynasty. Every actual situation where (15b) is true is then a situation where fortune cookies are served in precisely those three Chinese restaurants. But then (15b) lumps the proposition that fortune cookies are served with the check in exactly three Chinese restaurants: Amherst Chinese, Panda East, and China Dynasty. But that proposition is incompatible with the antecedent of the counterfactual in (14b), which adds another Chinese restaurant. The assumption of an additional Chinese restaurant leads to inconsistency.

A similar problem comes up with (15c), assuming the interpretation of existential quantification in (D4). At this very moment, every situation of our world where (15c) is true is a situation where the man who is the current king of Spain rules Spain. But the proposition that he rules Spain is incompatible with the antecedent of the counterfactual in (14c).

There is a difference between (15a) to (15c) on the one hand, and the cases of disjunction and quantification we discussed earlier. On their most natural interpretations, sentences (15a) to (15c) express non-accidental generalizations. That all Chinese restaurants serve fortune cookies with the check is a non-accidental generalization of our world. That all people in this room are painters is just an accidental fact. Likewise, that a king rules Spain is a non-accidental fact of our world, but not that a zebra escaped from the Hamburg zoo. It is a non-accidental generalization that the Queen or the Governor-General opens the New Zealand Parliament, but a mere accidental fact that Paula is buying a pound of apples or the moon is falling down.

Logical tautologies are non-accidental generalizations for sure, but which among the contingent truths of our world are non-accidental? I don't know, it's not a question a semantic theory should be expected to answer. The semantic question is what the observed ambiguity between accidental and non-accidental interpretations might consist in. A possible answer was already implicit in the preceding discussion: there are interpretations for disjunction and quantifier constructions that produce propositions with very strong lumping capacities. Those are the accidental interpretations. But there are also interpretations that create propositions that are very weak lumpers. Those are the non-accidental (or generic) interpretations. If sentences (15a) to (15c) are to support the counterfactuals (14a) to (14c), they need to be given non-accidental interpretations. For universally quantified sentences, we already have a candidate: the non-accidental interpretation (D7) in section 5.3.5. If (15b) is interpreted according to (D7), the resulting proposition no longer lumps any facts contradicting the antecedent of the counterfactual (14b). Non-accidental interpretations for disjunction and existential quantification can be produced in analogous fashion, and might look as follows:

(D10)   *Disjunction (non-accidental interpretation)*

$[[\alpha \ or \ \beta]]^g = \lambda s \ [\ [[\alpha]]^g(w_s) \vee [[\beta]]^g(w_s)]$.

(D11)   *Existential quantification (non-accidental interpretation)*

$[[(There \ is \ an \ x: \alpha)\beta]]^g = \lambda s \exists g' \ [g' \sim_x g \ \& \ [[\alpha]]^{g'}(w_s) \ \& \ [[\beta]]^{g'}(w_s)]$.

For a given sentence, its accidental and non-accidental interpretations always agree on the possible worlds part of the propositions assigned. Accidental generalizations and their non-accidental counterparts are logically equivalent, they only differ in the way their truth is distributed over the situations of a given world. As a consequence, they differ in lumping ability—a property that in turn affects their ability to support the truth of counterfactuals.

Non-Redundancy blocks the possibility that both members of a pair of logically equivalent accidental and non-accidental generalizations could be members of admissible Base Sets for counterfactuals. We need to make a choice. The non-accidental members of such pairs should only qualify if certain standards for lawhood are satisfied, whatever they are. Following David Lewis, we could think of lawlike propositions as propositions playing a privileged role within "some integrated system of truths that combines simplicity with strength in the best way possible." (Lewis 1986: 122; see also Lewis (1973a) reporting proposals by Ramsey).

The ambiguity between accidental and non-accidental interpretations is real, and has a major impact on counterfactual reasoning. Here is a dated Cold War example, which is a variation of one by Östen Dahl.[18] The sentence "All current superpowers are referred to by abbreviations the first letter of which is *U*" is ambiguous between an accidental and a non-accidental interpretation. We perceive both interpretations, but go by the accidental interpretation in this case, since the generalization doesn't satisfy the standards for lawhood in our world. If a Base Set for our world only contains the accidental generalization, we correctly predict the counterfactual "If Andorra was a current superpower, it would be referred to by an abbreviation the first letter of which is *U*" to be false.

The distinction between accidental and non-accidental generalizations is not always sharp. There are uncontroversial cases of laws like the laws of logic or the laws of gravity. But there is also a grey zone. There is indeterminacy

---

[18] Dahl's example was brought to my attention by an anonymous reviewer.

with respect to which generalizations have the status of laws, and that indeterminacy is bound to affect counterfactual reasoning.

5.5.2 *Hempel's Paradox and Goodman's Puzzle*

The preceding section showed how accidental and non-accidental generalizations can be distinguished in a situation semantics. I took non-accidental propositions to be propositions that are true in all or none of the situations of a world. Upon closer inspection, there is a problem with that proposal, however. It wouldn't allow us to draw finer distinctions between non-accidental propositions. What has been dubbed "Hempel's Paradox" or the "Raven Paradox" illustrates the problem (Hempel 1945):

(16)   a. All ravens are black.
        b. All non-black things are non-ravens.

(16a) and (16b) are logically equivalent—they are contrapositions of each other. What seems paradoxical about (16) relates to the observation that we very readily accept a black raven as counting towards confirming (16a), but are very reluctant to give that role to a green leaf or an orange chair. Moreover, humans are innately predisposed to come up with (16a), rather than (16b), as a generalization about the world they live in, where all ravens are black. If (16a) and (16b) are treated so differently by the human mind, there should be a semantic difference between the two. Unfortunately, neither standard possible worlds semantics nor our current account allows for any semantic difference between the propositions expressed by (16a) and (16b). If (16a) and (16b) are non-accidental generalizations, they are true in all or none of the situations of a world on our account. Since (16a) and (16b) are also logically equivalent, they are true in the same possible worlds. It now follows that (16a) and (16b) are true in the same possible situations, and hence express identical propositions.

According to what has been called "Nicod's Criterion" (Nicod 1924), (16a) is a generalization that is confirmed by black ravens, and (16b) is confirmed by non-ravens that are not black. Nicod's Criterion says that the generalization that all Fs are Gs is confirmed by Fs that are Gs, and that means that the generalization that all non-Gs are non-Fs is confirmed by non-Gs that are non-Fs. Nicod's Criterion is intuitive enough, but is hard to reconcile with the fact that (16a) and (16b) are logically equivalent. How can two logically equivalent generalizations have different confirmation sets? Situation semantics offers a way out of the dilemma: there can now be distinct logically equivalent propositions and logically equivalent generalizations with different confirmation sets. Here is a proposal for a non-accidental interpretation of universal quantification that hard-wires information about confirmation sets into the meanings of the generalizations themselves:

(D12) *Non-accidental universal quantification (another option)*

$[[(For\ all\ x: \alpha)\beta]]^g =$

$\lambda s\ [[\ \exists g'\ [g'\ \sim_x g\ \&\ [[\alpha]]^{g'}(w_s)]\ \rightarrow\ \exists g'\ [g'\ \sim_x g\ \&\ [[\alpha]]^{g'}(s)\ \&\ [[\beta]]^{g'}(s)\ ]]\ \&$
$\forall g'[[g'\ \sim_x g\ \&\ [[\alpha]]^{g'}(w_s)]\ \rightarrow\ [[\beta]]^{g'}(w_s)\ ]].$

According to (D12), (16a) is non-vacuously true in situations with black ravens in worlds where all ravens are black. (16a) is vacuously true in all situations of ravenless worlds. (16b), on the other hand, is non-vacuously true in situations with non-black non-ravens in worlds where all non-black things are non-ravens, and thus all ravens are black. (16b) is vacuously true in all situations of worlds where everything is black. (16a) and (16b) express distinct, but logically equivalent propositions, then. (D12) makes (16a) and (16b) logically equivalent—they wind up true in exactly the same possible worlds. But (D12) nevertheless equips (16a) and (16b) with different confirmation sets: the distribution of truth over the situations of the worlds where the two generalizations are true carries information about confirming situations.

Assuming (D12), (16a) and (16b) also wind up with different lumping properties. In a world that has ravens and where all ravens are black, (16a) lumps, and is lumped by, the proposition that some ravens are black. In contrast, in a world that has non-black non-ravens and where all non-black things are non-ravens, (16b) lumps, and is lumped by, the proposition that some non-black things are non-ravens. Moreover, if Nevermore is an actual raven, the singular proposition "Nevermore is a black raven" lumps (16a), but not (16b), in the actual world.[19] On the other hand, if Blanche is an actual dog that is not black, the singular proposition "Blanche is a non-black non-raven" lumps (16b), but not (16), in the actual world.

If confirmation sets are sets of situations, they are propositions, and we can use the lumping relation to define a relation of confirmation between propositions. Here is a first stab at such a definition:

Confirming propositions

A proposition p confirms a proposition q iff p lumps q in every world where both p and q are true.

---

[19] If Nevermore happens to be the only raven left in the actual world, (D12) has the effect that the proposition expressed by (16a) lumps the proposition that Nevermore is a black raven, as well as the proposition that there is exactly one raven. (16a) would then no longer show the behavior of a non-accidental generalization in counterfactual reasoning about the actual world. The confirmation-set-independent proposition produced by (D7) would be a more appropriate representation of the non-accidental generalization that all ravens are black in that case.

To illustrate, suppose p is the proposition that Nevermore is a black raven, and q is the proposition expressed by (16a) according to (D12). Then p confirms q. In each world where both p and q are true, q is true in precisely the situations that have black ravens in them. But then q is true in every situation where p is true, and p lumps q in all worlds where they are both true.

If non-accidental generalizations carry information about confirming situations, they can no longer be characterized as propositions that are true in all or none of the situations of a world. We need a weaker condition that exploits the fact that non-accidental generalizations are still vacuously true in all situations of at least some possible worlds.

Non-accidental generalizations

A non-accidental generalization is a proposition that is true in all situations of at least some possible worlds.

To illustrate, assuming (D12), the propositions expressed by (16a) and (16b) come out as non-accidental generalizations because they are vacuously true in all situations of any world that has no situation where the antecedent is true.

The assumption that non-accidental generalizations carry information about confirming situations may help with another famous puzzle: Goodman's Puzzle (Goodman 1947). Here is a version of the puzzle: King Ludwig of Bavaria likes to spend his weekends at Leoni Castle. Whenever the Royal Bavarian flag is up, and the lights in the castle are on, the King is home. As a matter of fact, the lights are on right now, the flag is down, and the King is away. Suppose now counterfactually that the flag were up. Well, then the King would be home and the lights would still be on. But why wouldn't the lights be out with the King still being away?

I deliberately picked a version of Goodman's Puzzle that would be a challenge if we tried to explain it by invoking causality or similarity. Goodman's original example is about a match. Would it light if it were struck? While striking a match in the right circumstances causes the match to light, the co-occurrence of the flag's being up and the lights being on doesn't cause the King to be home. That the asymmetry Goodman identified shows up in non-causal cases, too, tells us to stay away from explanations linking it to the asymmetry of causal relations. Appeal to similarity doesn't help either. Turning the lights off is no more of a departure from the actual world than bringing the King back to the castle. What, then, explains the asymmetrical treatment of factual premises in Goodman's Puzzle?

The asymmetry in counterfactual reasoning highlighted by Goodman's Puzzle has a parallel with indicative conditionals. Suppose that after hearing the King Ludwig story you are asked to answer the questions in (17):

(17) a. Q: Suppose the lights are on. What if the flag is up?
          A: Then the King must be home.

      b. Q: Suppose the King is away. What if the flag is up?
          A: Then the lights must be out.

(17) pairs each question with the correct answer, given our story. (17a) was easy; (17b) was harder. Why? I think that (17b) was hard because "whenever"-conditionals are universal generalizations, and universal generalizations have interpretations that carry information about confirming situations. When reasoning with "whenever"-conditionals and their kin, then, we seem to be guided by their confirmation sets. The way I told the King Ludwig story mentioned a generalization that is confirmed by situations where the flag is up, the lights are on, and the King is at home, not a generalization that is confirmed by situations where the King is away, the flag is up, and the lights are out. It seemed to have mattered, then, that the generalization mentioned was (18a), rather than the logically equivalent (18b), for example:

(18) a. Whenever the flag is up and the lights are on, the King is home.
      b. Whenever the King is away and the flag is up, the lights are out.

Since the questions in (17) are questions about what follows from the premises given, and hence about logical consequence relations, distinct but logically equivalent ways of representing the relevant generalization cannot possibly affect the truth of the answer. The differences only show up as processing difficulties. Processing difficulties with "whenever"-type conditionals have most famously been studied in the many versions of Wason's Selection Task:[20]

> The subjects (students) were presented with an array of cards and told that every card had a letter on one side and a number on the other side, and that either would be face upwards. They were then instructed to decide which cards they would need to turn over in order to determine whether the experimenter was lying in uttering the following statement: If a card has a vowel on one side then it has an even number on the other side.
>
> Wason (1966: 145).

---

[20] The generalization is stated with "if," rather than "whenever," in Wason's report on his experiment, but "if" could easily be replaced by "whenever" here. The connection between the Raven Paradox and the Wason Selection Task is made in Nickerson (1996).

The correct response was that both cards showing a vowel and cards showing an odd number needed to be turned over. Only a very small number of subjects gave the right answer. Most subjects selected cards that showed a vowel or an even number. From the current perspective, the results in Wason's experiment suggest that there is something about the mental representation of conditionals that pushes subjects towards confirming, rather than falsifying, situations. Cards with a vowel on one side and an even number on the other confirmed the generalization the subjects were given. Cards with a vowel on one side and an odd number on the other falsified it.

There has been much discussion in the literature about just what it is that the results in Wason's Selection Task show us about reasoning with conditionals.[21] What was bound to add an extra level of difficulty to the task was that subjects had to come up with an optimal verification strategy to pass the test. Cards with an even number on their visible side either confirmed the generalization or were irrelevant, and hence didn't *have to* be turned over when verifying the generalization. Subjects who turned over such irrelevant cards were not following an optimal verification strategy, then, and hence were considered as failing the test. Be this as it may, subjects showed a strong pull towards confirming situations in Wason's task, and if confirmation sets are hard-wired into the meaning of "whenever"-type conditionals, we have an explanation for this behavior.

I conclude that non-accidental "whenever"-conditionals have interpretations that carry information about confirmation sets. (D13) follows the model of (D12):

(D13) *Non-accidental conditionals*

$[[((whenever\ \alpha)\beta]]^g =$

$\lambda s\ [[\ [[\alpha]]^g\ (w_s) \rightarrow \exists s'\ \exists s''\ [s' \leq s\ \&\ s'' \leq s\ \&\ [[\alpha]]^g\ (s')\ \&\ [[\beta]]^g\ (s'')\ \&\ simul(s')(s'')]]\ \&\ \forall s'[[s' \leq w_s\ \&\ [[\alpha]]^g\ (s') \rightarrow \exists s''\ [simul(s')(s'')\ \&\ [[\beta]]^g\ (s')]]]].$

To illustrate, according to (D13), the proposition expressed by (18a) is true in all worlds where every situation where the flag is up and the lights are on can be matched with a simultaneous situation where the King is in the castle.[22] If vacuously true in a world, the proposition expressed by (18a) is true in all of its situations. If non-vacuously true in a world, it can only be true in

---

[21] See e.g. Sperber, Cara, and Girotto (1995) and Sperber and Girotto (2002).

[22] I am assuming that simultaneity is a relation between world mates, and hence no other condition needs to guarantee that *s'* and *s''* are world mates. For more complicated cases like *Whenever there is an A, there is a B*, we need to invoke Rothstein's Matching Function (Rothstein 1995) to make sure we get as many Bs as As.

subsituations where the flag is up, the lights are on, and the King is in the castle. (18a) is therefore confirmed by the following propositions, for example:

(19) a. There are occasions where the flag is up, the lights are on, and the King is home.

    b. Right now, the flag is up, the lights are on, and the King is home.

In contrast, (18b) is confirmed by the following propositions, among others:

(20) a. There are occasions where the King is away, the flag is up, and the lights are out.

    b. Right now, the King is away, the flag is up, and the lights are out.

(18a) and (18b) are confirmed by very different propositions, then. Those differences do not only explain the contrast between (17a) and (17b). I think they also hold the key to an explanation of Goodman's Puzzle. A difference that shows up as a mere processing difference with indicative conditionals may have a truth-conditional effect with counterfactuals.

To see how our analysis of counterfactuals might respond to differences in confirmation sets, look at the relevant propositions in the King Ludwig example:

(21) a. Whenever the flag is up and the lights are on, the King is home.

    b. The flag is down right now.

    c. The lights are on right now.

    d. The king is away right now.

The counterfactual assumption is (22):

(22) The flag is up right now.

Propositions from (21) can be consistently added to the counterfactual assumption (22) in two distinct ways while preserving the non-accidental generalization (21a):

Possibility 1:	Possibility 2:
(22)	(22)
(21a)	(21a)
(21c)	(21d)

Possibility 1 logically implies that the flag is up right now, the lights are on, and the King is home. Possibility 2 logically implies that the flag is up right now, the lights are out, and the King is away. We go for Possibility 1, and intuitions are very strong. What excludes Possibility 2, then, or makes it highly dispreferred?

The salient difference between Possibility 1 and Possibility 2 is that Possibility 1, but not Possibility 2, logically implies a confirming proposition for 2 (21a). (21a) is confirmed by the proposition that the flag is up right now, the lights are on, and the King is in the castle, but not by the proposition that the flag is up right now, the lights are out, and the King is away. When constructing the premise sets in the Crucial Set, then, we seem to privilege sets that logically imply confirming propositions for the non-accidental generalizations they contain.

Confirming Proposition Constraint (CPC)
When assembling the Crucial Set, privilege premise sets that logically imply confirming propositions for the non-accidental generalizations they contain.

The CPC instructs us to privilege premise sets that imply confirming propositions for the non-accidental generalizations they contain. Many more examples would have to be discussed before it would be wise to commit to a technically more explicit implementation of the CPC. I have to defer discussion of the various options that would have to be considered to another occasion—the informal statement above will have to do for now.

When presenting possibilities 1 and 2 above, I assumed without justification that the non-accidental generalization (21a) had to be preserved at all cost. Dropping it didn't seem an option. Containing no non-accidental generalization at all, Possibility 3 should be a non-starter:

Possibility 3:
(22)
(21c)
(21d)

Let us assume, then, that non-accidental generalizations are always privileged when constructing premise sets from a particular Base Set. On our account, the choice of non-accidental generalizations is momentous. Different choices of logically equivalent generalizations should be able to affect which counterfactuals we judge true. As a consequence, we should be able to manipulate judgments about counterfactuals by presenting different versions of logically equivalent generalizations. This is a very strong prediction of our account that needs to be checked out. We have to take care to construct the right test cases, though. We need to make sure that the different versions of the generalizations we want to compare are all sufficiently natural.

What are "natural" generalizations? We already know that logically equivalent generalizations are not necessarily equally good descriptions of a given regularity. That all non-black things are non-ravens is a bad way of saying that all ravens are black. What makes that generalization bad? As Quine (1969) points out, non-ravens and non-black things are not natural kinds, and this makes the set of non-black non-ravens an unnatural confirmation set. Unlike non-black non-ravens, black ravens have a lot in common with each other, and humans can effortlessly project the corresponding category from just a few positive instances. How do they do it? Murphy (2002) gives a comprehensive overview of contemporary research into human concepts and concept induction. Interestingly, non-black non-ravens do not figure in that research. They are uncontroversial non-starters.

On our account, Cognitive Viability is likely to exclude extremely unnatural generalizations from admissible Base Sets. If a generalization doesn't make it into the relevant Base Set, the engine assembling premise sets will not be able to use it. What if a very unnatural generalization is explicitly mentioned and thus made salient in the context? In that case, I could imagine that the reasoning engine might attempt to convert the generalization into a more natural, logically equivalent, counterpart. It's crucial, then, to keep an eye on the naturalness of confirmation sets when testing whether different logically equivalent non-accidental generalizations can trigger different truth-value judgments for affected counterfactuals. Here is a variation of the original King Ludwig example that experiments with a different presentation of the relevant generalization.

Whenever King Ludwig is away, the flag is down or the lights are out. Right now, the King is away, the flag is down and the lights are on. What if the flag were up?

In this context, it is no longer obvious that the King would be home. We also seem to be willing to entertain the possibility that the lights might be out with the King still being away. Judgments are no longer as firm as with the earlier King Ludwig example. We are unsure. That there should be a difference in judgment at all is noteworthy since neither the facts of the case nor the counterfactual assumption have changed. I only replaced the description of the regularity with a logically equivalent one. Instead of (23a), I used the equivalent (23b).

(23)   a. Whenever the flag is up and the lights are on, the King is home.
       b. Whenever the King is away, the flag is down or the lights are out.

The form of the generalizations relied on seems to have an effect on which counterfactuals we judge true, then.

If the generalization relied on was (23b), we have the following kinds of premise sets:

Possibility 1:	Possibility 2:
(22)	(22)
(23b)	(23b)
(21c)	(21d)

As before, Possibility 1 implies that the flag is up right now, the lights are on, and the King is home, and Possibility 2 implies that the flag is up right now, the lights are out, and the King is away. This time round, Possibility 2, not Possibility 1, logically implies a confirming proposition for the generalization relied on. Given the CPC, we expect Possibility 2 to be preferred. That's not quite what we find; judgments are insecure.

While (23b) is not a shockingly bad generalization, it is still a less natural way of describing the regularity in the King Ludwig case than (23a). (23a) is confirmed by situations where the flag is up right now, the lights are on, and the King is home. Those situations have a lot in common with each other. On the other hand, (23b) is confirmed by situations where the King is away right now, and the flag is down or the lights are out. Situations *s* where the King is away are situations that contain him wherever he is in the world of *s*, provided that's not home. If the King is actually in a boat on the lake, for example, then actual situations where he is away are situations where he is in that boat; if he is actually in his hunting hut, then actual situations where he is away are situations where he is in that hut. There is thus a lot of variation among situations where the King is away. The only thing those situations have in common is that the King is in some place that is not home. Confirming situations for (23b) also differ with respect to the flag and the lights: the flag may be up or down and the lights may be on or out, as long as the flag isn't down while the lights are out. Overall, (23b) is a less natural way of describing the regularity in the King Ludwig case than (23a). I suspect that that's the reason for the observed insecurities in judgment. My explicitly mentioning (23b) might not have been enough to overcome an inherent cognitive bias against it. A less natural, but explicitly mentioned, version of the generalization competed with a more natural default for inclusion in the Base Set. That there should be even a slight difference in judgment between the first and the second King Ludwig example is truly remarkable, though. It shows that the mere form of a salient generalization can affect which counterfactuals we judge true.

Schulz (2007) argues that the King Ludwig counterfactual and its kin are epistemic counterfactuals—a distinct, non-causal, type of counterfactuals that should be interpreted with respect to belief states, not facts. According to Schulz, the standard interpretation of the King Ludwig counterfactual is one where the speaker uttering the counterfactual is looking at the castle from a distance, where she can see that the lights are on and the flag is down, but has no direct evidence about the whereabouts of the King. Making the belief contravening assumption that the flag is up therefore only requires giving up the belief that the flag is down. The presence of the King in the castle follows from the retained beliefs and the assumed non-accidental generalization. What speaks against such an account is that judgments remain the same in contexts that would be non-standard for Schulz. Suppose the King and a friend are in a boat on the lake, from where they can see that the lights are on in the castle and the flag is down. They are obviously aware that the King is not in the castle. The King has just explained to the friend that he is in the castle whenever the flag is up and the lights are on. The friend asks: "Does this mean that if the flag were up over there, you would be in the castle?" The King replies: "Yes, that's right, you got it." Imagine the friend had asked instead: "Does this mean that if the flag were up over there, the lights would be out?" I would expect a slightly bewildered look from the King.

Veltman (2005) presents an example that he says has the same logical structure as the King Ludwig example without showing the mysterious asymmetry of Goodman's Puzzle:

Consider the case of three sisters who own just one bed, large enough for two of them, but too small for all three. Every night at least one of them has to sleep on the floor. Whenever Ann sleeps in the bed and Billie sleeps in the bed, Carol sleeps on the floor. At the moment Billie is sleeping in bed, Ann is sleeping on the floor, and Carol is sleeping in bed. Suppose now counterfactually that Ann had been in bed…

Veltman (2005: 178).

Veltman's assessment is that this time, we are not "prepared to say: 'Well, in that case Carol would be sleeping on the floor.' Indeed, why wouldn't Billie be on the floor?" I share Veltman's judgment, but I object to the suggestion that the Three Sisters example has the same logical structure as the King Ludwig example. It does not. The generalization in (24a) is just one of at least three equally relevant consequences of the salient generalization (24d). (24a) does not have any privileged status with respect to (24b) or (24c).

(24)   a.   Whenever Ann sleeps in the bed and Billie sleeps in the bed, Carol sleeps on the floor.

     b.   Whenever Ann sleeps in the bed and Carol sleeps in the bed, Billie sleeps on the floor.

    c. Whenever Billie sleeps in the bed and Carol sleeps in the bed, Ann sleeps on the floor.

    d. Whenever two of Ann, Billie, and Carol sleep in the bed, the third one sleeps on the floor.

On our account, not all of (24a) to (24d) can be in the Base Set because of Non-Redundancy. (24d) should be the winner since it logically implies (24a) to (24c), none of which is privileged with respect to the other two. Here are the relevant propositions for the Three Sisters example:

(25)   a. Whenever two of Ann, Billie, and Carol sleep in the bed, the third one sleeps on the floor.
        b. Ann is sleeping on the floor right now.
        c. Billie is sleeping in the bed right now.
        d. Carol is sleeping in the bed right now.

The counterfactual assumption is (26):

(26)   Ann is sleeping in the bed right now.

Propositions from (25) can be consistently added to the counterfactual assumption (26) in two distinct ways while preserving the non-accidental generalization (25a):

Possibility 1:	Possibility 2:
(26)	(26)
(25a)	(25a)
(25c)	(25d)

Possibility 1 logically implies that Carol is sleeping on the floor right now; Possibility 2 implies that Billie is sleeping on the floor right now. Both possibilities imply that two of Ann, Billie, and Carol are sleeping in the bed right now, and hence both possibilities satisfy the CPC. Neither possibility is privileged, then, and we correctly predict that Billie or Carol might be sleeping on the floor right now. The third possibility that excludes (25a), but includes both (25c) and (25d), is dispreferred since it has no non-accidental generalization to begin with.

    The CPC can privilege premise sets that describe worlds that are very clearly further away from reality than those described by some disfavored premise sets. Suppose we are looking at a barometer that correctly indicates that the current air pressure is 1005.2 millibars. Now consider the two counterfactuals (27a) and (27b) from Lewis (1973b):

(27) a. If the barometer reading had been higher, the air pressure would
          have been higher.

      b. If the barometer reading had been higher, the barometer would
          have been malfunctioning.

Lewis comments:

The barometer reading depends counterfactually on the pressure – that is as clear-cut
as counterfactuals ever get – but does the pressure depend counterfactually on the
reading? If the reading had been higher, would the pressure have been higher? Or
would the barometer have been malfunctioning? The second sounds better: a higher
reading would have been an incorrect reading.

Lewis (1973b: 564).

Intuitions are not that clear about this example, and, as Lewis observes,
context and wording matter:

Granted, there are contexts or changes of wording that would incline us the other
way. For some reason, "If the reading had been higher, that would have been because
the pressure was higher" invites my assent more than "If the reading had been higher,
the pressure would have been higher." The counterfactuals from readings to pressures
are much less clear-cut than those from pressures to readings. But it is enough that
some legitimate resolutions of vagueness give an irreversible dependence of readings
on pressures. Those are the resolutions we want at present, even if they are not
favored in all contexts.

Lewis (1973b: 565).

We can sharpen intuitions by spelling out the generalization that the example
relies on. The salient generalization is (28):

(28) Whenever the barometer reading is x and the barometer is function-
       ing, the air pressure is x.

Compare now the following two dialogues:

(29) a. Q: As a matter of fact, the air pressure is 1005.2 millibars right now,
             the barometer is functioning, and it reads 1005.2 millibars.
             What if the air pressure were 1010 millibars?
          A: Then the barometer would read 1010 millibars.

      b. Q: As a matter of fact, the air pressure is 1005.2 millibars right now,
             the barometer is functioning, and it reads 1005.2 millibars.
             What if the air pressure were 1010 millibars?
          A: Then the barometer would be malfunctioning.

(29b) is strongly dispreferred. Our analysis predicts this. The example has the same structure as the King Ludwig example. What is significant about this case is that a malfunctioning barometer would have required much less of a departure from reality than a change in air pressure:

> When something must give way to permit a higher reading, we find it less of a departure from actuality to hold the pressure fixed and sacrifice the accuracy, rather than vice versa. It is not hard to see why. The barometer, being more localized and more delicate than the weather, is more vulnerable to slight departures from actuality.
>
> Lewis (1973b: 565).

A naïve similarity theory of counterfactuals would wrongly predict (29b) to be preferred over (29a). Stalnaker's and Lewis's theories of counterfactuals are *not* naïve similarity theories of counterfactuals, of course. Their theories leave room for linguistic and non-linguistic context to influence the relevant similarity relation. But why should the wording of a salient generalization influence the similarity relation used for the evaluation of a particular counterfactual? As in the zebra example above, there is an undergeneration problem with the way Stalnaker or Lewis would deal with (29a) and (29b). Intuitions about the preference for (29a) over (29b) are clear. A theory of counterfactuals should thus predict them to be clear. Stalnaker's and Lewis's theories predict more vagueness and indeterminacy for those cases than we actually observe.

Pressure to match up non-accidental generalizations with confirming propositions also seems to affect the construction of admissible Base Sets. An often-discussed example, due to Pavel Tichý (Tichý 1976), illustrates.

> ... consider a man – call him Jones – who is possessed of the following dispositions as regards wearing his hat. Bad weather invariably induces him to wear his hat. Fine weather, on the other hand, affects him neither way: on fine days he puts his hat on or leaves it on the peg, completely at random. Suppose, moreover, that actually the weather is bad, so Jones is wearing his hat.
>
> Tichý (1976: 271).

On Tichý's scenario, (30a) is false, but (30b) and (30c) are both true.

(30)   a. If the weather were fine, Jones would be wearing his hat.
       b. If the weather were fine, Jones might be wearing his hat.
       c. If the weather were fine, Jones might not be wearing his hat.

As Tichý points out, a naïve similarity analysis of counterfactuals would predict (30a) to be true, since the closest worlds where the weather is fine would seem to be worlds where Jones is wearing a hat, given the fact that he is already wearing a hat. Tichý's example is a challenge for our analysis as well, since there doesn't seem to be any reason to discard the fact that Jones is wearing a hat under the counterfactual assumption that the weather is fine. But suppose there is pressure to construct admissible Base Sets for counterfactuals in such a way that non-accidental generalizations are matched up with confirming propositions if possible:

CPC for Base Sets

When constructing a Base Set, privilege confirming propositions for non-accidental generalizations.

If p is the proposition that the weather is bad right now, and q is the proposition that Jones is wearing his hat right now, then $p \cap q$ confirms the generalization that Jones wears his hat whenever the weather is bad. Neither p nor q alone confirms the generalization. If an admissible Base Set contains the generalization, then, the CPC for Base Sets tells us to privilege the conjunction $p \cap q$ over the individual propositions p and q when representing the facts of the world. Non-Redundancy excludes the possibility that a Base Set may contain all three of $p \cap q$, p, and q. But $p \cap q$ is incompatible with the counterfactual assumption that the weather is fine, and hence cannot appear in any premise set in the associated Crucial Set. The CPC for Base Sets guarantees that Jones's wearing a hat and the current bad weather is treated as a single fact in the evaluation of the counterfactuals in (30). Assuming that Tichý told us all relevant facts of this case, if the bad weather goes, so does Jones's hat.

The original CPC and the CPC for Base Sets are two sides of the same coin. In both cases, the reasoning engine looks for matches between non-accidental generalizations and propositions that confirm them. When assembling a Base Set, an important selection has to be made among logically equivalent non-accidental generalizations, and matches have to be found among the facts of the world of evaluation. When assembling premise sets for the Crucial Set, the engine is on the lookout for premise sets that logically imply certain confirming propositions.

We have seen that the truth of many counterfactuals depends on the choice of the right non-accidental generalizations. There is a fine line between accidental and non-accidental generalizations, though. Change the King Ludwig scenario just a little bit. Everything stays the same except now you and I are passing by the castle. Seized by some childish inclination, I say to you: "Suppose I hoisted the flag"... the consequences could be dramatic. Would my hoisting the flag bring the King back into the castle? No. The counterfactual expressed by (31) is false.

(31)   If I hoisted the flag, the King would appear in the castle.

The earlier King Ludwig generalization was a generalization about the habits of the King and his staff. It has been true for as long as anybody can remember that whenever the flag was up and the lights were on, the King was in the castle. The King announced that the flag and the lights would be signs of his presence. The King's staff is reliable. No irregularities. Yet I could destroy the regularity with a single action. Our second scenario suggests that this may indeed be my intention.

What was treated as a non-accidental generalization before has now been demoted to a simple accidental one. The relevant facts are listed in (32):

(32)   a. Each occasion where the flag is up and the lights are on is an occasion where the King is in the castle.
       b. The flag is down right now.
       c. The lights are on right now.
       d. The King is away right now.

(32a) is meant to expresses an accidental generalization. As a consequence, it cannot be added consistently to the antecedent of the counterfactual expressed by (32). Being a mere accidental generalization, (32a) is only true in situations that are big enough to contain all occasions where the flag is up and the lights are on. It therefore lumps, among others, the propositions in (33):

(33)   On occasion 1, the flag is up.
       On occasion 2, the flag is up.
       On occasion 3, the flag is up.
       . . . .
       On occasion 115, the flag is up.
       The flag is up on exactly 115 occasions.

The antecedent of the counterfactual (31) adds yet another occasion to this collection which leads to inconsistency. Among the propositions mentioned, only (32c) and (32d) can be consistently added to the antecedent of our counterfactual. But then the flag would be up, the lights would be on, and the King would still be away.

5.6 Negation

5.6.1 *In search of an accidental interpretation*

In many ways, negation confronts us with the same issues as universal quantification. Try to formulate the truth-conditions for negated sentences in the way familiar from classical logic. The result is (D14).

(D14) *Non-persistent negation*

$$[[\,not\;\alpha\,]]^g = \lambda s \; \neg[[\alpha]]^g(s).$$

(D14) produces propositions that violate the Persistence Constraint. To see this, suppose the Hampshire Gazette has been delivered today and is lying on the kitchen table. The proposition "a paper is lying on a table" is then true in our world right now. It is also true in some of its parts, but there are other parts where it is not true.[23] Zoom in on s_{sink}—that part of our world that consists of the sink and nothing else. The proposition "a paper is lying on a table" is not true in s_{sink}. According to (D14) the proposition expressed by (34)

(34)   There isn't a paper lying on a table.

should then be true in s_{sink}. That proposition is not true in our world, however, since the Hampshire Gazette is actually lying on the kitchen table. Persistence is violated.

Next, consider a Kripke-style interpretation for negation (Kripke 1965):

(D15) *Generic negation*

$$[[\,not\;\alpha\,]]^g = \lambda s \; \forall s'[s \le s' \rightarrow \neg\;[[\alpha]]^g\;(s')].$$

(D15) produces persistent propositions that are true in all or none of the situations of a world. Those propositions are generic. Negated sentences *can* certainly have generic interpretations, as when I claim "Cats don't bark." But they don't *have to* be generic. Moreover, section 5.5.2 argued for a more differentiated representation of generic sentences. (D15) is not an option, then.[24]

To make progress towards figuring out accidental interpretations for negated sentences, it may be helpful to recall the accidental interpretation for universal quantification spelled out in (D8): to account for the strong lumping properties of accidental universal generalizations, we made sure that, in the non-vacuous case, the propositions assigned could only be true in situations that satisfied a condition supplied by the restrictive clause of the construction. Maybe negative sentences come with restrictive clauses, too. Since Jackendoff (1972), it has often been noted that negation has a special relation with focus. This has been taken to mean that the semantic interpretation of focus constructions involves a mechanism that isolates the unfocused part from the rest of the sentence. In one way or other, some such procedure

---

[23] I haven't used the word "false" so far. Saying that a proposition is false in a situation suggests that its negation is true in that situation. This is not what I mean when I talk about propositions being "not true."

[24] Once an accidental interpretation for negation is in place, the generic interpretation could follow the model of (D12). I will not investigate generic negated sentences here.

is at the heart of a variety of approaches to focus: Jackendoff (1972), von Stechow (1981), Cresswell and von Stechow (1982), Jacobs (1982, 1983), Kadmon and Roberts (1986), Hajičová, Partee, and Sgall (1998), and many others. I want to suggest that we should think of negation as an operator that associates with focus, and that the standard tripartite Logical Forms for quantifier constructions are also right for negative sentences.[25]

5.6.2 *Negation and restrictive clauses*

At the end of the preceding section, I suggested that negated sentences have the tripartite Logical Forms of quantifier constructions, which becomes apparent when negation interacts with focus. In English, focused constituents can be distinguished phonetically by the presence of particular pitch accents, or syntactically by cleft constructions. Those tools are usually not sufficient to determine unambiguous focus assignments to sentences, however (see Jackendoff (1972) and Selkirk (1984) for discussion). In what follows I am assuming that we are given appropriate focus assignments for sentences. I will use capital letters to indicate what the intended focused constituents are, regardless of what the actual means for focusing may have been. (35) and (36) illustrate:

(35)   Paula isn't registered in PARIS.

(36)   PAULA isn't registered in Paris.

Preserving the spirit of previous analyses of focus while emphasizing the similarity with restricted quantifier structures, we are led to the following Logical Forms for (35) and (36):

(35′)   (Not: x is a place and Paula is registered in x)
         Paula is registered in Paris.

(36′)   (Not: x is a person and x is registered in Paris)
         Paula is registered in Paris.

---

[25] My views on focus and its role in restricting the domains of quantifiers have changed during the last twenty years. Rooth (1985), (1992), and von Fintel (1994) argued convincingly that the impact of topic and focus on domain restrictions is only indirect and is mediated by domain restriction variables. Beaver and Clark (2008) have clarified the various ways expressions can associate with focus. Kratzer and Selkirk (2007) and Kratzer and Selkirk (in preparation) have made a case for distinguishing between information focus and the different varieties of "contrastive" or "alternative" focus. Information focus is not represented in the grammar at all, according to Kratzer and Selkirk, only givenness and alternative focus is. The prosody traditionally associated with information focus is a reflex of default prosody. Incorporating those views into this chapter would have required a complete rewrite of this section without much gain for the plot as a whole, which still stands: negation depends on domain restrictions in the very same way adverbial quantifiers do, and focus has a systematic impact on what those restrictions are.

In (35′) and (36′), the restrictive clause corresponds to the unfocused part of the sentence. In addition to the material contained in the original sentences, the restrictive clause contains some sortal for the variable to be provided by the context of use. Here is a first attempt at a meaning definition that will do for now:

(D16) *Accidental negation*

$$[[(Not\,\alpha)\,\beta]]^g =$$
$$\lambda s\forall g'[[g' \sim_x g \,\&\, [[\alpha]]^{g'}(w_s)] \rightarrow [\, [[\alpha]]^{g'}(s) \,\&\, \neg\, [[\beta]]^{g'}(s)\,]].$$

According to (D16), the proposition expressed by (35) can be true in a proper, non-world, situation s only if Paula is registered somewhere[26], and whenever Paula is registered anywhere in the world of s, she is registered at that place in s. In contrast, the proposition expressed by (36) can be true in a situation s only if somebody is registered in Paris[27], and whenever anybody is registered in Paris in the world of s, that person is registered in Paris in s. In both cases, there is the invariant requirement that Paula not be registered in Paris in s.

(D16) treats negation syntactically like an adverbial quantifier. It suggests that there is no such thing as a one-place negation operator. Every negation operator has a restrictive clause that results from the original clause by replacing the focused phrase by an appropriate variable. Richly typed languages like Cresswell's lambda categorial language (Cresswell 1973) or Montague's intensional logic (Montague 1974) have variables for each syntactic category that are interpreted via variable assignments assigning them appropriate entities. A variable of category S, for example, is assigned a proposition. In the extreme case, where a whole sentence is focused, we have logical forms of the following kind:

(37) $(Not:\, x_S)\beta$

The proposition expressed by sentences of this form can only be true in a situation s if all propositions that are true in the world of s are true in s. But this means that the propositions expressed by such sentences can only be true in worlds.

If negation is connected to focus, as suggested here, the Logical Forms for negated sentences are not a simple matter. Sentence negation and verb phrase negation are just special cases out of a much broader range of possibilities. Work on negation will have to pay close attention to work on focus and intonation, an area that is under active investigation in linguistics. The above

---

[26] This requirement should ultimately be a presupposition. I will neglect this issue here.
[27] See the previous footnote.

thoughts suggest a possible road for further research, but cannot do justice to the full range of questions we might want to ask.

I have made a proposal for accidental interpretations of negated sentences. What still needs to be shown is that (D16) produces propositions with the correct lumping properties. The following section will take up this question.

5.6.3 *Negation and counterfactual reasoning*

You have probably heard of Clyde, a sweet young man who eventually married Bertha (Dretske 1972). Suppose now counterfactually that he hadn't married BERTHA. Might he have married somebody else? If there weren't such a thing as lumping, life would look grim for Clyde. In the actual world, he didn't marry CATHERINE, for example. The proposition expressed by

(38)   Clyde didn't marry CATHERINE.
       (Not: Clyde married x_N and x_N is a woman) Clyde married Catherine.

can be consistently added to the antecedent of our counterfactual and the proposition that Clyde didn't marry CATHERINE follows from the resulting set. Without lumping, there would be the danger that each and every way of adding propositions that are facts of this world to the antecedent of our counterfactual while preserving consistency would eventually reach a point where the resulting set implies the proposition that Clyde didn't marry CATHERINE. Hence Clyde wouldn't marry CATHERINE. Clyde wouldn't have more luck with other women. Analogous reasoning would show that he wouldn't marry EVANGELINE, he wouldn't marry GUINEVERE, he wouldn't marry ISOLDE, he wouldn't marry KIRI, he wouldn't marry MIR-IAM, he wouldn't marry OLGA, he wouldn't marry QUILLA, he wouldn't marry STEPHANIE, he wouldn't marry URSULA, he wouldn't marry WIL-HELMINA, he wouldn't marry YVONNE, . . . (Cresswell 1981). But fortunately, there is lumping. Every situation of our world where the proposition expressed by (38) is true is a situation where Clyde married Bertha (assuming that (38) is given an accidental interpretation and that Clyde married only Bertha). Hence the proposition expressed by (38) lumps the proposition that Clyde married Bertha in our world. As a consequence the proposition expressed by (38) cannot be added consistently to the antecedent of a counterfactual of the form "If Clyde hadn't married Bertha. . . ." But then, it seems, Clyde might have married Catherine, he might have married Evangeline, he might have married Guinevere, and all the rest, provided only that there weren't other facts preventing this (supposing that no man marries his sister in our world, and this is a non-accidental generalization, Clyde wouldn't have married his sister, for example).

At this point, you may wonder what will happen with a proposition like the one expressed by the following sentence.

(39)   Clyde didn't MARRY Catherine.
        (Not: Clyde x_V Catherine) Clyde married Catherine.

The propositions expressed by (38) and (39) are logically equivalent. They are true in exactly the same possible worlds. In particular, they are both true in the actual world. But unlike the proposition expressed by (38), that expressed by (39) does not lump the fact that Clyde married Bertha in the actual world. If we try to add the proposition expressed by (38) to the antecedent of a counterfactual like (40), no inconsistency is likely to arise via lumping.

(40)   If Clyde hadn't married BERTHA, he might have married Catherine.

But then (40) might very well come out false (the exact outcome depends on the complete array of facts, of course). Similar points could be made with respect to all the other women in the list. But then Clyde would be likely to stay unmarried after all.

The example of Clyde and Bertha suggests that foregrounding and back-grounding of information may sometimes play a role in selecting or rejecting a proposition as relevant for the evaluation of a given counterfactual. In our case, we would have to assume that the proposition expressed by (38) is selected, while the logically equivalent proposition expressed by (39) is rejected. The proposition expressed by (38), but not that expressed by (39) would be in the relevant Base Set. It is actually not difficult to see why this should be so. The focus structure of the antecedent of (40) conveys that we are discussing alternatives as to who Clyde might have married. The focus structure of (38) conveys that we are discussing precisely those alternatives. This information is not only encoded by the restrictive clause of the Logical Form of (38). It is also hard-wired into the corresponding proposition on our account. The proposition expressed by (38) can only be true in a situation s if s contains all the women who Clyde married in the world of s. In contrast, the focus structure of (39) conveys that we are discussing alternatives as to what Clyde might have done with respect to Catherine. Again, this information is retrievable from the restrictive clause of the logical form of (39), as well as from the proposition expressed. We may assume, then, that sometimes the focus structure of a counterfactual sentence may guide admission into the Base Set, and lead to the rejection of "non-matching" logically equivalent propositions as relevant for its evaluation. The exact mechanism of this process will have to be explored in future work.

Let us turn to another example. You may remember those lines that might have been longer or shorter than they actually are (Lewis 1973a). Take this clothesline here. It is thirty feet long. Suppose now counterfactually that it were longer than it actually is. How long might it be? I think it might be 35 feet long, for example. On Lewis's account, that couldn't be. Given his interpretation of "might"-counterfactuals (Lewis 1973a: 21), the proposition expressed by (41)

(41)   If this clothesline were longer than it actually is, it might be 35 feet long.

could only be true in a world if there is no world in which the line is longer than it actually is and is not 35 feet long which is closer to the actual world than any world in which the line is longer than it actually is and is 35 feet long. But there are plenty of such worlds: all the worlds in which the clothesline is longer than 30 feet but shorter than 35 feet. A proponent of the similarity theory would now have to argue that for some reason, trying to stay as close as possible to the actual length of the line isn't a consideration guiding the evaluation of counterfactuals of this sort. But why should this be so? On the present account, we can explain this rather puzzling fact. The explanation is similar to the one we gave in the case of the zebra. If closeness to the actual length of the line were to play a role in the evaluation of counterfactual sentences of the form "If this clothesline were longer than it actually is...," then this would mainly be due to the presence of a host of relevant negative facts like the ones expressed by sentences of the following kind (let us forget about units smaller than feet):

(42)   (Not: x_N is a number and this clothesline is longer than x_N feet) this clothesline is longer than 31 feet
(Not: x_N is a number and this clothesline is longer than x_N feet) this clothesline is longer than 32 feet
(Not: x_N is a number and this clothesline is longer than x_N feet) this clothesline is longer than 33 feet

. . . .

The propositions expressed by the Logical Forms in (42) are true in all those situations of our world where this clothesline is present and is longer than 1, 2, . . . , 29 feet. But all of those situations are situations where this clothesline is actually 30 feet long. Hence the propositions expressed by the Logical Forms in (42) all lump the proposition that this clothesline is 30 feet long in our world. Adding any of those propositions to the antecedent of the counterfactual in (42), then, always leads to inconsistency.

The examples we have examined in this section were all examples where negative propositions had to be eliminated. They were in the way and had to be knocked out by lumping. Or else they had to be considered as irrelevant for the evaluation of the counterfactual under consideration. Doesn't this suggest that, maybe, negative propositions are *never* relevant for the evaluation of a counterfactual? Why should we admit negative propositions as relevant only to eliminate them later on through lumping? Are there ever any occasions where negative propositions are crucial for the truth of a counterfactual? I don't know about "crucial," but I do know that there are pieces of counterfactual reasoning where negative propositions enter at least naturally. Here is an example: I am not wearing MY GLASSES right now. Suppose counterfactually that I tried to read the sign over there. I couldn't do it. My eyes are bad and I am not wearing GLASSES, and I am not wearing CONTACT LENSES, and I am not.... and there are laws stating under which circumstances a person like me can read signs which are that far away. It seems, then, that sometimes we do want to use negative propositions in counterfactual reasoning. A proposition like the one that I am not wearing GLASSES will bring along other propositions: that I am wearing earrings, that I am not wearing SHOES, that I am wearing a sweater, that I am not wearing A SCARF, ... All these propositions will peacefully join the antecedent of our last counterfactual. If I tried to read the sign over there, I couldn't do it.

5.7 Conclusion

This chapter has been a *tour de force* navigating around some of the hardest topics in contemporary semantic theory: situation semantics, counterfactual reasoning, non-accidental generalizations and their confirmation sets, focus, and negation. That so many apparently unconnected topics showed up with their classical puzzles on our way is a good sign. We may be digging into a cognitive domain with a rich structure that may be explored with similar success as syntactic structures have been during the last fifty years or so.

If a theory of counterfactuals of the kind presented here is correct, all semantic complexities of natural languages could potentially add to the complexity of counterfactual reasoning: the Logical Forms of particular constructions produce propositions with particular lumping properties that affect counterfactual reasoning in particular ways. The investigation of counterfactuals could therefore give us invaluable insights into the semantics of natural languages. This enterprise could keep us busy for many years to come.

Introducing Chapter 6

This chapter is about a connection between knowledge ascriptions and counterfactual reasoning. In both cases, facts are central. And in neither case can we get away with facts that are merely true propositions. A more specific notion is needed.

The unifying theme of the chapter are variations of Gettier puzzles (Gettier 1963). Gettier puzzles are widely discussed with knowledge ascriptions, but we also find them in other areas. There are Gettier-analogs of mere belief ascriptions, of content ascriptions without mental attitudes, and of counterfactual reasoning.

In the first part of the chapter, I suggest that what makes a Gettier example a Gettier example in knowledge ascriptions is that the propositional content of the belief is described correctly, but it so happens that the content is exemplified by a fact that the believer has no belief about. A true description of the propositional content of the belief picks out the wrong *res*. The second part of the chapter shows that an analogous mismatch between propositions and exemplifying facts is a potential source of trouble for counterfactual reasoning. In counterfactual reasoning, too, we have to keep an eye on the exemplifying facts of true propositions. This is why premise sets were closed under Lumping in *An Investigation of the Lumps of Thought* (chapter 5). The chapter concludes with the suggestion that Closure under Lumping can be dispensed with if accidental facts for premise sets are projected at the right level of specificity from the very start.

Chapter 6 is a revised and updated version of *Facts: Particulars or Information Units?*, which appeared in 2002 in *Linguistics and Philosophy* 25, 655–70. The *Linguistics and Philosophy* article was itself a revised version of *How Specific is a Fact?*, which was included in the *Proceedings of the Conference on Theories of Partial Information* held at the Center for Cognitive Science, University of Texas at Austin, January 25–7 1990. For the current re-edition of the paper, I also used bits and pieces from my 2007 article on *Situations in Natural Languages* in the *Stanford Encyclopedia of Philosophy*, and from *Constraining Premise Sets for Counterfactuals*, a short note published in 2005 in the *Journal of Semantics* 22, 153–8.

Chapter 6

Facts: Particulars or Information Units?*

Why are the same intellectual battles fought over and over again? Why aren't there arguments good enough to settle those debates once and for good?

What are facts, situations, or events? When Situation Semantics was born in the eighties, I objected because I could not warm up to the idea that situations might be chunks of information. For me, they had to be particulars like sticks or bricks. I could not imagine otherwise. The first manuscript of *An investigation of the Lumps of Thought* that I submitted to *Linguistics and Philosophy* had a footnote where I distanced myself from all those who took possible situations to be units of information. In that context and at that time, this meant Jon Barwise and John Perry.

I eventually met Jon Barwise at a colloquium at MIT. When we had a drink together afterwards, he asked me: "Why did you put that footnote in your paper?" I don't remember what I replied, but Jon invited me to Stanford for a talk. I accepted the invitation. I have been ashamed about the footnote ever since. I took it out. It never made it into the printed version of my paper. However, I am sad that I was never able to pay back Jon's generosity. Like the original article, this chapter is dedicated to his memory.

6.1 Worldly facts

I know of two areas in semantics where we seem to need a notion of "fact" that cannot be identified with "true proposition." One is the semantics of the verb *to know*. The other is the semantics of counterfactuals. If facts are not merely true propositions, what kind of creatures could they be? Take Charles Baylis:

* I want to thank Thomas Ede Zimmermann, Irene Heim, and in particular two anonymous reviewers for *Linguistics and Philosophy* for comments and suggestions that were so substantial that it took me 10 years to digest them. The topic I am dealing with here might be around forever, though. Why hurry, then?

In the case of ordinary empirical knowledge these facts are fully concrete and particular. Going out in a rainstorm, for example, we become acquainted with some few aspects of the highly complex fact of fully particularized rain falling in a completely particularized way. Though we notice, and perhaps talk about, only certain features of this complex particular event, we believe that it has an indefinitely large number of characteristics. It is raining at a definite rate. Each raindrop is of a definite size and composition. The condition of the clouds above and of the ground beneath is also determinate. The spatiotemporal relation of each raindrop to every other object in the world is specific. There seem always to be further questions about the rainstorm that can be asked.[1]

On this view, facts are particulars. The facts of our world are parts of our world. Facts, then, are not at all like propositions. Propositions apply to facts as properties apply to things. Facts exemplify propositions as things exemplify properties.

> ...and these facts embody or exemplify the abstract propositional meanings they make true. The relation meant by the term *exemplify* is the one commonly signified in the literature of symbolic logic by $\in$. The relation symbolized by *characterize* is the converse of the epsilon relation.[2]

In this chapter, I will first look at possible motivations for positing facts that are particulars. Such "worldly" facts, as I will call them, play a role in the semantics of the verb *to know*. The second part of the chapter will then show that we cannot get away with worldly facts alone. Worldly facts have closely related propositional analogs that are needed in the semantics of counterfactuals. Sometimes, then, the things we might want to call "facts" might be more like information units after all.

6.2 Facts and the semantics of the verb *to know*

There was a time when knowledge was thought to be justified true belief. That view was done away with by Edmund Gettier.[3] There is, I think, a way of rescuing the traditional view, however. We could understand "justified true belief" in a slightly different way. What if justified true beliefs were justified true beliefs of facts? Instead of ❶, we would have ❷:

❶   Justified true beliefs are justified beliefs of true propositions.

❷   Justified true beliefs are justified true beliefs of facts.

If facts are just true propositions, justified true beliefs are bound to be justified true beliefs of facts, of course. But if we take the worldly view of

---

[1] Baylis (1948: 459).   [2] Baylis (1948: 460).   [3] Gettier (1963).

facts, adopting ❷ might make Gettier's threat go away. Let us see why. The earliest Gettier example I know of is by Bertrand Russell:[4]

> If a man believes that the late Prime Minister's name began with a B, he believes what is true, since the late Prime Minister's last name was Sir Henry Campbell Bannerman. But if he believes that Mr. Balfour was the late Prime Minister, he will still believe that the late Prime Minister's last name began with a B, yet this belief though true, would not be thought to constitute knowledge.

Russell's example is arguably not a *real* Gettier example, since Russell's man is not necessarily justified in believing that the late Prime Minister's last name began with a "B." Satisfaction of the justification or reliability condition is an issue with the original Gettier examples as well, however, as pointed out by one of the referees for the original version of this chapter. For my present concerns, the question whether Russell's example is or isn't a true Gettier example is not relevant. The justification condition is not what I think is at stake here to begin with. Something else is going wrong. Suppose Russell's man is Jones, and look at the following sentences:

(1)   Jones knows that the late Prime Minister's name began with a "B."

(2)   The late Prime Minister's name began with a "B."

On Russell's story, (1) is false, even though Jones believes (2), and (2) is true. Jones believes a true proposition, then. Does Jones also believe (2) of a fact? To answer this question, we have to know more about just what it means to believe something of a fact. In Alvin I. Goldman's *A Causal Theory of Knowing*, we find the following truth-conditions for knowledge ascriptions:[5]

❸   A person knows *p* iff the fact *p* is causally connected in an "appropriate" way with the person's believing *p*.

If facts are particulars, it might be tempting to depart a little from Goldman's original definition, and reinterpret it as involving true *de re* beliefs of facts. We have then:

❹   A person knows *p* iff the person believes *p* *de re* of some fact exemplifying *p*.

What has dropped out in ❹ is any explicit mention of a causal connection between *S*'s belief that *p* and some fact exemplifying *p*. The reason why I eliminated that part from Goldman's definition is that for *de re* beliefs to

---

[4] Russell (1912). Quoted from the 1959 Oxford University Press paperback edition, 131–2.
[5] Goldman (1967). Reprinted in Davis (1983: 150).

be possible, some causal connection between believers and the *res* of their beliefs is required as well. David Kaplan requires some causal rapport between believer and *res*, for example, and David Lewis posits a suitable relation of acquaintance.[6] It might be, then, that the acquaintance relation that is necessary for *de re* belief ascriptions is already sufficient to give us the "appropriate" causal connection for knowledge ascriptions. We'll see shortly that that last conjecture is false, but let us set the issue aside for just now, and see what ❹ (as is) buys us for the Russell example.

According to ❹, (1) can only be true if Jones's belief is a *de re* belief about an actual fact exemplifying the proposition that the late Prime Minister's name began with a "B." In our case, that fact is the fact that Henry Campbell Bannerman's name began with a "B." But that fact is not a fact that Jones has a *de re* belief about. Hence ❹ correctly predicts that Jones doesn't know that the late Prime Minister's name began with a "B." Good.

❹ also does well with other Gettier examples. Here is one of Gettier's own.[7] Smith has strong evidence for the proposition expressed by (3).

(3)   Jones owns a Ford.

Smith's evidence is that Jones has owned a Ford for many years and has just offered Smith a ride while driving a Ford. Smith has another friend, Brown, of whose whereabouts he is totally ignorant. Smith selects a place name at random and constructs the following sentence.

(4)   Either Jones owns a Ford, or Brown is in Barcelona.

The proposition expressed by (3) logically implies the proposition expressed by (4). Smith is aware of the entailment, and accepts (4) on the basis of (3). But unknown to Smith, Jones doesn't own a Ford but is driving a rented car. And by sheer coincidence, Brown is in fact in Barcelona. On this scenario, Smith believes the proposition expressed by (4), he is justified in believing it, and it is true. Yet the proposition expressed by (5) is false.

(5)   Smith knows that either Jones owns a Ford, or Brown is in Barcelona.

On Gettier's story, the actual fact exemplifying the proposition expressed by (4) is the fact that Brown is in Barcelona. But Smith's belief is not a *de re* belief about that fact. Consequently, ❹ correctly classifies (5) as false.

---

[6] Kaplan (1968), Lewis (1979c). A useful collection of papers on causal accounts of reference, knowledge, perception, and memory is Davis (1983).

[7] Gettier (1963). Reprinted in Davis (1983: 135–7).

Some notions in Goldman's definition ❸ and its successor ❹ need further thought. While Goldman explores possibilities for appropriate causal connections,[8] he takes the notion "fact that p" for granted. My version of Goldman's definition does the same with the notion "fact that exemplifies p." What is a "fact that exemplifies p"? In the two examples just discussed, the facts the attitudes were about were very specific, while the content of the attitudes ascribed was very general. The "mismatch" between highly specific facts and the much more general propositional contents of beliefs is what produces a typical Gettier example on the analysis I am proposing. In knowledge ascriptions, the "that"-clause seems to have a double function. One is to characterize the information content of the belief ascribed.[9] The other one is to characterize a fact that the belief ascribed is a belief of. That is, the "that"-clause also helps pick out the *res* of the belief. This *res* is not a proposition. It is a worldly thing—a situation. Our next task, then, is to elucidate the notion "fact that exemplifies the proposition p," and this is where situation semantics comes in.

6.3 Facts that exemplify propositions

As in chapter 5, our starting point is a set S of possible situations. Possible situations are parts of possible worlds. A subset of S is singled out as the set of possible individuals. The members of S are particulars. Consider this shirt. It is striped in a very particular way. This very particular way of being striped is an actual state of my shirt. It is a state so particular that it is a state that only my shirt can be in. Its particular way of being striped is just one of the states of my shirt. There are others. Its very particular way of being cotton, its very particular way of being as long as it is, and its very particular way of being from Italy. All of those states are fairly permanent. But there are also more fugitive states that my shirt might be in. Its very particular spinning in the washing machine this morning. Its very particular drying on the line. Its very particular way of being folded and placed in the drawer. Particular states like these, whether actual or merely possible, I suggest, are the kind of situations that are in S.

Situations stand in part-whole relations to each other. The part-whole relationship $\leq$ that we are interested in here is a partial ordering on S satisfying at least the following additional condition:

---

[8] He does not see the connection with *de re* belief, however.

[9] The relationship between the "that"-clause and the information content of the belief ascribed is not trivial. Moreover, the information content of beliefs may not be propositions at all. See Lewis (1979c). I will ignore these complications in what follows.

❺   For all $s \in S$ there is a unique $s' \in S$ such that $s \leq s'$ and for all $s'' \in S$, if $s' \leq s''$, then $s'' = s'$.

Condition ❺ says that every possible situation s is related to a unique maximal element: the world of s. As a consequence, no possible situation can be part of more than one possible world. Situations may be related across possible worlds via counterpart relations as proposed in D. K. Lewis (1968, 1986). Intuitively, $\leq$ corresponds to a part relation that is restricted to world mates. The set of all maximal elements with respect to the ordering $\leq$ is the set W of possible worlds.

Propositions are sets of possible situations, and hence classify situations. They are properties of situations. A proposition p is true in a situation s iff s is a member of p. If p is not true in s, then p is not necessarily "false" in s. It may be that p is "not yet" true in s, but will become true in some situation of which s is a part. To keep the semantics classical, the logical relations depend only on the possible worlds in which propositions are true. Two propositions are logically equivalent, for example, just in case they are true in the same possible worlds. And a proposition p logically implies a proposition q, just in case $p \cap W \subseteq q \cap W$. There are constraints for sets of possible situations to qualify as viable propositions for natural languages, and persistence might be one of them. A proposition is persistent iff whenever it is true in a situation s, it remains true in all situations of which s is a part.

The crucial definition we are after in this section tells us what it means for a situation to be a fact that exemplifies a proposition. Here is a proposal:

❻   A possible situation s (is a fact that) exemplifies a proposition p iff whenever there is a part of s where p is not true, s is a minimal situation where p is true.

Intuitively, a situation that (is a fact that) exemplifies a proposition p is a situation that does not contain anything that does not contribute to the truth of p. ❻ encodes two options for a situation s to exemplify p. Either p is true in all subsituations of s, or s is a minimal situation where p is true. The notion of minimality appealed to in ❻ is the standard one: a situation where p is true is a minimal situation where p is true just in case it has no proper parts where p is true. The situation Mud (Case One below) gives a first illustration of what ❻ does.

Assuming that Mud and all of its parts are mud, Mud and all of its parts exemplify the proposition in (6)[10], since there are no parts of Mud where there is no mud.

---

[10] Here and in what follows, I will take the liberty to use example numbers to refer to either the sentences given in the example or the propositions expressed by those sentences. This will make for

Case One: Mud

Mud is a situation that consists of mud and only mud.

(6)   There is mud.

(6) is not exemplified by Mud & Snow (Case Two below), however:

Case Two: Mud & Snow

Mud & Snow is a situation that consists of some mud and some snow
and nothing else.

Mud & Snow has parts where (6) is not true: the white parts where there is
only snow. But Mud & Snow is not a minimal situation where (6) is true.
   Next, consider the proposition in (7):

(7)   There are three teapots.

(7) describes situations that have at least three teapots in them. (7) seems to
be exemplified by the situation Teapots (Case Three below).

---

less cumbersome prose. A caveat is needed, though. We have seen in the previous chapter that in a
situation semantics, it is not always obvious what the proposition expressed by a given sentence is.
There can be different logically equivalent propositions, for example, and the proposition expressed
by a particular sentence in a context might not always be the one we first think of. This will become
relevant shortly.

Case Three: Teapots

Teapots has three teapots and nothing else in it.

There is no proper subsituation of Teapots where (7) is true. Since Teapots has nothing but three teapots in it, any proper subsituation of Teapots would have to be one where a part of at least one of the three teapots is missing. But (7) is true in Teapots itself, and Teapots is thus a minimal situation where (7) is true.

There is a potential glitch in the above piece of reasoning. It assumes that when an individual is a teapot in a world, no proper part of that individual is also a teapot in that world. This assumption can be questioned, however. Following the reasoning in Geach's story of the 1001 cats (1980: 215), we might reason as follows: my teapot would remain a teapot if we chipped off a tiny piece. Chipping off pieces from teapots doesn't create new teapots, so there must have been smaller teapots all along. We might feel that there is just a single teapot sitting on the table, but upon reflection we might have to acknowledge that there are in fact many overlapping entities that all have legitimate claims to teapothood. The unexpected multitude of teapots is a source of headaches when it comes to counting. A fundamental principle of counting says that a domain for counting cannot contain non-identical overlapping individuals (Casati and Varzi 1999: 112; Chierchia 2010):

❼ *Counting Principle*

A counting domain cannot contain non-identical overlapping individuals.

❼ tells me that just one of the many overlapping teapots on my shelf can be counted, and the question is which one. If we are that liberal with teapothood, we need a counting criterion that tells us which of the many teapots in our overpopulated inventory of teapots we are allowed to count.

With spatio-temporal objects like teapots, humans seem to rely on counting criteria that privilege maximal self-connected entities (Spelke 1990; Casati and Varzi 1999). A self-connected teapot is one that cannot be split into two parts that are not connected. In contrast to parthood, which is a mereological concept, connectedness is a topological notion.[11] The maximality require-ment prevents counting teapots that are proper parts of other teapots, and the self-connectedness requirement disqualifies sums of parts from different teapots. Casati and Varzi point out that not all kinds of entities, not even all kinds of spatio-temporal entities, come with counting criteria that involve topological self-connectedness. Obvious counterexamples include bikinis, three-piece suits, and broken glasses that are shattered all over the floor. We have to recognize a wider range of counting criteria, then, that guarantee compliance with ❼ in one way or other.

Assuming counting criteria, (7) would still be exemplified by Teapots, even if we grant that teapots can in principle have proper parts that are also teapots. The specification of denotations for sentences with numerals now needs to make reference to "numerical" teapots—teapots that can be counted. The proposition in (7) could then be represented by the formula in (8):

(8) $\lambda s \; \exists x \; [x \leq s \; \& \; /\{y: y \leq x \; \& \; \text{numerical-teapot}(y)(w_s)\}/ = 3]$

If Teapots contains nothing but three individuals that are numerical teapots in the actual world, (8) is true in Teapots. But none of the proper subsitua-tions of Teapots can contain three individuals that are numerical teapots. Any such situation contains at least one teapot that is a proper part of one of the teapots in Teapots, and hence cannot contain three numerical teapots.

In contrast to Teapots, Teapots & Scissors (Case Four below) does not exemplify (8). Teapots & Scissors has parts where (8) is not true: take any part that has just the scissors or just a part of the scissors in it, for example. But Teapots & Scissors is not a minimal situation where (8) is true.

Case Four: Teapots & Scissors

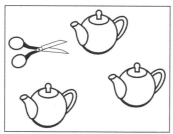

Teapots & Scissors has three teapots and a pair of scissors and nothing else in it.

---

[11] See Casati and Varzi (1999) for discussion of various postulates for a "mereotopology"—a theory that combines mereology and topology.

Definition ❼ has the consequence that Teapots does not exemplify the proposition in (9) below, even though (9) is true in Teapots.

(9)   There are two teapots.

(9) is true in Teapots, since Teapots does have two teapots in it. However, (9) is not exemplified by Teapots. Teapots has parts where (9) is not true without being a minimal situation where (9) is true. (9) can only be exemplified by situations that have exactly two teapots, then.

If any situation that has any amount of mud and nothing else in it exemplifies (6), what kind of situations exemplify the following propositions?

(10)   a. There is furniture.
        b. There are teapots.

Intuitively, any situation with any amount of furniture and nothing else in it should exemplify (10a), and any situation with any number of teapots and nothing else in it should exemplify (10b). But then a situation that has furniture and nothing else in it should *not* have subsituations without furniture, and a situation with teapots and nothing else in it should *not* have subsituations without teapots. How so? Think about the following case. An apple tree is growing on the property line between my and my neighbor's yards. Half of it is on my property; the other half on his. There are no other apple trees in my yard. Do I have a yard without apple trees? No! But then, how many apple trees are in my yard? Not even one! Here is another case. The first two movements of the symphony were performed on Monday before 12:00 a.m. The last two movements were performed on the following Tuesday right after 12:00 a.m. Were Monday or Tuesday days without symphony performances? No. But how many symphonies were performed on each of those days? Not even one! Suppose the extension of *furniture* contains pieces of furniture and their sums (Chierchia 1998, 2010), and the extension of *teapots* contains teapots and their sums. The partitive uses of those nouns illustrated in (10a) and (10b) could then be mediated by a partitive operator with the denotation in (11a).

(11)   a. $[[Part]] = \lambda P \lambda x \lambda s\ [P(x)(w_s)\ \&\ \text{overlap}(x)(s)]$
        b. $[[\ [_{VP}(are)\ Part\ furniture]\ ]] = \lambda x \lambda s\ [\text{furniture}(x)(w_s)\ \&\ \text{overlap}(x)(s)]$
        c. $[[\ [_{VP}\ (are)\ Part\ teapots]\ ]] = \lambda x \lambda s\ [\text{teapots}(x)(w_s)\ \&\ \text{overlap}(x)(s)]$
        d. $[[there]] = \lambda P \lambda s\ \exists x\ P(x)(s)$
        e. $[[there\ [_{VP}\ are\ Part\ teapots]\ ]] = \lambda s\ \exists x\ [\text{teapots}(x)(w_s)\ \&\ \text{overlap}(x)(s)]$

Our analysis now says that the proposition in (10a) is exemplified by any situation that is part of a situation with any amount of furniture and nothing else in it, and the proposition in (10b) is exemplified by any situation that is part of a situation that has any number of teapots and nothing else in it. Teapots and all of its parts are situations of this kind.

Definition ❻ may still appear problematic in view of (12):

(12)   There are infinitely many stars.

If (12) is the proposition p that is true in any possible situation that has infinitely many stars, we are in trouble. Definition ❻ would say that there couldn't be a fact that exemplifies p. Whenever p is true in a situation s, s has parts where p is not true. Take situations with five or six stars, for example. But such situations are not part of any minimal situation where p is true.

Similar issues come up with (13):

(13)   There is more than 5 tons of mud.

Whenever there is a situation that has more than five tons of mud in it, there are parts that have just five tons or less. But none of those parts can be part of any minimal situation with more than five tons of mud, since there are no such situations.

I don't think we have to be alarmed about cases like (12) or (13). One of the major insights of the previous chapter was that in a situation semantics, the relation between an English sentence and the proposition it expresses is no longer that obvious. There are subtleties of meaning to pay attention to. Who says that the proposition expressed by the English sentence in (12) *has to* be p, for example? Sentence (12) could also be understood as making a claim about our world, and might then say that it has an infinite number of stars in it. The proposition expressed by the sentence in (12) could then be the proposition q that is true in a situation s iff s contains all the stars in the world of s and there are infinitely many of them. Consequently, if q is true in a world at all, there is always a minimal situation where it is true, and hence there is always a fact that exemplifies it.

In a similar vein, the sentence in (13) has an interpretation where it makes a claim about a contextually salient situation c, which could be the actual world in the limiting case. On that interpretation, sentence (13) expresses the proposition that is true in any situation that contains a counterpart of c with the right amount of mud in it. That proposition is then exemplified by counterparts of c, as long as they have more than five tons of mud in them.

Exemplification is a notion that plays a central role in natural language semantics. It is at the heart of just about any phenomenon involving "minimal interpretations," including adverbial quantification, donkey sentences, exhaustiveness implicatures, and Davidsonian event semantics (see Kratzer

(2007) for an overview). There are thus many windows that let us probe into the relationship between sentences, the propositions they express, and the situations exemplified. Donkey sentences are a good illustration. The crucial feature of any analysis of donkey sentences within a situation semantics is that quantification is over minimal situations where the antecedent of the conditional is true. Take (14), for example:

(14)   Whenever a man spotted a donkey, the man greeted the donkey.

Suppose I use (14) to talk about a particular situation—call it "Donkey Parade." The situations that *whenever* quantifies over are the minimal sub-situations of Donkey Parade where the antecedent of (14) is true. Those situations are precisely the subsituations of Donkey Parade that exemplify the proposition in (15):

(15)   A man spotted a donkey.

Some kind of minimality requirement is crucial for the analysis of donkey sentences like (14). We have to make sure that the situations quantified over have just one man and just one donkey in them, because definite descriptions have to be unique with respect to the situations they are evaluated in. Finding the right minimality condition for donkey conditionals has proven far from trivial, however. Consider (16), for example:

(16)   Whenever snow falls around here, it takes 10 volunteers to remove it.

(16) shows that a naïve notion of minimality won't do. We can't just quantify over minimal situations where snow falls around here. It's not clear whether there ever are such situations, but even if there are, (16) does not quantify over them. A more flexible notion of minimality is needed. The notion of exemplification in ❻ provides such a notion. (16) can now be taken to quantify over situations *exemplifying* (17).

(17)   Snow falls around here.

Paying attention to Casati and Varzi's Counting Principle, the domain of quantification for (16) should be further restricted to include only maximal spatio-temporally connected situations that exemplify (17). This gives us a set of maximal spatio-temporally connected snowfalls. More research is needed to find out which situations exemplify which propositions on a case-by-case basis. I have given some illustrations here. Kratzer (2007) discusses a few more complicated cases.

   The definition of knowledge that we are currently working with says that knowledge of a proposition p requires a *de re* belief of a fact that exemplifies *p*. Isn't that way too strong? I know that a child was born yesterday. I know it, because I know that a child is born every day in the world I live in. Suppose Ashley, Beverly, and Kimberley were the children born yesterday. I do not know about any of those births. But then I do not seem to have a *de re* belief about any fact exemplifying the proposition that a child was born yesterday. How come I still know the proposition expressed by (18)?

(18)   A child was born yesterday.

Again, who says that (18) *has to* express the proposition we thought it did, namely the one that is true in any situation *s* just in case *s* is temporally located within yesterday, and a child was born in *s*? The subject of (18) is a weak indefinite, and this makes it possible for (18) to be interpreted as a thetic statement.[12] In a thetic statement, the predication is about a temporal or spatial location, and in our case, the location should be the world as a whole. On the intended reading, (18) should have a non-overt locative, then, corresponding to the overt locative in (19).

(19)   In this house, a child was born yesterday.

Understood in this way, (18) expresses a proposition that can only be true in worlds, just as (19) expresses a proposition that can only be true in situations that contain (a counterpart of) this house. Knowing the proposition expressed by (18) would then rely on a *de re* belief about the actual world, since a proposition that is only true in worlds can only be exemplified by worlds.

We are all well acquainted with the world we live in. It's therefore easy to have a *de re* belief about it. But wouldn't it now become too easy to also have knowledge about it? What if I believed that exactly 2001 children were born yesterday and I just happened to be right? We don't *yet* have to worry. We knew that something is still missing in definition ❹. We still have to make sure that in order for us to have knowledge, it can't be a mere accident that our beliefs are true.

6.4 Reliability in knowledge ascriptions

Goldman's (1967) definition that ❹ is based on has no justification or reliability condition. That some such condition is needed is shown by the following example from Goldman (1976):[13]

---

[12] For discussion of thetic statements and implicit locative topics, see Ladusaw (2000), Jäger (2001), or Kratzer and Selkirk (2007).
[13] Goldman (1976). Reprinted in Davis (1983: 175–6). Barn examples exist in many varieties in the philosophical literature. Carl Ginet is usually credited for inventing the original barn example.

Henry is driving in the countryside with his son. For the boy's edification Henry identifies various objects on the landscape as they come into view. "That's a cow", says Henry, "That's a tractor", "That's a silo", "That's a barn", etc. Henry has no doubt about the identity of these objects; in particular, he has no doubt that the last-mentioned object is a barn, which indeed it is. Each of the identified objects has features characteristic of its type. Moreover, each object is fully in view, Henry has excellent eyesight, and he has enough time to look at them reasonably carefully, since there is little traffic to distract him. Given this information, would we say that Henry *knows* that the object is a barn? Most of us would have little hesitation in saying this, so long as we were not in a certain philosophical frame of mind. Contrast our inclination here with the inclination we would have if we were given some additional information. Suppose we are told that, unknown to Henry, the district he has just entered is full of papier-mâché facsimiles of barns. These facsimiles look from the road exactly like barns, but are really just facades, without back walls or interiors, quite incapable of being used as barns. They are so cleverly constructed that travelers invariably mistake them for barns. Having just entered the district, Henry has not encountered any facsimiles; the object he sees is a genuine barn. But if the object on that site were a facsimile, Henry would mistake it for a barn. Given this new information, we would be strongly inclined to withdraw the claim that Henry *knows* the object is a barn.

On Goldman's scenario, there is a situation *s* that exemplifies the proposition *p* in (20), where we take *p* to be true in any possible situation *s* where the (counterpart of the) thing Henry is actually referring to is a barn:

(20)   That's a barn.

Henry correctly believes *p* of *s*. Yet Henry doesn't know that *p*. Why? The usual reaction in the face of examples of this kind is that Henry's belief hasn't been acquired through a reliable method. Usually, our visual perception apparatus is a reliable method for gaining knowledge. But Henry had bad luck and found himself in a situation of trickery. As long as trickery is a possibility, visual perception is not a good enough method for gaining knowledge. The story of Henry shows that if definition ❹ is on the right track at all, an additional condition is needed. We also need to require that all relevant possibilities that are compatible with Henry's evidence have counterparts of the situation *s* he is looking at with (real) barns in them. Following Lewis (1996) and setting aside knowledge *de se et nunc*, we can think of the possibilities that are compatible with Henry's evidence as the set of worlds where his perceptual experience and memory at the time considered are exactly what they are in the actual world. In the terminology of chapter 2, we would say that knowledge ascriptions have a modal semantics with realistic, rather than informational, conversational backgrounds. The evidence at stake is "evidence of things"—that is, the existence, rather than the content, of Henry's perceptual experience and memory. Lewis (1996) is very clear about this:

When perceptual experience E (or memory) eliminates a possibility W, that is not because the propositional content of the experience conflicts with W. (Not even if it is the narrow content.) The propositional content of our experience could, after all, be false. Rather, it is the existence of the experience that conflicts with W: W is a possibility in which the subject is not having experience E. Else we would need to tell some fishy story of how the experience has some sort of infallible, ineffable, purely phenomenal propositional content... Who needs that? Let E have propositional content P. Suppose even – something I take to be an open question – that E is, in some sense, fully characterized by P. Then I say that E eliminates W iff W is a possibility in which the subject's experience or memory has content different from P. I do *not* say that E eliminates W iff W is a possibility in which P is false.[14]

Our final analysis of knowledge ascriptions could now look as follows:

❽ A person knows *p* iff (i) to (iii) are satisfied:
   (i) Truth: there is a situation *s* that exemplifies *p*.
   (ii) Belief: the person believes *p* *de re* of *s*.
   (iii) Reliability: all relevant possible worlds that are not eliminated by the person's evidence have counterparts of *s* where *p* is true.

❽ has almost the familiar three conditions: (i) requires truth, (ii) belief, and (iii) some form of reliability. Bringing in the notion of "relevant alternatives," condition (iii) introduces context dependency and indeterminacy into the semantics of knowledge ascriptions. What is or isn't a relevant alternative may depend on a variety of contextual factors. If the fake barns are further away, or just a possibility mentioned by a nearby skeptic, our intuitions about what Henry does or doesn't know start fading away. The fake barns become less and less relevant. The exact type of context-dependency for knowledge ascriptions is a matter of debate and has given rise to a staggering variety of *–isms*—most prominently a whole range of contextualist versus relativist positions. Both types of positions acknowledge the context dependency of epistemic standards for knowledge attributions. What is being debated is whether the context at stake is the utterance context or the context of assessment.[15] The account I sketched in ❽ is presented at an informal, non-technical, level that allows me to remain neutral with respect to contextualist versus relativist positions. For the purposes of this chapter, it

---

[14] Lewis (1996: 553).   [15] See MacFarlane (2005).

doesn't matter whether it is the context of utterance or the context of assessment that is responsible for the indeterminacy and variability of epistemic standards for knowledge ascriptions, as long as we agree that there is indeterminacy and variability at all.

What does matter for my proposal is that for a successful knowledge ascription, a cluster of three conditions has to be satisfied. We might therefore expect to find those conditions to play a role in generating a typology of possible verbs related to ascriptions of content. In the best of all possible worlds, any suitable combination of conditions, should be found with some verb or other. Moreover, we should be able to distinguish different types of failures for knowledge ascriptions, depending on which of the three conditions are not satisfied. The proposed analysis groups together Russell's example and Gettier's examples because condition (ii) is not satisfied. The believers are not acquainted with any facts exemplifying the proposition at stake. Judgments are very robust in those cases. Knowledge ascriptions clearly fail. On the other hand, in barn examples, conditions (i) and (ii) are both satisfied, and the only question is whether condition (iii) is satisfied as well, which depends on contextually variable epistemic standards. As a result, judgments are volatile, and can be manipulated by evoking skeptical scenarios, changing practical interests (Stanley 2007), and what have you. Definition ❸ thus draws a fundamental distinction between "true" Gettier examples and barn examples, and correctly predicts the observed differences in the robustness of judgments.

If "true" Gettier examples are characterized by the failure of condition (ii), as our analysis has it, we should be able to find Gettier-analogs of mere belief ascriptions. Gettier examples should not be confined to knowledge ascriptions. There should be examples of belief ascriptions that are false, not because the propositional content of the belief is characterized incorrectly, but because of a problem relating to the *res* of the belief ascribed. This expectation is borne out, as shown by the story of the Butler and the Judge from Kratzer (1998a):

The judge was in financial trouble. He told his butler that he had been ready to commit suicide, when a wealthy man, who chose to remain anonymous, offered to pay off his debts. The butler suspected that Milford was the man who saved his master's life by protecting him from financial ruin and suicide. While the butler was away on a short vacation, the judge fell into a ditch, drunk. Unconscious and close to death, he was pulled out by a stranger and taken to the local hospital, where he recovered. When the butler returned to the village, he ran into a group of women who were speculating about the identity of the stranger who saved the judge's life by taking him to the hospital. One of the women said she thought that Milford saved the judge's life. The butler, who hadn't yet heard about the accident and thought the women were talking about the judge's financial traumas, reacted with (21):

(21) I agree. I, too, suspect that Milford saved the judge's life.

The next day, when discussion of the judge's accident continued, somebody said:

(22) The butler suspects that Milford saved the judge's life.

There is a sense where the belief attribution in (22) is not true. It seems infelicitous, if not outright false, even though the butler does indeed suspect that Milford saved the judge's life. In the context of our story, the imagined utterance of (22) ascribes to the butler a belief about a particular situation s where the judge was rescued from the ditch. Since the butler had no belief about s, the person who uttered (22) said something infelicitous or false. Belief ascriptions like (22) can be *de re* about particular situations, then, and they can wind up false or infelicitous because of a mix-up in *res* situations.

It may be objected that there is another possible take on the example of the Butler and the Judge. Couldn't the past tense in the embedded sentence in (22) be an indexical tense referring to a particular past time, as many have claimed since Partee (1973)? The mix-up would then not be about the *res* of the belief ascribed, but about the proposition claimed to be the content of the belief. While there are languages with referential past tenses, English doesn't seem to be one of them. A referential past tense is expected to be infelicitous in contexts that do not provide a salient past time for the tense to refer to. It should be infelicitous in out-of-the-blue utterances, then. Suppose we are looking at churches in Italy and are wondering who built the church in front of us. The use of the English simple past is fine in such situations, but the use of the German simple past is not. In German, the present perfect has to be used in such contexts:

(23) a. Who built this church?
      b. # Wer baute diese Kirche?
          Who built this   church?
      c. Wer hat diese Kirche gebaut?
          Who has this   church built?

Or imagine an award ceremony for doctors in a hospital who all saved a patient's life at some time or other during their tenure at the hospital. In English we can describe the doctor's achievements with the simple past, as in (24a). In German, the present perfect has to be used. The simple past would require a particular contextually salient time when the patients' lives were saved—all at the same time.

(24) a.   Each of those doctors saved a patient's life.

b. # Jeder von diesen Ärzten   rettete einem Patienten   das Leben.
    Each of   those doctors saved a-DAT patient-DAT the life.

c.   Jeder von diesen Ärzten hat einem Patienten   das Leben
    Each of   those doctors has a-DAT patient-DAT the life
    gerettet.
    saved.

In contrast to the German simple past, the English past is not referential, then. It merely places a temporal constraint on the situations described. Glossing over issues that are not crucial for our current discussion, the proposition expressed by the embedded sentence in (22) could be that in (25):

(25) λs [precede(s)(s$_0$) & save-life (the judge)(Milford)(s)].

Given our story, (25) seems the correct characterization of the propositional content of the butler's belief.[16] The claim made with (22) is false because the butler is claimed to believe (25) of the wrong situation.

Belief ascriptions can be *de re* with respect to particular situations, then. On my account, the characteristic property of Gettier analogs of belief ascriptions is that the propositional content of the belief is characterized correctly, but there is a mix-up about the *res*. If there are Gettier analogs of mere belief ascriptions, it would be wrong to invoke a condition that is specific to knowledge ascriptions to explain both Gettier examples and barn-style examples. Definition ❽ separates the cases.

Unlike *know*, verbs like *believe* or *suspect* are not factive, and there is thus no requirement that the embedded proposition be exemplified by the *res* situation. The *res* situation can be contextually provided, and, in the absence of contextual overrides, will be the actual world as a whole. The Butler and the Judge example aggressively manipulated *res* situations, and was constructed so as to make two particular smaller situations stand out, thus allowing for a mix-up.

---

[16] This particular claim may not hold up in the end. I do not want to exclude the possibility that the correct analysis of the belief ascription we are interested in would say that the butler believes the temporally indefinite proposition λs save-life (the judge)(Milford)(s) of a contextually salient situation that precedes the utterance time. I am ignoring this possibility because the point is not crucial here and the apparent discrepancy between surface syntax and interpretation would require argumentation that would take us far beyond what I want to achieve in this chapter. Kratzer (1998b) considers this possibility within a framework where a tense that is embedded under an attitude verb can be represented as an uninterpretable temporal feature that enters into an agreement relation with an inaudible, but interpretable, temporal feature carried by a matrix sentence representation of the *res* situation.

We can create Gettier analogs for content ascriptions that do not involve attitudes at all. Imagine a surveillance camera that reliably records who enters South College at any given time, except for a unique one-time prank: its creator preprogrammed it to briefly stop recording at 5 p.m. yesterday and show me entering South College with the time stamp for that time, wiping out any record of who actually entered then. Suppose that, by sheer coincidence, I did enter South College at 5 p.m. yesterday. Even though the camera correctly conveyed that information, there is a sense where (26) is false:

(26)   The surveillance camera revealed who entered South College yesterday at 5 p.m.

We judge (26) false because there is no appropriate causal relationship between the pictures the camera produced for 5 p.m. yesterday and my entering South College at that time. Those pictures were not about the fact exemplifying the proposition that I entered South College at 5 p.m. Judgments are robust in this case, just as with the original Gettier examples. Judgments become shakier if it is just, say, the camera's accuracy with time stamps that is compromised. Suppose the camera occasionally mixes up time stamps, but recorded my 5 p.m. entrance to South College correctly. Is (26) still true? What if the camera generally mixes up time stamps, but by sheer accident, happened to record my 5 p.m. entrance correctly? As with knowledge ascriptions, problems with reliability lead to gradient judgments about what a surveillance camera can reveal. Problems with *res* situations tend to produce clearer judgments.

There are also counterfactual analogs of Gettier puzzles. Counterfactual reasoning and knowledge ascriptions resemble each other in that in counterfactual reasoning, too, we have to keep an eye on the exemplifying facts of true propositions. This was one of the major insights from *Lumps of Thought*. The parallel with knowledge ascriptions opens up new ways of thinking about facts that can be exploited for a slightly different account of how to construct Base Sets representing the facts of the world of evaluation for counterfactuals.

6.5 Facts and counterfactuals

The preceding section showed that knowledge ascriptions require a highly specific notion of "fact." In this section, we will see that the truth-conditions for counterfactuals rely on facts that are almost equally specific. But this time round, those facts have to be propositional. They can no longer be particulars.

In a premise semantics, a "would"-counterfactual is true in a world w iff every way of adding as many facts of w to the antecedent as consistency allows reaches a point where the resulting set logically implies the consequent. On the other hand, a "might"-counterfactual is true in a world w iff not every way of adding as many facts of w to the antecedent as consistency allows reaches a point where adding the consequent would result in an inconsistent set.

Facts figure prominently in those truth-conditions. What kind of facts? If facts are to be compatible or incompatible with propositions, they must themselves be propositions. However, while being propositions, they must still be highly specific. This is shown by examples that are directly modeled after Russell's and Gettier's examples. Look at (27):

(27)   If Whitehead had been the Prime Minister, his name might have started with a "B."

(27) is false on Russell's scenario. Yet if facts were simply true propositions, our analysis would predict (27) to be true. We have:

(28)   Whitehead is the Prime Minister (Counterfactual Antecedent).

(29)   The Prime Minister's name starts with a "B" (Fact).

(30)   Whitehead's name starts with a "B" (Counterfactual Consequent).

(28) is the antecedent of our counterfactual. (29) is true, and hence a fact by assumption. (28) and (29) together logically imply (30). Hence every superset of $\{(28), (29)\}$ logically implies (30). This means that there is a way of adding as many facts to the antecedent of our counterfactual as consistency allows such that there will never come a point where adding the consequent would result in an inconsistent set. A very similar example can be constructed using Gettier's scenario. Consider the following counterfactual:

(31)   If Brown hadn't been in Barcelona, Jones might have owned a Ford.

(31) is false on Gettier's story. Yet if facts were just true propositions, it would be predicted to be true. We have:

(32)   Brown is not in Barcelona (Counterfactual Antecedent).

(33)   Jones owns a Ford or Brown is in Barcelona (Fact).

(34)   Jones owns a Ford (Counterfactual Consequent).

As before, the counterfactual antecedent and the fact mentioned jointly imply the counterfactual consequent. But this is sufficient to predict that (31) should come out true.

The two examples we have just examined show that the facts involved in the evaluation of a counterfactual must be highly specific. While they have to be propositions, and have to be true, they can't be identified with true propositions. Let us investigate some alternative possibilities.

6.6 Propositional facts and natural propositions

We have seen that the facts in Base Sets for counterfactuals must be rather specific. But they cannot be too specific. They must be capable of being true in merely possible situations. Otherwise they could never be compatible with an assumption that is actually false. Which possible situations are we going to include, then? Here is a way of thinking about this question. Let a natural proposition be a persistent proposition that doesn't distinguish between maximally similar situations. Whenever it is true in a situation s, it is also true in any situation that is maximally similar to s. Applying strictest standards of similarity, we may think of maximally similar situations as isomorphic situations, very much like the isomorphic worlds of Kit Fine.[17]

Intuitively speaking, two worlds are isomorphic if they are qualitatively the same, i.e., if they are the same but for the identity of the individuals in the world.

Take the fact that Thomas picked roses in my yard yesterday at five o'clock. Take it as a worldly fact—a particular; a situation. Let us say that a merely possible situation is isomorphic to that actual situation if it is qualitatively the same and preserves counterpart relationships. It can't contain Thomas or the roses he picked if individuals cannot exist in different possible worlds. But it must contain maximally similar counterparts of Thomas and his roses. And the roses' counterparts must be picked by Thomas's counterpart at five o'clock in a maximally similar way. Now consider (34):

(35)   Thomas was picking roses.

Suppose there is just one fact f that exemplifies (35) in the actual world. $\{f\}$ is a proposition. It is a proposition all right, but not a very interesting one. For once, it is not persistent. Take the smallest persistent superset then. This gives us $p = \{s: f \leq s\}$. Since f is a fact of the actual world, and p is persistent, the actual world is in p. Since f is only part of a single world, no other world

---

[17] Fine (1977). See also Rabinowicz (1979). Thanks to Ede Zimmermann for the references.

is in *p*. The proposition *p* is still highly specific, then. Too specific, that is. It is useless for the evaluation of counterfactuals, since the antecedents of counterfactuals are typically false.

To extend *p* into a natural proposition, we have to add all situations that are maximally similar to some situation in *p*. Assuming persistence then forces us to add all situations that contain any one of the recently added situations as parts. Naturalness requires us to add all situations that are maximally similar to the situations we just added, ... you got the idea. We eventually end up with a set of situations that have one property in common: they are all situations in which an indistinguishable counterpart of Thomas is picking indistinguishable counterparts of actual roses in a way that is indistinguishable from the way Thomas was picking roses in our world.

Counterpart relationships between individuals are based on overall similarity with respect to worlds, not situations. This guarantees persistence of propositions like the one in (35). (35) is true in any situation *s* iff *s* contains a rose-picking individual that is a counterpart of Thomas in the world of *s*. If the similarity relation involved in naturalness preserves all counterpart relations, propositions like the one expressed by (35) are guaranteed to come out as natural as well. Requiring maximal qualitative similarity alone isn't sufficient, since two individuals that inhabit different worlds and are qualitatively indistinguishable in some situations don't have to be counterparts of each other. They may be quite different in other situations, and hence lack overall similarity. But then it may happen that a proposition like (34) is true in a situation without being true in all situations that are qualitatively the same.

For any possible situation *s*, let the *natural extension* of *s* be the proposition generated by *s* in the manner I described above. We can now consider the following definition of the propositional facts of a world:

❾   A proposition *p* is a propositional fact of a world *w* iff there is an $s \leq w$ such that *p* is the natural extension of *s*.

Let me briefly review what ❾ does by looking at the counterfactual version of Russell's example. What went wrong there was the possibility of using (29) as a fact for the evaluation of the counterfactual (27). According to ❾, (29) is not a propositional fact of our world. It is too general. The propositional fact corresponding to (29) is the natural extension of the particular fact exemplifying (29). But that proposition is incompatible with the antecedent of (27). A parallel story can be told about the counterfactual analog of Gettier's example. (33) itself is not a propositional fact. The propositional fact corresponding to (33) is the natural extension of the particular fact exemplifying

(33), but that proposition is incompatible with the antecedent of the counterfactual (31).

If all facts that are not non-accidental generalizations were propositional facts in premise sets for counterfactuals, "dangerous" propositions like (29) or (33) would be automatically excluded. Premise sets would no longer have to be closed under Lumping, since propositional facts already come with the right level of specificity. Apart from the choice of non-accidental generalizations, a major source of vagueness for counterfactuals would now be underspecification of the initial set of "starter" situations, which could be big or small, depending on context. Invariant conditions on the set of starter situations might include the requirement that they shouldn't overlap, and that their sum should be the world of evaluation. The partitions relevant for counterfactuals would now be partitions of worlds: a partition of a world w is a set of non-overlapping situations whose sum is w.

The accidental facts in Base Sets for counterfactuals might very well be propositional facts, then. Propositional facts are sets of possible situations of a highly specific kind. Yet they still allow for possibilities. If the standards for "maximal qualitative similarity" are lowered, they become information units. This gets us closer and closer towards C. I. Lewis, whose views on facts his student Charles Baylis found so hard to swallow:[18]

Charles Baylis is minded to pin a theory of fact on me, taking advantage of a momentary lapse of my verbal defense-mechanisms in an old article. I account this pure wickedness on his part; he knows that 'fact' is one of the trickiest words in any language; and he knows that I know it. But I shall foil him yet: I shall now pronounce the final and authoritative Lewis theory of fact. A fact is an actual state of affairs. But 'fact' is a crypto-relative term, like 'landscape'. A landscape is a terrain, but a terrain as seeable by an eye. And a fact is a state of affairs, but a state of affairs as knowable by a mind and stateable by a statement.

[18] C. I. Lewis (1968: 660).

References

Abrusán, Márta. 2007. 'Contradiction and Grammar: The Case of Weak Islands'. Ph.D. dissertation. MIT, Cambridge, Mass.

Abusch, Dorit. Forthcoming. 'Circumstantial and Temporal Dependence in Counterfactual Modals'. *Natural Language Semantics*.

Adams, Ernest W. 1965. 'The Logic of Conditionals'. *Inquiry* 8: 166–97.

—— 1970. 'Subjunctive and Indicative Conditionals'. *Foundations of Language* 6: 89–94.

Aikhenvald, Alexandra. 2004. *Evidentiality*. Oxford: Oxford University Press.

Alchourròn, Carlos E., Peter Gärdenfors and David Makinson. 1985. 'On the Logic of Theory Change: Partial Meet Contraction and Revision Functions'. *Journal of Symbolic Logic* 50: 510–30.

Alonso-Ovalle, Luis. 2008. 'Innocent Exclusion in an Alternative Semantics'. *Natural Language Semantics* 16: 115–28.

Anscombe, Gertrude E. M. 1957. *Intention*. Oxford: Blackwell.

Armstrong, David M. 1978. *Nominalism and Realism: Universals and Scientific Realism*. Cambridge: Cambridge University Press.

Arregui, Ana. 2005. 'On the Accessibility of Possible Worlds: The Role of Tense and Aspect'. Ph.D. dissertation. University of Massachusetts, Amherst.

—— 2007. 'When Aspect Matters: The Case of "would" Conditionals'. *Natural Language Semantics* 15: 221–64.

—— 2009. 'On Similarity in Counterfactuals'. *Linguistics and Philosophy* 32: 245–78.

—— 2010. 'Detaching *If*-Clauses from *Should*'. *Natural Language Semantics* 18: 241–93.

Bach, Emmon. 1986. 'Natural Language Metaphysics'. In R. B. Marcus, G. J. W Dorn, and P. Weingartner (eds.), *Logic, Methodology and Philosophy of Science*. Vol. VII Amsterdam: Elsevier, 573–95.

Barwise, Jon and Robin Cooper. 1981. 'Generalized Quantifiers and Natural Language'. *Linguistics and Philosophy* 4: 159–219.

—— and John Perry. 1983. *Situations and Attitudes*. Cambridge, Mass.: The MIT Press.

Baylis, Charles A. 1948. 'Facts, Propositions, Exemplification and Truth'. *Mind, New Series* 57: 459–79.

Beaver, David and Brady Clark. 2008. *Sense and Sensitivity: How Focus Determines Meaning*. Oxford: Wiley-Blackwell.

Bech, Gunnar. 1949. 'Das semantische System der deutschen Modalverba'. *Travaux du Cercle Linguistique de Copenhague* 4: 3–46.

Belnap, Nuel D. 1979. 'Rescher's Hypothetical Reasoning: An Amendment'. In E. Sosa (ed.), *The Philosophy of Nicholas Rescher*. Dordrecht: Reidel, 19–28.

Bhatt, Rajesh. 1999. 'Covert Modality in Non-finite Contexts'. Ph.D. dissertation. University of Pennsylvania, Philadelphia. Published 2006. Berlin: de Gruyter Mouton.

—— and Roumyana Pancheva. 2006. 'Conditionals'. In M. Everaert and H. v. Riemsdijk (eds.), *The Blackwell Companion to Syntax*. Oxford: Blackwell Publishers, 638–87.

Bittner, Maria. 2005. 'Future Discourse in a Tenseless Language'. *Journal of Semantics* 22: 339–87.

—— Forthcoming. 'Time and Modality without Tenses or Modals'. In R. Musan and M. Rathert (eds.), *Tense across Languages*. Tübingen: Niemeyer.

Boole, George. 1854. *An Investigation of the Laws of Thought.* London: Macmillan. Reprinted 1958, New York: Dover.

Brennan, Virginia. 1993. 'Root and Epistemic Modal Auxiliary Verbs'. Ph.D. dissertation. University of Massachusetts, Amherst.

Burgess, John. 1981. 'Quick Completeness Proofs for Some Logics of Conditionals'. *Notre Dame Journal of Formal Logic* 22: 76–84.

Büring, Daniel. 1997. *The Meaning of Topic and Focus: The 59th Street Bridge Accent.* London and New York: Routledge.

Butler, Jonny. 2004. 'Phase structure, Phrase structure, and Quantification'. Ph.D. dissertation. University of York, York.

Carlson, Gregory N. 1977. 'Reference to Kinds in English'. Ph.D. dissertation. University of Massachusetts, Amherst. Published 1980 as *Outstanding Dissertation in Linguistics*. New York: Garland Publishers.

—— and Jeffrey Pelletier. 1995. *The Generic Book.* Chicago: Chicago University Press.

Casati, Roberto and Achille Varzi. 1999. *Parts and Places: The Structures of Spatial Representation.* Cambridge, Mass.: The MIT Press.

Chemla, Emmanuel. In press. 'Expressible Semantics for Expressible Counterfactuals'. *The Review of Symbolic Logic* 2.

Chierchia, Gennaro. 1998. 'Plurality of Mass Nouns and the Notion of Semantic Parameter'. In S. Rothstein (ed.), *Events and Grammar*. Dordrecht: Kluwer Academic Publishers, 53–104.

—— 2004. 'Scalar Implicatures, Polarity Phenomena, and the Syntax/Pragmatics Interface'. In A. Belletti (ed.), *Structures and Beyond*. Oxford: Oxford University Press, 39–103

—— 2010. 'Mass Nouns, Vagueness and Semantic Variation'. *Synthese* 174: 99–149.

—— Danny Fox and Benjamin Spector. Forthcoming. 'The Grammatical View of Scalar Implicatures and the Relationship between Semantics and Pragmatics'. In K. v. Heusinger, C. Maienborn, and P. Portner (eds.), *An International Handbook of Natural Language Meaning*. Berlin: Mouton de Gruyter.

Chomsky, Noam. 1981. *Lectures on Government and Binding.* Dordrecht: Foris.

Chung, Kyung-Sook. 2005. 'Space in Tense: The Interaction of Tense, Aspect, Evidentiality, and Speech Acts in Korean'. Ph.D. dissertation. Simon Fraser University, Vancouver.

—— 2007. 'Spatial Deictic Tense and Evidentials in Korean'. *Natural Language Semantics* 15: 187–219.

Cohen, Shai. 2009. 'On the Semantics of "too" and "only": Distinctness and Subsumption'. Ph.D. dissertation. University of Massachusetts, Amherst.

Condoravdi, Cleo. 2002. 'Temporal Interpretation of Modals: Modals for the Present and for the Past'. In D. Beaver, S. Kaufmann, B. Clark, and L. Casillas (eds.), *The Construction of Meaning*. Stanford: CSLI Publications, 59–88.

—— and Stefan Kaufmann. 2005. 'Modality and Temporality'. *Journal of Semantics* 22: 119–28.

Cover, Rebecca. 2010. 'Aspect, Modality, and Tense in Badiaranke'. Ph.D. dissertation. University of California, Berkeley.

Cresswell, Maxwell J. 1973. *Logics and Languages*. London: Methuen.

—— 1981. 'Adverbs of Causation'. In H. J. Eikmeyer and H. Rieser (eds.), *Words, Worlds, and Contexts*. Berlin: de Gruyter, 21–37.

—— and Arnim von Stechow. 1982. '*De Re* Belief Generalized'. *Linguistics and Philosophy* 5: 503–35.

Culicover, Peter. 1970. 'One More Can of Beer'. *Linguistic Inquiry* 1: 366–69.

Cushing, Stephen. 1976. *The Formal Semantics of Quantification*. Los Angeles: UCLA.

Dahl, Östen. 1975. 'On Generics'. In E. Keenan (ed.), *Formal Semantics of Natural Language*. Cambridge: Cambridge University Press. 99–111.

Davis, Henry, Lisa Matthewson, and Hotze Rullmann. 2009. 'A Unified Modal Semantics for Out-of-Control in St'át'imcets'. In L. Hogeweg, H. d. Hoop, and A. Malchukov (eds.), *Cross-Linguistics Semantics of Tense, Aspect, and Modality*. Amsterdam: John Benjamins, 205–44.

Davis, Steven (ed.). 1983. *Causal Theories of Mind: Action, Knowledge, Memory, Perception, and Reference*. Berlin and New York: de Gruyter.

Deal, Amy Rose. 2010a. 'Topics in the Nez Perce Verb'. Ph.D. dissertation. University of Massachusetts, Amherst.

—— 2010b. 'Modals without Scales'. Unpublished MS. Department of Linguistics, Harvard University, Cambridge, Mass.

Deggau, Gustav. 1907. *Über den Gebrauch und die Bedeutungsentwicklung der Hilfsverben "können" und "mögen"*. Giessen: Universität Giessen.

Dretske, Fred. 1972. 'Contrastive Statements'. *Philosophical Review* 81: 411–37.

Drubig, Hans Bernhard. 2001. 'On the Syntactic Form of Epistemic Modality'. Unpublished MS. Universität Tübingen, Tübingen.

Edgington, Dorothy. 1986. 'Do Conditionals Have Truth Conditions?' *Critica* 18: 3–30.

—— 1995. 'On Conditionals'. *Mind, New Series* 104: 235–329.

Egan, Andy, John Hawthorne, and Brian Weatherson. 2005. 'Epistemic Modals in Context'. In G. Preyer and G. Peter (eds.), *Contextualism in Philosophy: Knowledge, Meaning, and Truth*. Oxford: Oxford University Press, 131–70.

Égré, Paul and Mikael Cozic. 2010. '*If*-Clauses and Probability Operators'. Unpublished MS. Institut Jean Nicod, Paris.

Ehrich, Veronika. 2001. 'Was nicht müssen und nicht können (nicht) bedeuten können: Zum Skopus der Negation bei den Modalverben des Deutschen'. In R. Müller and M. Reis (eds.), *Modalität und Modalverben im Deutschen*. Hamburg: Hermann Buske Verlag, 149–76.

Faller, Martina. 2002. 'Semantics and Pragmatics of Evidentials in Cuzco Quechua'. Ph.D. dissertation. Stanford University, Stanford.

—— 2004. 'The Deictic Core of Non-Experienced Past in Cuzco Quechua'. *Journal of Semantics* 21: 45–85.

Farkas, Donka and Yoko Sugioka. 1983. 'Restrictive *If / When* Clauses'. *Linguistics and Philosophy* 6: 225–58.

Fine, Kit. 1977. 'Properties, Propositions, and Sets'. *Journal of Philosophical Logic* 6: 135–91.

Fintel, Kai von. 1994. 'Restrictions on Quantifier Domains'. Ph.D. dissertation. University of Massachusetts, Amherst.

—— 2003. 'Epistemic Modals and Conditionals Revisited'. Paper presented at the Department Colloquium, Department of Linguistics, University of Massachusetts, Amherst.

—— 2007. '*If*: The Biggest Little Word'. Paper presented at the Georgetown University Roundtable, Washington DC.

—— and Anthony S. Gillies. 2010. 'Must . . . Stay . . . Strong!' *Natural Language Semantics* 18: 351–83.

—— —— Forthcoming. '"Might" Made Right'. In A. Egan and B. Weatherson (eds.), *Epistemic Modality*. Oxford: Oxford University Press.

—— and Sabine Iatridou. 2007. 'Anatomy of a Modal Construction'. *Linguistic Inquiry* 38: 445–83.

—— —— 2008. 'How to Say *ought* in Foreign: The Composition of Weak Necessity Modals'. In J. Guéron and J. Lecarme (eds.), *Time and Modality*. Berlin: Springer. 115–41.

Fox, Danny. 2007. 'Free Choice and the Theory of Scalar Implicatures'. In U. Sauerland and P. Stateva (eds.), *Presupposition and Implicature in Compositional Semantics*. New York: Palgrave MacMillan, 71–120.

Fraassen, Bas van. 1969. 'Presuppositions, Supervaluations, and Free Logic'. In K. Lambert (ed.), *The Logical Way of Doing Things*. New Haven: Yale University Press, 67–92.

—— 1972. 'The Logic of Conditional Obligation'. *Journal of Philosophical Logic* 1: 417–38.

Frank, Anette. 1996. 'Context Dependence and Modal Constructions'. Ph.D. dissertation. Institut für Maschinelle Sprachverarbeitung, Stuttgart.

Frege, Gottlob. 1923. *Logische Untersuchungen. Dritter Teil: Gedankengefüge*. Göttingen: Vandenhoeck and Ruprecht.

Gajewski, Jon. 2002. 'L-Analyticity and Natural Language'. Unpublished MS. MIT, Cambridge, Mass.

Garrett, Edward. 2001. 'Evidentiality and Assertion in Tibetan'. Ph.D. dissertation. UCLA, Los Angeles.

Gazdar, Gerald. 1979. *Pragmatics: Implicature, Presupposition, and Logical Form*. New York: Academic Press.

Geach, Peter. 1980. *Reference and Generality*. 3rd edn. Ithaca: Cornell University Press.

Geis, Michael L. 1970. 'Adverbial Subordinate Clauses in English'. Ph.D. dissertation. MIT, Cambridge, Mass.

—— 1985. 'The Syntax of Conditional Sentences'. In M. L. Geis (ed.), *Working Papers in Linguistics* 31. Columbus, Ohio: Department of Linguistics, Ohio State University, 130–59.

Gettier, Edmund. 1963. 'Is Justified True Belief Knowledge?' *Analysis* 23: 121–3.

Geurts, Bart. 1995. 'Presupposing'. Ph.D. dissertation. Universität Stuttgart, Stuttgart.

Gibbard, Allan. 1981. 'Two Recent Theories of Conditionals'. In W. L. Harper, R. Stalnaker, and G. Pearce (eds.), *Ifs: Conditionals, Belief, Decision, Chance, and Time*. Dordrecht: Reidel, 211–48.

Goldman, Alvin I. 1967. 'A Causal Theory of Knowing'. *The Journal of Philosophy* 64: 357–72.

—— 1976. 'Discrimination and Perceptual Knowledge'. *The Journal of Philosophy* 73: 771–91.

Goodman, Nelson. 1947. 'The Problem of Counterfactual Conditionals'. *Journal of Philosophy* 44: 113–28.

—— 1955. *Fact, Fiction, and Forecast*. Cambridge, Mass.: Harvard University Press.

Grabski, Michael. 1974. 'Syntax und Semantik der Modalverben in Aussagesätzen des Deutschen'. Ph.D. dissertation. Universität Stuttgart, Stuttgart.

Graf, Oskar Maria. 1978. *Das Leben meiner Mutter*. München: Süddeutscher Verlag. 1st German edn: 1946. München: Verlag Kurt Desch.

Grice, H. Paul. 1989. *Studies in the Way of Words*. Cambridge, Mass.: Harvard University Press.

Groenendijk, Jeroen and Martin Stokhof. 1984. 'Studies on the Semantics of Questions and the Pragmatics of Answers'. Ph.D. dissertation. Universiteit van Amsterdam, Amsterdam.

Grove, Adam. 1988. 'Two Modellings for Theory Change'. *Journal of Philosophical Logic* 17: 157–70.

Haan, Ferdinand de. 1999. 'Evidentiality and Epistemic Modality: Setting the Boundaries'. *Southwest Journal of Linguistics* 18: 83–101.

Hacking, Ian. 1975. *The Emergence of Probability*. Cambridge: Cambridge University Press.

Hackl, Martin. 1998. 'On the Semantics of Ability Attributions'. Unpublished MS. MIT, Cambridge, Mass.

Hacquard, Valentine. 2006. 'Aspects of Modality'. Ph.D. dissertation. MIT, Cambridge, Mass.

—— 2009. 'On the Interaction of Aspect and Modal Auxiliaries'. *Linguistics and Philosophy* 32: 279–312.

—— 2010. 'On the Event Relativity of Modal Auxiliaries'. *Natural Language Semantics* 18: 79–114.

Haegeman, Liliane. 2010. 'The Movement Derivation of Conditional Clauses'. *Linguistic Inquiry* 41: 595–621.

Hajičová, Eva, Barbara Hall Partee, and Eric Sgall. 1998. *Topic-focus Articulation, Tripartite Structures, and Semantic Content*. Dordrecht: Kluwer Publishers.

Halpern, Joseph Y. 1997. 'Defining Relative Likelihood in Partially-Ordered Preferential Structures'. *Journal of Artificial Intelligence Research* 7: 1–24.

—— 2003. *Reasoning about Uncertainty*. Cambridge, Mass.: The MIT Press.

Hamblin, Charles L. 1959. 'The Modal "Probably"'. *Mind, New Series* 68: 234–40.

Hansson, Bengt. 1969. 'An Analysis of Some Deontic Logics'. *Noûs* 3: 373–98.

Hansson, Sven Ove. 2006. 'Logic of Belief Revision'. In E. N. Zalta (ed.), *The Stanford Encyclopedia of Philosophy*. Stanford, Calif.: Metaphysics Research Lab, CLSI, Stanford University.

Heim, Irene R. 1982. 'The Semantics of Definite and Indefinite Noun Phrases'. Ph.D. dissertation. University of Massachusetts, Amherst.

Hempel, Carl G. 1945. 'Studies in the Logic of Confirmation I'. *Mind, New Series* 54: 1–26.

Hintikka, Jaakko. 1962. *Knowledge and Belief: An Introduction to the Logic of the Two Notions*. Ithaca: Cornell University Press.

Horgan, Terence. 1979. '"Could", Possible Worlds, and Moral Responsibility'. *Southern Journal of Philosophy* 17: 345–58.

Huitink, Janneke. 2008. 'Modals, Conditionals, and Compositionality'. Ph.D. dissertation. Radboud Universiteit Nijmegen, Nijmegen.

Iatridou, Sabine. 1991. 'Topics in Conditionals'. Ph.D. dissertation. MIT, Cambridge, Mass.

—— 2000. 'The Grammatical Ingredients of Counterfactuality'. *Linguistic Inquiry* 31: 231–70.

Ippolito, Michela. 2002. 'The Time of Possibilities: Truth and Felicity of Subjunctive Conditionals'. Ph.D. dissertation. MIT, Cambridge, Mass.

Izvorski, Roumyana. 1997. 'The Present Perfect as an Epistemic Modal'. Paper presented to Semantics and Linguistic Theory 7, Stanford University, Stanford, Calif.

Jackendoff, Ray. 1972. *Semantic Interpretation in Generative Grammar*. Cambridge, Mass.: The MIT Press.

Jacobs, Joachim. 1982. *Syntax und Semantik der Negation im Deutschen*. München: Fink.

—— 1983. *Fokus und Skalen: Zur Syntax und Semantik der Gradpartikeln im Deutschen*. Tübingen: Niemeyer.

Jäger, Gerhard. 2001. 'Topic-Comment Structure and the Contrast Between Stage Level and Individual Level Predicates'. *Journal of Semantics* 18: 83–126.

Kadmon, Nirit. 1987. 'On Unique and Non-Unique Reference and Asymmetric Quantification'. Ph.D. dissertation. University of Massachusetts, Amherst.

—— and Craige Roberts. 1986. 'Prosody and Scope: The Role of Discourse Structure'. Paper presented to the CLS 22: Parasession on Pragmatics and Grammatical Theory, University of Chicago, Chicago, Ill.

Kamp, Hans. 1975. 'Two Theories About Adjectives'. In E. Keenan (ed.), *Formal Semantics of Natural Language*. Cambridge: Cambridge University Press, 123–55.

Kanazawa, Makoto, Stefan Kaufmann, and Stanley Peters. 2005. 'On the Lumping Semantics of Counterfactuals'. *Journal of Semantics* 10: 201–16.

Kaplan, David. 1968. 'Quantifying In'. *Synthese* 19: 178–214.

—— 1978. 'On the Logic of Demonstratives'. *Journal of Philosophical Logic* 8: 81–98.

Kaufmann, Stefan. 2005. 'Conditional Truth and Future Reference'. *Journal of Semantics* 22: 231–80.

Kiefer, Ferenc. 1983. 'What is Possible in Hungarian'. *Acta Linguistica Hungarica* 33: 149–87.

Klein, Wolfgang. 1982. 'Local Deixis in Route Directions'. In R. J. Jarvella and W. Klein (eds.), *Speech, Place, and Action: Studies in Deixis and Related Topics*. New York: Wiley, 161–82.

Kratzer, Angelika. 1977. 'What "must" and "can" Must and Can Mean'. *Linguistics and Philosophy* 1: 337–55.

—— 1978. *Semantik der Rede: Kontexttheorie, Modalwörter, Konditionalsätze*. Kronberg: Scriptor.

—— 1979. 'Conditional Necessity and Possibility'. In R. Bäuerle, U. Egli, and A. v. Stechow (eds.), *Semantics from Different Points of View*. Berlin, Heidelberg, and New York: Springer, 117–47.

—— 1981a. 'Partition and Revision: The Semantics of Counterfactuals'. *Journal of Philosophical Logic* 10: 201–16.

—— 1981b. 'The Notional Category of Modality'. In H. J. Eikmeyer and H. Rieser (eds.), *Words, Worlds, and Contexts*. Berlin and New York: de Gruyter. Reprinted 2002 in P. Portner and B. Partee (eds.), *Formal Semantics: The Essential Readings*. Oxford: Blackwell, 289–323; and 2003 in J. Gutiérrez-Rexach (ed.), *Semantics: Critical Concepts*, Vol. iv. London: Routledge. 365–403.

—— 1986. 'Conditionals'. In A. M. Farley, P. Farley, and K. E. McCollough (eds.), *Papers from the Parasession on Pragmatics and Grammatical Theory*. Chigago: Chigago Lingustics Society, 115–35.

—— 1989. 'An Investigation of the Lumps of Thought'. *Linguistics and Philosophy* 12: 607–53.

—— 1990. 'How Specific is a Fact?' Proceedings of the Conference on Theories of Partial Information held at the Center for Cognitive Science, University of Texas, Austin, Jan. 25–7, 1990.

—— 1998a. 'Scope or Pseudoscope? Are there Wide-scope Indefinites?' In S. Rothstein (ed.), *Events in Grammar*. Dordrecht: Kluwer, 163–96.

—— 1998b. 'More Structural Analogies Between Pronouns and Tenses'. Paper presented at Semantics and Linguistic Theory (SALT) 8, MIT, Cambridge, Mass.

—— 2002. 'Facts: Particulars or Information Units?' *Linguistics and Philosophy* 25: 655–70.

—— 2005. 'Constraining Premise Sets for Counterfactuals'. *Journal of Semantics* 22: 153–8.

Kratzer, Angelika. 2007. 'Situations in Natural Language Semantics'. In E. N. Zalta (ed.), *Stanford Encyclopedia of Philosophy*. Stanford, Calif.: Metaphysics Research Lab, CSLI, Stanford University.

—— Forthcoming. *Modality in Context*. Oxford: Oxford University Press.

—— and Elisabeth Selkirk. 2007. 'Default Phrase Stress, Prosodic Phrasing and the Spellout Edge'. *The Linguistic Review* 24: 93–135.

—— —— In preparation. 'Representing Contrastive, New, and Given Information'.

Krifka, Manfred. 2009. 'Counting Configurations'. Paper presented at Sinn and Bedeutung 13, Stuttgart.

Kripke, Saul. 1965. 'Semantical Analysis of Intuitionistic Logic 1'. In J. N. Crossley and M. A. E. Dummett (eds.), *Formal Systems and Recursive Functions*. Amsterdam: North Holland, 92–130.

Ladusaw, William. 2000. 'Thetic and Categorical, Stage and Individual, Weak and Strong'. In L. R. Horn and Y. Kato (eds.), *Negation and Polarity: Syntactic and Semantic Perspectives*. Oxford: Oxford University Press, 232–42.

Landman, Fred. 1986. 'Towards a Theory of Information'. Ph.D. dissertation. Universiteit van Amsterdam, Amsterdam.

Lassiter, Daniel. 2010. 'Gradable Epistemic Modals, Probability, and Scale Structure'. Paper presented at Semantics and Linguistic Theory 20, Vancouver.

Lee, Jungmee. 2009. 'The Korean Evidential "-te": A Modal Analysis'. Paper presented at the Colloque de Syntaxe et Sémantique à Paris, Paris.

Lewis, Clarence I. 1968. 'Reply to My Critics'. In P. A. Schilpp (ed.), *The Philosophy of C. I. Lewis*. LaSalle, Ill.: Open Court, 653–76.

Lewis, David K. 1968. 'Counterpart Theory and Quantified Modal Logic'. *Journal of Philosophy* 65: 113–26.

—— 1972. 'General Semantics'. In D. Davidson and G. Harman (eds.), *Semantics of Natural Language*. Dordrecht: Reidel, 169–218.

—— 1973a. *Counterfactuals*. Cambridge, Mass.: Harvard University Press.

—— 1973b. 'Causation'. *Journal of Philosophy* 70: 556–67.

—— 1975. 'Adverbs of Quantification'. In E. Keenan (ed.), *Semantics of Natural Language*. Cambridge: Cambridge University Press, 3–15.

—— 1976. 'Probabilities of Conditionals and Conditional Probabilities'. *Philosophical Review* 85: 297–315.

—— 1979a. 'Scorekeeping in a Language Game'. *Journal of Philosophical Logic* 8: 339–59.

—— 1979b. 'Counterfactual Dependence and Time's Arrow'. *Noûs* 13: 455–76.

—— 1979c. 'Attitudes *De Dicto* and *De Se*'. *Philosophical Review* 88: 513–43.

—— 1980. 'Index, Context, and Content'. In S. Kanger and S. Öhmann (eds.), *Philosophy and Grammar*. Dordrecht: Reidel, 79–100.

—— 1981. 'Ordering Semantics and Premise Semantics for Counterfactuals'. *Journal of Philosophical Logic* 10: 217–34.

—— 1986. *On the Plurality of Worlds*. Oxford: Blackwell.

—— 1996. 'Elusive Knowledge'. *Australasian Journal of Philosophy* 74: 549–67.

McCawley, James. 1981. *Everything that Linguists Have Always Wanted to Know About Logic But Were Ashamed to Ask.* Chicago: Chicago University Press.

MacFarlane, John. 2005. 'The Assessment Sensitivity of Knowledge Attributions'. *Oxford Studies in Epistemology* 1: 197–233.

Makinson, David. 2003. 'Ways of Doing Logic: What Was Different About AGM 1985?' *Journal of Logic and Computation* 13: 5–15.

Matthewson, Lisa, Hotze Rullmann, and Henry Davis. 2007. 'Evidentials as Epistemic Modals: Evidence from St'át'imcets'. *The Linguistic Variation Yearbook* 7: 201–54.

Montague, Richard. 1974. *Formal Philosophy: Selected Papers of Richard Montague*, ed. R. H. Thomason. New Haven: Yale University Press.

Mosteller, Frederick and Cleo Youtz. 1990. 'Quantifying Probabilistic Expressions'. *Statistical Science* 5: 2–12.

Murphy, Gregory L. 2002. *The Big Book of Concepts.* Cambridge, Mass.: The MIT Press.

Murray, Sarah. 2010. 'Evidentiality and the Structure of Speech Acts'. Ph.D. dissertation. Rutgers University, New Brunswick, New Jersey.

Nauze, Fabrice D. 2008. 'Modality in Typological Perspective'. Ph.D. dissertation. Universiteit van Amsterdam, Amsterdam.

Nickerson, Raymond S. 1996. 'Hempel's Paradox and Wason's Selection Task: Logical and Psychological Puzzles of Confirmation'. *Thinking and Reasoning* 2: 1–31.

Nicod, Jean. 1924. *Le Problème Logique de l'Induction.* Paris: Félix Alcan.

Partee, Barbara. 1973. 'Some Structural Analogies Between Tenses and Pronouns in English'. *The Journal of Philosophy* 70: 601–9.

Paul, Hermann. 1920. *Deutsche Grammatik*, Band 5: *Wortbildungslehre*. Halle an der Saale: Max Niemeyer.

Peirce, Charles Sanders. 1933. *Collected Papers of Charles Sanders Peirce*, vol. iv: *The Simplest Mathematics*. Cambridge, Mass.: Harvard University Press.

Peterson, Tyler. 2008. 'The Ordering Source and Graded Modality in Gitksan Epistemic Modals'. Paper presented at Sinn und Bedeutung 13, Universität Stuttgart, Stuttgart.

Pinkal, Manfred. 1977. *Kontext und Bedeutung.* Tübingen: Gunter Narr.

—— 1979. 'How to Refer with Vague Descriptions'. In R. Bäuerle, U. Egli, and A. v. Stechow (eds.), *Semantics from Different Points of View.* Berlin, Heidelberg, and New York: Springer, 32–50.

Pollock, John L. 1976. *Subjunctive Reasoning.* Dordrecht: Reidel.

—— 1984. *The Foundations of Philosophical Semantics.* Princeton, New Jersey: Princeton University Press.

Portner, Paul. 1998. 'The Progressive in Modal Semantics'. *Language and Linguistics Compass* 74: 760–87.

—— 1999. 'The Semantics of Mood'. *GLOT International* 4: 3–9.

—— 2003. 'The Temporal Semantics and Modal Pragmatics of the Perfect'. *Linguistics and Philosophy* 26: 459–510.

Portner, Paul. 2009. *Modality*. Oxford: Oxford University Press.

Prince, Alan and Paul Smolensky. 1993. 'Optimality Theory: Constraint Interaction in Generative Grammar'. Rutgers University Center for Cognitive Science Technical Report 2. 2002 version available in Rutgers Optimality Archive.

Quine, Willard Van Orman. 1969. *Ontological Relativity and Other Essays*. New York: Columbia University Press.

Rabinowicz, Wlodek. 1979. *Universalizability: A Study in Morals and Metaphysics*. Dordrecht: Reidel.

Raynaud, Franziska. 1974. 'Les verbes de modalité en allemand contemporain'. Ph.D. dissertation. Université de Paris IV, Paris.

Recanati, François. 2007. *Perspectival Thought: A Plea for (Moderate) Relativism*. Oxford: Oxford University Press.

Rescher, Nicholas. 1964. *Hypothetical Reasoning*. Amsterdam: North Holland.

—— 1973. *The Coherence Theory of Truth*. Oxford: Clarendon Press.

—— 1979. 'Reply to Belnap'. In E. Sosa (ed.), *The Philosophy of Nicholas Rescher: Discussion and Replies*. Dordrecht: Reidel, 29–31.

Roberts, Craige, 1987. 'Modal Subordination, Anaphora, and Distributivity'. Ph.D. dissertation. University of Massachusetts, Amherst.

—— 1989. 'Modal Subordination and Pronomial Anaphora in Discourse'. *Linguistics and Philosophy* 12: 683–721.

—— 1996. 'Information Structure: Towards an Integrated Theory of Formal Pragmatics'. In J.-H Yoon and A. Kathol (eds.), *OSU Papers in Linguistics* 48. Columbus, Ohio: Linguistics Department, Ohio State University, 91–136.

Rooth, Mats. 1985. 'Association with Focus'. Ph.D. dissertation. University of Massachusetts, Amherst.

—— 1992. 'A Theory of Focus Interpretation'. *Natural Language Semantics* 1: 75–110.

Rothschild, Daniel. 2009. 'Conditionals and Probability: A Classical Approach'. Paper presented at Sinn and Bedeutung 2009, University of Vienna, Vienna.

Rothstein, Susan. 1995. 'Adverbial Quantification over Events'. *Natural Language Semantics* 3: 1–31.

Rott, Hans. 2001. *Change, Choice, and Inference: A Study in Belief Revision and Nonmonotonic Reasoning*. Oxford: Oxford University Press.

Rubinstein, Aynat. Forthcoming. 'Roots of Modality'. Ph.D. dissertation. University of Massachusetts, Amherst.

Rullmann, Hotze, Lisa Matthewson, and Henry Davis. 2008. 'Modals as Distributive Indefinites'. *Natural Language Semantics* 16: 317–57.

Russell, Bertrand. 1912. *The Problems of Philosophy*. Oxford: Oxford University Press.

Sauerland, Uli. 2004. 'Scalar Implicatures in Complex Sentences'. *Linguistics and Philosophy* 27: 367–91.

Schein, Barry. 1993. *Plurals and Events*. Cambridge, Mass.: The MIT Press.

Schlenker, Philippe. 2004. 'Conditionals as Definite Descriptions (a Referential Analysis)'. *Research on Language and Computation* 2: 279–304.

Schulz, Katrin. 2007. 'Minimal Models in Semantics and Pragmatics: Free Choice, Exhaustivity, and Conditionals'. Ph.D. dissertation. Universiteit van Amsterdam, Amsterdam.

—— 2008. 'Non-Deictic Tenses in Conditionals'. Paper presented at Semantics and Linguistic Theory 18, Amherst, Mass.

Selkirk, Elisabeth O. 1984. *Phonology and Syntax: The Relation between Sound and Structure*. Cambridge, Mass.: The MIT Press.

Sider, Theodore. 2006. 'Bare Particulars'. *Philosophical Perspectives* 20: 387–97.

Simons, Mandy. 2000. *Issues in the Semantics and Pragmatics of Disjunction*. New York: Garland.

Speas, Peggy. 2008. 'On the Syntax and Semantics of Evidentials'. *Language and Linguistics Compass* 2: 940–65.

Spelke, Elizabeth. 1990. 'Principles of Object Perception'. *Cognitive Science* 14: 29–56.

Sperber, Dan, Francesco Cara, and Vittorio Girotto. 1995. 'Relevance Theory Explains the Selection Task'. *Cognition* 85: 277–90.

—— and Vittorio Girotto. 2002. 'Use or Misuse of the Selection Task? Rejoinder to Fiddick, Cosmides, and Tooby'. *Cognition* 57: 31–95.

Stalnaker, Robert. 1968. 'A Theory of Conditionals'. In N. Rescher (ed.), *American Philosophical Quarterly Monograph*, vol. ii: Studies in Logical Theory. Oxford: Basil Blackwell, 98–112.

—— 1970. 'Pragmatics'. *Synthese* 22: 272–89.

—— 1981. 'A Defense of Conditional Excluded Middle'. In W. L. Harper, R. Stalnaker, and G. Pearce (eds.), *Ifs*. Dordrecht: Reidel, 87–104.

Stanley, Jason. 2007. *Knowledge and Practical Interests*. Oxford: Oxford University Press.

Stechow, Arnim von. 1981. 'Topic, Focus, and Local Relevance'. In W. Klein and W. Levelt (eds.), *Crossing the Boundaries in Linguistics*. Dordrecht: Reidel, 95–130.

Stone, Matthew. 1999. 'Reference to Possible Worlds'. Unpublished MS. Rutgers University, New Brunswick, New Jersey.

Stowell, Timothy. 2004. 'Tense and Modals'. In J. Guéron and J. Lecarme (eds.), *The Syntax of Time*. Cambridge, Mass.: The MIT Press.

Tichý, Pavel. 1976. 'A Counterexample to the Stalnaker–Lewis Analysis of Counterfactuals'. *Philosophical Studies* 29: 271–3.

Veltman, Frank. 1976. 'Prejudices, Presuppositions and the Theory of Conditionals'. In J. Groenendijk and M. Stokhof (eds.), *Amsterdam Papers in Formal Grammar*, vol. i. Amsterdam: Centrale Interfaculteit, University of Amsterdam.

—— 1984. 'Data Semantics'. In J. Groenendijk and M. Stokhof (eds.), *Truth, Interpretation, and Information*. Dordrecht: Foris, 43–64.

—— 1985. 'Logics for Conditionals'. Ph.D. dissertation. Universiteit van Amsterdam, Amsterdam.

—— 2005. 'Making Counterfactual Assumptions'. *Journal of Semantics* 22: 159–80.

Villalta, Elisabeth. 2008. 'Mood and Gradability: An Investigation of the Subjunctive Mood in Spanish'. *Linguistics and Philosophy* 31: 467–522.

Wason, Peter. 1966. 'Reasoning'. In B. M. Foss (ed.), *New Horizons in Psychology* 1. Harmondsworth: Penguin, 135–51.

Werner, Thomas. 2003. 'Deducing the Future and Distinguishing the Past: Temporal Interpretation in Modal Sentences in English'. Ph.D. dissertation. Rutgers University, New Brunswick, New Jersey.

Westmoreland, Robert R. 1998. 'Information and Intonation in Natural Language Modality'. Ph.D. dissertation. Indiana University, Bloomington.

Willett, Thomas. 1988. 'A Cross-Linguistic Survey of the Grammaticization of Evidentiality'. *Studies in Language* 12: 51–97.

Wright, Georg Henrik von. 1963. 'Practical Inference'. *The Philosophical Review* 72: 159–79.

—— 1972. 'On So-called Practical Inference'. *Acta Sociologica* 15: 39–53.

Yablo, Stephen. 2006. 'Non-Catastrophic Presupposition Failure'. In A. Byrne and J. J. Thompson (eds.), *Content and Modality: Themes from the Philosophy of Robert Stalnaker*. Oxford: Oxford University Press, 164–90.

Yalcin, Seth. 2008. 'Modality and Inquiry'. Ph.D. dissertation. MIT, Cambridge, Mass.

—— 2010. 'Probability Operators'. *Philosophy Compass* 5: 916–37.

Zvolenszky, Zsófia. 2002. 'Is a Possible Worlds Semantics for Modality Possible?' Paper presented at Semantics and Linguistic Theory 12, University of California, San Diego, and San Diego State University.

Index

OXFORD STUDIES IN THEORETICAL LINGUISTICS

Lightning Source UK Ltd.
Milton Keynes UK
UKOW06f0627040315

247245UK00001B/1/P